ROMANTIC LONGINGS

ROMANTIC LONGINGS

LOVE IN AMERICA, 1830–1980

STEVEN SEIDMAN

Routledge · New York & London

Published in 1991 by

Routledge
An imprint of Routledge, Chapman and Hall, Inc.
29 West 35 Street
New York, NY 10001

Published in Great Britain by

Routledge
11 New Fetter Lane
London EC4P 4EE

Library of Congress Cataloging in Publication Data

Seidman, Steven.
    Romantic longings : love in America, 1830–1980 / Steven Seidman.
        p.   cm.
    Includes bibliographical references and index.
    ISBN 0-415-90404-8
    1. Sex customs—United States—History.   2. Love—History.
    3. Sexual ethics—United States—History.   4. Intimacy (Psychology)
    I. Title.
    HQ18.U5S43   1991
    306.7'0973—dc20   90-8875

British Library Cataloguing in Publication Data

Seidman, Steven
    Romantic longings : love in America 1830–1980.
    1. Interpersonal relationships, Role of love
    I. Title
    302

    ISBN 0-415-90404-8

For Linda Nicholson,
my romantic friend

Contents

Preface

The disciplinary organization of knowledge is collapsing. Disciplinary boundaries are becoming more and more fluid and porous. This is, in my view, a welcome development as disciplines, at least the human sciences, are drifting into a sterile insularity. Interdisciplinary projects, such as gender studies, urban studies, literary analysis, are flourishing. More and more scholars address social themes that draw on conceptual strategies, methodologies and data from diverse disciplines. Social studies increasingly incorporates literature from sociology, psychology, geography, history, anthropology, literary studies, gender studies and so on. The innovators of our times—figures such as Foucault, Habermas, Fredric Jameson, Manuel Castells, Mary Douglas, Joan Scott, Jeffrey Weeks, Clifford Geertz—are often either outside the conventional disciplines or working in their interstices.

Romantic Longings falls squarely in this movement against narrowly discipline-bounded social inquiry. I am a sociologist, indeed trained as a sociological theorist. I have felt compelled to break away from the conventions of my discipline which I find, at times, constricting and obscure. Nor does this book represent a conversion to "history," whose disciplinary codes exhibit their own compulsive narrowing and parochialism. I prefer to think of social inquiry, at its best, as offering narratives, sometimes small or local, at other times, such as in this book, broad and synthetic. Ideally, a social narrative should be deeply historical, attending to the changes in the meaning and form of the subject matter under study and attentive to the historicity of the categories of social analysis. In my view, storytelling of the type the human sciences do always carries ideological significance. Discourses, as we often say today, are social practices, no less socially consequential than, say, political, gender or economic factors. This is particularly true of the human sciences whose discourses carry the public authority of science and whose topics are already sites of social and political conflict. The producers of social narratives should own up to the moral and political significance of their creations. Accordingly, I believe that social narratives ought to incorporate some reflection on their work as moral and political interventions.

Romantic Longings is a response to current intellectual and social conflicts around intimate life in the United States. I offer a narrative of the development and current meaning of American intimate culture. I wish to propose a broad perspective on the present that will move public discussion in a particular direction. The wish to affect the outcome of current conflicts is the moral hope behind this work. My standpoint will become clear in the narrative. Put simply, I remain hopeful of our ability to shape a future for ourselves that permits a wide latitude of choice. In the end, I prefer to be a friend of choice, with all its attendant ills, than to side with the advocates of restraint and discipline, with its costly sacrifices in the present for a future hope.

Acknowledgments

Linda Nicholson provided sustained intellectual and personal support for this project. She read the manuscript several times, and her comments always proved helpful. I was fortunate to have had recourse to the sharp historical minds of Ron Berger and Peter Stearns. Eileen Pellegrino and Sharon Baumgardner typed and retyped the manuscript, almost always in good spirits and always with care and competence. The interlibrary loan staff at the State University of New York at Albany were outstanding in helping me gain access to documents spanning two centuries. Finally, during the years this book was in the making I shared the special pleasures of a modern romance with Aaron Roth. I have learned much about romantic longings from this sweet soul.

Introduction

Intimate norms and practices in twentieth-century America which have valued an expansive notion of sexual choice, diversity and erotic pleasure are today under assault. The value placed upon sex as a domain of pleasure and self-expression is being held responsible for a variety of contemporary personal and social ills. Our expanded sexual freedom, it is argued, has eroded relational commitments; it has created unrealistic expectations for personal happiness; it has uncoupled sex from stable social bonds. The yield of this intimate culture, some critics contend, has not been sexual and intimate fulfillment but an anomic and narcissistic culture. AIDS, herpes, escalating rates of divorce, illegitimacy and teen pregnancies, loneliness, violence against women, and the impoverishment and abandonment of our children are claimed as its bitter fruit. This critique of current sexual trends often carries a nostalgia for an idealized nineteenth-century intimate culture. In this period, it is assumed, sex was firmly embedded in permanent social bonds and intimacy was not dependent on fleeting sexual pleasures but anchored in a deep spiritual kinship and a range of social responsibilities. Although this critique is especially prevalent among conservatives, it has surfaced among liberals and the left, including feminists.

I take issue with this critical perspective on contemporary American intimate culture. Embedded in my historical narrative is a cautious defense of certain trends in middle-class intimate culture. I relate a story of successively unique epochs of intimate culture. The Victorian period cannot serve as a standard to judge contemporary intimate life. Although the myth of the "repressed Victorian" may have been put to rest, reinventing the Victorians as moderns who successfully integrated desire and affect is no less a simplification. Our contemporary intimate conventions are anchored primarily in twentieth-century developments. In the early decades of this century an intimate

1

culture formed which framed sex as a medium of love. By sexualizing love, this culture encouraged a heightened attention to the body, sensual pleasure and sex technique. One consequence of the "sexualization of love" was that eroticism was conceived of as a source of romantic bonding. Mutual erotic fulfillment was intended to enhance intimate solidarity in a social context where other unifying forces (e.g., kinship, patriarchy, economic dependency) were losing their power to do so. A second consequence of the development of the erotic aspects of sex was that the pleasurable and expressive qualities of sex gradually acquired legitimacy apart from settings of romantic intimacy. In the post–World War II years, discourses appeared in mainstream culture that constructed sex as having multiple meanings (procreation, love and pleasure) and diverse legitimate social contexts. Although this development has been bewailed by some critics for causing many current ills, it has, in my view, been crucial to the expansion of sexual choice and diversity. In short, there materialized in twentieth-century United States an intimate culture that framed sex as a sphere of love and romantic bonding as well as a domain of self-expression and sensual happiness.

My aim, however, is not to celebrate the American intimate culture. Discourses and representations promoting the joys and social uses of eroticism have sometimes neglected the dangers of sex; they have not adequately examined the emotional and moral context of sex; they have, at times, overloaded sex with excessive expectations of self-fulfillment. Finally, the culture of eroticism has imbued sex with ambiguous, often conflicting meanings: sex is projected as a sphere of love and romance and, alternatively, as a medium of pleasure and self-expression.

My reserved endorsement of American intimate culture forms, if you will, the moral and ideological underpinnings of this book. My principal agenda, however, is to offer a unique perspective on the development of this intimate culture. I aim to document a series of changes in the meaning of romantic love in the United States from 1830 to 1980. Specifically, I intend to analyze the changing conceptions and norms which define sex in relation to love in American culture.

I offer primarily a cultural analysis of love.[1] I intend to describe the meanings Americans attach to love or the beliefs, ideals and norms Americans hold regarding the relation between sex and love. Sex and love are not simply psychological or social facts but are cultural phenomena as well. We imbue sex and love with layers of meaning that are emotionally and morally charged. These meanings are part of broader symbolic configurations as well as implicated in complex

social structural dynamics related to kinship, gender or class dynamics. At various points in my argument, I suggest structural accounts
of these changing cultural meanings. I have found the Marxian analysis of the commodification of everyday life, the feminist focus on
gender dynamics and the Foucauldian notion of discursive formations
helpful in explaining the structural sources of cultural change. My
principal interest, however, is to analyze sex and love as cultural
constructs or symbols. From a cultural perspective, sex and love suggest less a set of practices to be explained by psychological or sociological processes than a symbolic complex. I study sex and love by analyzing them as part of a system of meanings or symbols.[2] Their meaning
is comprehended by situating them in a dense network of interrelated
categories including the body, maleness and femaleness, reproduction, sensuality, health, selfhood and so on. I am unapologetic about
the cultural and descriptive focus of this study. All too often, especially
in sociology, the urge to explain crowds out the phenomenon under
study. Proving the power or elegance of an analytical explanation
takes precedence over understanding the subject matter. Enhancing
control over social reality is a driving force behind explanation. My
aim, however, is to clarify what is unique about the present in order
to contribute to understanding ourselves.

The meanings and purposes we invest in love are, in part, a product
of diverse discourses, representations, traditions, and legal and moral
customs. These cultural forces construct love as a domain about which
we hold a range of beliefs and judgments. These meanings shape the
way we imagine and experience love. They define what we expect or
hope for from love and how it relates to self-fulfillment as well as the
welfare and future of our society. These public representations change
over time. We should not assume that change occurs in a uniform,
continuous or evolutionary way. Indeed, I have emphasized breaks
and disjunctions in the development of intimate mores in America.
Although my narrative features alterations in the dominant cultural
codes of intimate life, past configurations often persist as symbolic
resources in the present. Moreover, I have tried to avoid both a Whiggish tale of progress and a Tory story of woe and sorrow. I take the
early nineteenth century as my starting point. This is not entirely
arbitrary, since historians seem to agree that during these years a
distinctive culture of intimacy had come into existence. The period,
roughly between 1830 and 1890, represents the crucial decades of
American Victorian culture. The AIDS epidemic, beginning in the
early 1980s, seems a compelling, logical endpoint. Although it is too
early to tell, AIDS may signify a turning point in our collective intimate life.

This study assumes that love has no essential or unitary identity. Not only does its meaning change over time, but within a given society at a fixed time there will be variations in its meaning. A sociology of love would, I think, show how social factors such as gender, class, education or social status shape cultural meanings and practices. The social population that I study is primarily the nonimmigrant, white middle class that resides chiefly in the Northeast. Although I am not as convinced as others that this social group is the pacesetter of culture in modern societies, its size, social position and social impact justify its study. I leave it to other researchers to determine whether or to what extent my conclusions bear on other social groups.

I have made some effort to assess how gender impacts on the image and experience of middle-class love. I caution readers, though, not to interpret my remarks on the different patterns of love between men and women in an essentialist manner. I use the categories "man" and "woman" as analytical constructs that are useful in highlighting certain typical, though by no means uniform, cultural and behavioral patterns. I am, in addition, aware that not all love among the white middle class is heterosexual. Same-sex love—men loving men and women loving women—is all too frequently neglected or relegated to a marginal scholarly place. This is not only bad scholarship but it reinforces the public perception of the marginal and devalued status of same-gender love. The reader will find an analysis of the changing meaning of "homosexual" love alongside of my account of "heterosexual" love.

THE SEXUALIZATION OF LOVE
The Eroticization of Sex

The principal theme of this book can be stated fairly simply. Between the early part of the nineteenth century and the later part of the twentieth century, the meaning and place of sex in relation to love, and therefore the meaning of love, underwent important changes. Love changed from having an essentially spiritual meaning to being conceived in a way that made it inseparable from the erotic longings and pleasures of sex. By the early decades of the twentieth century, the desires and pleasures associated with the erotic aspects of sex were imagined as a chief motivation and sustaining source of love. The Victorian language of love as a spiritual communion was either marginalized or fused with the language of sensual desire and joy. I chart a process of the progressive "sexualization of love" in which the erotic dimensions of sex assume an expanded role in proving and maintaining love.

Paralleling the sexualization of love is an equally momentous dynamic, namely, the legitimation of the erotic aspects of sex. To the extent that erotic pleasure was viewed as a medium of love, the pursuit of sensual pleasure received public legitimation. I am suggesting, in other words, an account of the rise in the twentieth century of an intimate culture in which sex was valued for its sensually pleasurable and expressive qualities. It became legitimate to pursue sex for carnal pleasure to the extent that eroticism acquired a higher meaning as a symbol or vehicle of love.

The sexualization of love made possible the legitimation of the erotic aspects of sex. Ironically, while the eroticization of sex was initially accepted only in a context of love, by the post–World War II period the pleasurable and expressive qualities of eroticism acquired value apart from a context of love. This development introduced new possibilities and complexities into America's intimate culture. For example, if sex now carried multiple legitimate meanings, individuals had more opportunities to design their own sexual and intimate lifestyles. Yet, expanded sexual choice and the pursuit of erotic pleasure raised fears about negatively impacting on the stability of intimate bonds; concerns were voiced regarding the morality of sexual objectification and the reduction of individuals to vessels of pleasure. Moreover, sex was now invested with conflicting meanings. Despite even the most enthusiastic efforts to deromanticize sex and construct it as merely a domain of pleasure and self-expression, it remains culturally entangled with emotional and moral resonances of love. As both an expression and medium of love and a domain of pleasure and self-expression, sex carries ambiguous meanings and behavioral directives. The possibilities for expanded choice and lifestyle diversity as well as the new dangers and strains presented by these developments define the ambiguous moral meaning of contemporary American intimate culture.

DOCUMENTS AND EVIDENCE
Methodological Issues

I aim, foremost, to document American's beliefs and norms about sex and love. Accordingly, I am most interested in evidence that gives me the most direct access to mainstream public meanings. With this consideration in mind, I have chosen to rely heavily upon advice literature and popular medical texts. I have, in addition, drawn extensively from personal documents (diaries, letters and autobiographies), novels, and sex surveys and research.

An explanation is perhaps necessary in light of the recent caution

issued by historians against too much dependence upon advice literature.[3] The reservations regarding these documents relate to their supposedly prescriptive status. Advice literature, so the argument goes,
tells us what people ought to believe or do, not what people actually
think or do. Hence, it is not a trustworthy guide to actual behavior.
At first glance this critique seems irrelevant to this work, since my
chief aim is precisely to describe cultural ideals and norms, not to
explain behavior. The critique becomes relevant when it is further
claimed that even as a guide to norms and ideals these documents
are only minimally reliable because of their reformist intent. The
presumption is that advice literature is indicative of the culture of
disaffected and marginal segments of the population. In other words,
if sex advice literature is peripheral to mainstream intimate culture,
what is the value of studying it? A response to this query is crucial.

Two related points seem to render this argument less compelling.
First, it is often not possible to distinguish in a meaningful way between a prescriptive and a descriptive discourse. To know whether a
discourse, not a specific statement or utterance, is prescriptive or
not, we need to be able to unambiguously describe practices as they
actually are. This is difficult even when available evidence is substantial and clear; in the case of sexual and intimate mores and behavior,
where data is lacking and highly ambiguous, it is impossible.[4] A second consideration relates to the point that the connecting tie between
a discourse and social practices is complex. Insofar as the domains of
sex and love cover norms, ideals, beliefs, feelings and wishes as well as
behavior, any description is likely to include normative and cognitive
elements that derive from prescriptive discourses. In addition, intimate conventions and practices change under the impact of and sometimes in the direction desired by prescriptive discourses. In other
words, reformers are often successful; what was prescriptive becomes
descriptive.

Historians are surely right to issue a caution against using advice
literature uncritically or relying exclusively upon it as evidence for
cultural meanings or behavior. Yet, advice literature may be profitably used if it is approached in a more deliberate way. Guiding my
selection and use of advice literature have been the following considerations: An advice text must be typical or exhibit the standard themes
of this literary genre; it should have achieved a certain public credibility. I take references to a text in other texts and public popularity as
measured by sales indicators of a text's social currency. In addition,
the credibility of advice texts are enhanced if their basic themes
surface in other public documents, e.g., scientific, medical, literary or
political texts.

Knowing the problems associated with advice texts, I have drawn from other sources of documentation. In particular, I have relied upon diaries, letters and especially autobiographies. While autobiographies are often less candid and reliable for discovering private feelings and behavior, they are quite useful for gaining access to public culture. I have, moreover, made use of novels where other evidence seemed limited. Finally, I have read virtually all the relevant sex surveys and research that bear on my theme. Some of this research uses interviews which contain highly pertinent material; other research allows me to make inferences about cultural meaning or to make some loose connection between meanings and behavior. It hardly needs to be added that any study covering 150 years is, in essence, a sketch to be filled in and revised by subsequent research.

OVERVIEW AND IMPLICATIONS

This book is divided into three parts, each relating to a specific time period. Part One covers the Victorian period, 1830–1890. In white, middle-class, Victorian culture, a spiritual ideal of love figured prominently. Love referred to a spiritual affinity and spiritual companionship. The Victorians, however, were by no means prudes. They affirmed the power and beneficial qualities of sex. Sex was an expected, obligatory and healthy part of marriage. However, we can discern an antagonism between sex and love in Victorian culture. Love was considered an ideal basis and the essential state of marriage. Yet, sex was thought of as an equally vital part of marriage. It is the nature of sex, so many Victorians thought, to incite sensuality which threatens to destroy the spiritual essence of marriage by engulfing it in a sea of lust. Accordingly, Victorians sought to control the place of sex in marriage. They did this by urging the desexualization of love and the desensualization of sex. At times, Victorians defended the desexualization of marriage itself, but this contradicted their belief in the omnipresence and beneficent power of the sex instinct. Curiously, the desexualization of love and the desensualization of sex made same-sex love more acceptable. Romantic friendships or love between women and, to a lesser extent, love between men was fairly typical and carried no trace of wrongdoing or shame. The antithesis today between a pure and ennobled heterosexuality and an impure and ignoble homosexuality was absent. Love between members of the same sex and between members of the opposite sex were often viewed as complementary, not mutually exclusive.

Part Two covers the post-Victorian, "modern" years from 1890 to 1960. I chart a change in the direction of the sexualization of love. The language of love now intermingles with that of sex. Sexual attraction is taken as a sign of love; the giving and receiving of sexual pleasures are viewed as demonstrations of love; sustained sexual longing and satisfaction is thought to be a condition for maintaining love. It is, moreover, the sensual side of sex that is valued. Sensuality is legitimated as a vehicle of love. Hence, the Victorian antithesis between love and sex and especially between love and sensuality disappears. Of course, love means more than sex. The Victorian ideal of spiritual companionship is transfigured into an idealized solidarity of lovers based upon personal, social and cultural companionship. True love is thought to combine sexual fulfillment and this idealized solidarity. The sexualization of love was paralleled by the exaltation of heterosexual love and the pollution of homosexual love. Under the impact of a scientific-medical discourse of homosexuality, the nineteenth-century paradigm of romantic friendship was replaced by that of homosexual or lesbian love. Heterosexuality and homosexuality were now described as mutually exclusive categories of desire, identity and love.

In Part Three we move into the contemporary period, 1960–1980. My focus shifts here. In chapter 5 I am less interested in further detailing the sexualization of love than in showing how this process inadvertently led to legitimating the erotic aspects of sex. In the early decades of the twentieth century, sensual pleasures were imbued with a higher value and purpose. Erotic fulfillment sustained, enhanced and revitalized love. This implied a heightened focus and value placed upon erotic technique and fulfillment. Although the value placed on eroticism was legitimated initially only for the purpose of strengthening romantic bonds, by the 1960s the pleasurable and expressive qualities of sex were appealed to as a sufficient justification of sex. Discourses and representations appeared that constructed sex as a domain of pleasure and self-expression requiring no higher purpose so long as the interpersonal context was one of consent and mutuality. Eros was released from the culture of romance that gave birth to it.

In chapter 6 my attention turns to the gay culture. In the post–World War II years we can observe a third dramatic change in the meaning of same sex intimacy. The Victorian model of romantic friendship, we recall, gave way to the model of homosexual or lesbian love in the early decades of the twentieth century. In the contemporary period, "gay love" emerges as a new, positive model of same sex intimacy. I examine the meanings and patterns of gay love in the pre-AIDS era. I am particularly interested in how the combining of sex, love and intimacy in the gay culture overlaps and differs from that of middle-class heterosexual men and women.

In the Epilogue I return to the moral and political implications of this study. I take issue with critics who relate current disturbances in American intimate culture to the expansion of sexual choice and diversity. Although a liberal intimate culture may occasion excesses or discontents associated with sexual objectification, vulgarity, emotional callousness, even sexual disease, these are acceptable costs for expanded choice and an intimate culture that values erotic pleasure and variety.[5] In addition, I explore, very tentatively, the immediate and possible long-term impact of AIDS on our intimate conventions. In the short term, I see only limited cultural and behavioral changes. In the long run, the desexualization of pleasure and perhaps the deeroticizing of sex are possible responses to a desire that is increasingly identified as dangerous. I detect, as well, a trend toward a more restrictive intimate culture. To the extent that a politics of restriction gains public authority, nonconventional sexual groups (e.g., gays and lesbians, swingers, sadomasochists) and oppositional groups (e.g., feminists) will play an important role in the defense of an expanded notion of sexual choice and variety in the 1990s.

Part One

*The Victorian World
1830–1890*

1

The Power of Desire and the Danger of Pleasure

The Antinomy of Eroticism and Love

The Victorian era was dominated by Protestantism. Despite successive waves of non-Protestant immigrants to American shores, Protestants wielded enormous political and cultural authority. They managed, moreover, to more or less successfully forge an identification between Protestantism and being an American. Throughout the nineteenth century, Protestantism was strongly influenced by those Puritan dissenters and divines who have fascinated subsequent generations of Americans. What, we may ask, is the relation between Puritanism and the Victorian conventions of intimacy?

The Puritans have acquired a bad reputation. In popular American culture, Puritanism continues to be associated with excessive sexual renunciation and asceticism. This stereotype seems to have been the invention of modernist rebels in the early decades of the twentieth century.[1] In the struggle of self-described "moderns" for sexual freedom, they labeled their Victorian opponents as puritans. "Puritan" came to stand for a style of sexual prudishness that was presumed to be dominant from the colonial period through the late nineteenth century. Victorianism was viewed as a continuation of Puritan intimate culture.

Contemporary historians have objected to this flattened, Whiggish popular history. They have distinguished between Puritan and Victorian sexual conventions. They found in Puritan intimate culture a unique and complex configuration of beliefs and conventions. In addition, contemporary scholars have related Puritanism to Victorianism in a much more nuanced way than observing either simple continuity or discontinuity. Some recent scholarly perspectives on Puritanism and Victorianism are virtually antithetical to the popular view.

According to a recent study of English Puritanism, the popular stereotype of the sexually repressed Puritan is grossly misleading. "Within the confines of the marriage bed, sexuality and sexual pleasure were . . . seen as good things. Sex was not simply for procreation or to avoid fornication but was good in itself to the degree that it gave pleasure and comfort to both husband and wife."[2] Edmund Leites argues that the distinctively Puritan ideal of intimacy centered around an ethic of moral constancy. The Puritans valued moral and emotional steadiness. This included an ideal of self-control and sobriety but also emotional warmth and erotic delight. "Mainstream Puritans did not see marital sexuality as a threat to moral constancy; in fact, they saw it as a remarkable and happy harmony of carnal, moral, and spiritual bonds."[3] Yet, Leites introduces some serious qualifications to his thesis of the modernity of the Puritans. The sexual pleasures these Puritan preachers endorsed were not romantic passions or carnal desires, but "a moderate feeling which did not originally lead to extremes of passion."[4] And even these "moderate feelings" were subject to strict control. "The ethic of mainstream Puritanism placed severe constraints upon erotic pleasures."[5]

The dangers of eroticism for the Puritan were twofold. First, sensual motivations were thought to disturb the emotional and moral constancy the Puritan sought. Sex was thought to easily incite lust which propelled the individual down the path of perdition. Carnal feelings were legitimate only if they were tightly controlled and carefully regulated. Second, eroticism anticipated the danger of idolatry.[6] The Puritan's supreme duty and devotion was to serve God. "The highest love of all Christians was reserved for God himself; and since human beings, husbands and wives, were only the creation of God, they could not take his place. . . . To prize them too highly was to upset the order of creation and descend to idolatry." Marriage was not to be approached as an end in itself. In a truly Christian marriage, the husband and wife are brought nearer to God by loving God in the image of their spouse. "A woman who truly loved God would be sure to love God's image in her husband, as a godly man would be sure to love the image of God mirrored back to him from his wife."[7] In a word, conjugal love and marriage drew its highest legitimacy from its capacity to elevate the individual into a better Christian.

Sex for the Puritans had value only within marriage. Sexual expression outside of marriage was severely condemned. Harsh punishments were meted out for masturbation and fornication. In many New England colonies, bestiality, buggery and sodomy were capital crimes.[8] Puritan law imposed the death penalty for adultery.[9] Although such drastic measures were rarely taken, harsh punishments, from rituals of degradation (e.g., public whippings or confessions) to heavy fines, ridicule, ostracism and banishment from the community, indicate a dominant Puritan marital-centered sexual norm.

Within marriage, Puritans accepted sexual expression. Sex was as much a duty as, say, a husband's responsibility to provide economic support for the household or the obligation of the spouses to establish a peaceful, comfortable home. No marriage was considered complete unless consummated in sexual union. Marital sex was, in part, justified to prevent the individual from becoming preoccupied with carnal desires and from engaging in improper sex. The Puritans also accepted erotic pleasure so long as it promoted the mutual comfort and affection of the conjugal pair. Recently, the historians John D'Emilio and Estelle Freedman have argued that, though the Puritans may have permitted sexual pleasure in marriage, the procreative function of sex was its chief rationale. "Sex became a duty that husband and wife owed to one another; it also could be a means of enhancing the marriage. Nonetheless, pleasure alone did not justify sexual union, which remained closely tied to procreation. ... The regulation of sexual behavior reinforced the primacy of marital, reproductive sex and the need for the legitimacy of children."[10]

Marriage for the Puritans was no practical, businesslike arrangement. It involved mutual affection and respect. Puritans were religiously enjoined to fashion a marriage on the basis of love. The Puritan divine Benjamin Wadsworth offered the following characterization of conjugal love.

> This duty of love is mutual, it should be performed by each, to each of them. They should endeavor to have their affections really, cordially and closely knit, to each other. If therefore the *Husband* is bitter against his wife, beating or striking of her (as some vile wretches do) or in any unkind carriage, ill language, hard words, morose, peevish, surly behavior; nay if he is not kind, loving, tender in his words and carriage to her; he then shames his profession of Christianity, he breaks the Divine Law, he dishonors God and himself too, by this ill behavior. The same is true of the Wife too. If she strikes her Husband (as some shameless, impudent wretches will) if she's unkind in her carriage, given to ill language, is sullen, pouty, so cross that she'll scare eat or speak sometimes; nay if she neglects to manifest real love and kindness, in her words or carriage either; she's then a shame to her profession of Christianity, she dishonors and provokes the glorious God, tramples his Authority under her feet; she not only affronts her Husband, but also God her Maker, Lawgiver and Judge, by this her wicked behavior. The indisputable Authority, the plain Command of the Great God, required Husbands and Wives, to have and manifest very great affection, love and kindness to one another. They should (out of Conscience to God) study and strive to render each others life, easy, quiet and comfortable; to please, gratifie and oblige one another, as far as lawfully then can.[11]

Puritan love meant less a driving romantic passion than a steady, deepening reciprocal respect and affection. This ideal of love explains why the Puritans were not enjoined to marry for love but to marry someone they could learn to love.[12] Love evolved after marriage, not as its originating force. This ensured, presumably, that the Puritan would not confuse romantic or carnal attraction for true love.

Mainstream American Puritanism as described by recent historians bears little resemblance to the popular stereotype. Puritans were not, in the main, antisexual, prudish or ascetic.[13] Puritan intimate culture revolved around a marriage-centered, procreative sexual ideal. Puritans aspired to create in marriage a domain of love that symbolically mirrored their love of God. Although the dominant imagery of conjugal love is religious, Puritan love was not a wholly spiritual affair. Sex was expected, not only to produce legitimate offspring but to bring mutual comfort and pleasure. Erotic pleasures were acknowledged so long as they did not threaten to incite lust or anticipate idolatry. This possibility, however, imbued sex with powerful resonances of danger. This anticipation of danger prompted Puritans to place severe restrictions on eroticism; for some Puritans, argues one historian, it led to a dread of and hostility toward sex. "The Puritan was encouraged to marry but obliged even within marriage to treat his sexuality, as well as his emotions, with suspicion and mistrust."[14] The Puritan may not have been the excessively repressed figure depicted in popular stereotypes, but neither was he or she especially comfortable with an eroticism that was linked to atheism, paganism and idolatry.[15]

Until recently, the overwhelming weight of opinion among historians supported the notion that Victorianism marked a break from the Puritan culture of intimacy. Under the impact of successive waves of Protestant evangelical revitalization movements or, as other historians claim, reflecting the emerging hegemonic status of a bourgeois class, American sexual culture turned decidedly prudish and repressive. The Victorians, so the argument goes, denied that women possess sexual feelings; they sought to purge sex of its sensuality and restrict its role to a procreative one; Victorian marriage was, finally, described as characteristically cold as the relations between husband and wife were emotionally distant and formal. The Victorians, in other words, were thought to be responsible for creating the sex-negative culture against which twentieth-century "moderns" have rebelled.[16]

The view of the Victorians as the "real Puritans" has been challenged in the last decade or so. Several historians, most notably Carl Degler, Peter Gay and Ellen Rothman, have proposed major reinterpretations of Victorian intimate conventions.[17] Restricting themselves primarily to the white middle class, they have highlighted the role of personal choice in mate selection and the informality of courting among Victorians. They describe Victorian marriage as a consensual arrangement based on love. Husband and wife sought—and frequently found—companionship and personal happiness in marriage. Sexual expression was typically accepted by Victorians as an integral part of love and marriage. Sex was not, moreover, restricted to a procreative function but was valued as a sign of love and as a domain of sensual pleasure. Finally, although heterosexuality was normative, same-sex intimacy and love was tolerated as long as it was discreet and private. This revisionist view of Victorianism underscores important continuities between the Puritans and their successors. "Puritan divines asserted the importance of affection, intimacy, and companionship within marriage, elements that would become central to the ideal of marriage in America in the nineteenth century."[18] Victorianism represents, for these revisionist historians, less a departure or break from Puritanism than a continuous development of its intimate culture.

My own point of departure accepts, in general terms, this revisionist account. I see the Victorians as endorsing a marital-centered sexual ethic. Like their Puritan predecessors, Victorians hoped for a marriage based upon love. However, love figured even more prominently as a reason to marry and as its overriding rationale. As love assumed a central place in legitimating marriage, the reproductive rationale lost some of its cultural salience. Although Victorians continued to emphasize a reproductive norm, hygienic and spiritual rationales for sex were quite salient. The stereotype of the Victorian as repressed is as much in need of correction as the popular stereotype of the Puritan.

Unfortunately, corrective exercises all too often produce their own stereotypes. Thus, according to at least one historian, there has been a tendency to replace the popular stereotype of the Puritan with an overly sanguine, modern image.[19] I believe the same is true of revisionist accounts of Victorian intimate culture. Some of these interpretations flatten Victorian experience, purge it of its complexity and contradictory impulses, or ignore the ways in which inner conflicts in this culture frustrated the individual's quest for love. There is, I feel, a noticeably nostalgic or romanticized quality to these revisionist historical accounts.

Despite these shortcomings, the work of revisionist historians offers the most promising approach to understanding intimate affairs in nineteenth-century America. I aim to build on this already impressive body of scholarship. I do not, of course, intend to comment on all aspects of Victorian sexual and intimate life. My focus is on the beliefs and norms or meanings white, middle-class Victorians attached to sex and its relation to love. In this chapter I rely exclusively upon popular medical texts and marital advice literature. In chapter 2, I will draw on personal documents (diaries, letters and autobiographies) to further explore Victorian images of love.

In the remainder of this chapter, I propose to detail a set of assumptions and contradictory pulls that are at the core of Victorian intimate culture. The Victorians held that the sex instinct is a powerful force that needs to be channeled in the proper way to be beneficial to humanity. Because marriage was thought to involve a relationship of love and permanent responsibilities, it was considered the ideal sphere for sexual expression. Sex was, accordingly, an expected and necessary part of marriage. Yet, marriage was not simply an arrangement for the purpose of satisfying sexual needs or creating a family. Marriage was, ideally, a relationship of love. And love, the Victorian insisted, is essentially a spiritual phenomenon involving moral and religious affinities and bonds. Thus, ideally, marriage should be based upon love but include sexual expression as an obligatory and integral component. Problems arise, however, due to the belief in the omnipresence and power of the sexual instinct. The Victorians believed that arousing sexual feelings easily elicits sensuality which, in turn, threatens to dominate intimate feelings. To preserve the spiritual essence of marriage, the Victorians felt compelled to de-eroticize sex or to erect elaborate barriers to contain erotic desires. At times this urge to control eroticism passed into a demand to desexualize marriage itself. This, however, conflicted with their nearly ubiquitous belief in the power and beneficial effects of proper sexual expression.

THE DIALECTIC OF SEX
The Power of the Sex Instinct

Far from denying and devaluing the importance of the sex instinct, the Victorians believed in its omnipresence and power. Indeed, they exalted it as a benevolent power. The obverse side to assuming the power of sex is its potential danger. A Victorian discourse on the danger of sex was intended to restrict desire and, ultimately, to provide a rationale for sublimating carnal impulses into spiritual love. The Victorians imagined a drama of an omnipresent powerful sex drive propelled toward pleasure but susceptible to the dangers of excess and ruin. Self-control and the spiritualization of desire would make possible an autonomous self and civilized society.

The Victorians originated the modern idea of a sexual instinct that is natural and powerful. Most Victorians would have agreed with Dr.

Frederick Hollick's observation that "the [sexual] instinct . . . is innate in all beings, and exercises a most powerful influence, both upon individual action and upon the destinies of nations."[20] Dr. Elizabeth Blackwell was even more certain about the power of the sex instinct. "The instinct of sex always exists as the indispensable condition of life, and the foundation of society. It is the strongest force in human nature."[21] The sex drive was not only a powerful force but a benevolent one. Typically, advice writers advanced hygienic justifications of sex. "Sexual intercourse is no doubt beneficial to health in all fully developed persons," commented William Ashton.[22] This belief was reiterated by William Action. "Regular and moderate sexual intercourse is, on the whole, of advantage to the [physical] system at large."[23] The proper exercise of the sexual function was thought to contribute to the mental health and vigor of the individual. "Sexual matters," wrote Henry Guernsey, "are so thoroughly interwoven with the highest destinies of the human race, physically, mentally, and spiritually, there is scarcely any concern of higher import . . . than that assigned to the genital organs. No functions more deeply concerns the healthiness of the body, the clearness and brilliancy of the intellect."[24] Dr. Edward Foote connected the proper use of the sex instinct to individual industriousness. "It gives vigor [and] . . . stimulates ambition."[25] In one of the first popular medical books of the nineteenth century, Robert Dale Owen took issue with the Shakers and other detractors of the sexual instinct. "I think its influence [is] moral, humanizing, polishing, beneficent."[26] Almost fifty years later the physician Russell Trall echoed this ideal. "Normally exercised, no act of an intelligent being is more holy, more humaning, more ennobling."[27] These Victorians believed that the very progress of humanity was anchored in the sex instinct. "Sexual feelings exercise a directive power over most of the activities of life—moulding our religion, our literature, our art, our etiquette."[28] Guided by reason, declared James Scott, the sexual instinct will "advance civilization to its . . . highest destiny."[29] To the Victorians, sex was a natural instinct whose significance for the individual and society was far-reaching and powerful.

The sexual instinct was not only a benevolent power but potentially a principal source of misfortune and evil. Its very capacity to shape the destiny of humanity rendered sex a potentially menacing force. Advice writers would not have needed to alert contemporaries to the grave dangers of abusing the sex instinct unless it was assumed to be a powerful force.

A prominent motif found in these texts is that sexual feelings are dangerous because they easily stimulate sensual or erotic feelings. Sensuality was thought to be governed by an internal logic whose dynamic force is lust and whose outcome is personal ruin. The logic of sexual desire, as Victorians imagined it, can be described as a sort of domino theory of sex. Once sensual desires are stimulated they become insatiable. "Indulgence inflames," declared Orson Fowler. "The more it is indulged, the more it demands."[30] Gradually, carnal motivations may come to monopolize the unconscious and conscious life of the individual. Once the pleasures of sensual gratification are tasted, "these become habitual and haunt him, until at last the sexual passion absorbs not only his working thoughts, but his very dreams."[31] The individual becomes trapped in a life of sexual excess and perversion; he becomes unwittingly the "slave of his passions."[32] The result is moral degradation, unimaginable suffering and personal ruin. Speaking of the dangers of autoeroticism, Dr. Samuel Woodward rehearsed this insidious logic whereby the temptations of pleasure bring inevitable ruin. "It [masturbation] is a vice which excites . . . the strongest and most uncontrollable propensities of animal nature; these are rendered more active by indulgence, while the power of . . . restraint is lessened by it in a tenfold degree. The moral sensitivity becomes so blunted as to retain no ascendancy in the character to control and regulate conduct. Under such circumstances, the best resolutions to reform . . . fail of accomplishment. In spite of himself, the victim sinks deeper and deeper in pollution, till he is overwhelmed at last in irretrievable ruin and disgrace."[33]

The dangers of sex were highlighted by the fact that the consequences of sensual indulgence were generalized. Ashton related excess to male impotence. "Long continued excesses in venery, whether with women or by means of onanism, is a frequent cause of barrenness or impotence in men."[34] Sylvester Graham linked excess to a general deterioration of the nervous system. "All the organs and tissues of the body . . . become extremely debilitated; and their functional powers exceedingly weak."[35] Physical enfeeblement renders the body vulnerable to a host of diseases. "Venereal excesses occasion the most loathsome, and horrible, and calamitous diseases that human nature is capable of suffering."[36] After describing in detail the physical degeneration that accompanies sexual excess, Graham provided a succinct review of its costs. "Languor, lassitude, . . . general debility and heaviness, depression of spirits, loss of appetite, indigestion, feebleness of circulation, chilliness, headache, melancholy, hypochondria, hysteria, feebleness of all the senses, impaired vision, loss of sight . . . disorders of the liver and kidneys, urinary difficulties, disorders of the genital organs, weakness of the brain, loss of memory, epilepsy, insanity, apoplexy,—and extreme feebleness and early death of offspring—are among the common evils which are caused by sexual excesses."[37] As Graham's chilling statement indicates, sexual excess was thought to be not only physically debilitating but to "[impair] the intellectual and moral faculties, and [debase] the mind."[38] Depression, sleeplessness, devitalization, melancholy, impotence, insanity and suicide were considered the fateful consequences of sexual excess. Indeed, Augustus Gardner connected excess to death. "We know that excess is premature death."[39] Typically, sexual excess was invoked to explain various social problems. Dr. Trall observed the "prevalence of vice, crime, disease and degradation resulting from perverted amativeness [sexuality]."[40] Dr. Henry Kellogg linked sexual excess to social decline. "What is it that is undermining the health of the race, and sapping the constitution of our American men? . . . There can be no doubt that vice is the most active case (particularly) secret sin [i.e., masturbation] and its kindred vices."[41]

The causal link between sexual excess and decline was not confined to behavioral acts.[42] Sensual indulgence did not refer solely to actual conduct. Sensual thoughts or fantasies were considered sufficient to activate the mechanical causality linking sensuality to deterioration. "Hence, therefore, SEXUAL DESIRE, cherished by the mind and dwelt on by the imagination, not only increases the excitability . . . of the genital organs themselves, but always throws an influence . . . over the whole nervous domain; disturbing all the functions depending on the nerves for vital energy. . . . And, hence, . . . Lascivious Day-dreams, and amorous reveries . . . are often the sources of general debility, effeminacy, disordered functions, and permanent disease, and even premature death, without the actual exercise of the genital organs."[43] This statement by Graham is typical and commonplace among popular medical and advice writers. Almost fifty years later, the same notion surfaced in Dio Lewis. "Where one person is injured by sexual commerce, many are made feverish and nervous by harboring lewd thoughts. Rioting in visions of nude women may exhaust one as much as an excess in actual intercourse."[44] And Dr. Kellogg wrote, "It is vain for a man to suppose himself chaste who allows his imagination to run riot amid scenes of amorous associations. . . . Though he may never have committed an overt act of unchastity, if he cannot pass a handsome female in the street without, in imagination, approaching the secrets of her person, he is but one grade above the open libertine, and is as truly unchaste as the veriest debauchee."[45]

Many Victorians believed that sexual excess can be a mental as well as a behavioral reality. This suggests that the claim of historians that Victorians assumed a causal link between excess and decline solely through the loss of semen needs to be qualified. To be sure, "spermatozza" or the excessive loss of semen through masturbation or too much coitus was widely invoked as an explanation of personal or social decline.[46] Semen was frequently considered to be a major source of vigor in men and women. Its excessive loss was believed to result in physical and mental debility and disease. "Where we find the general health suffering, the disposition to intellectual employment almost lost or impaired, exercise becoming a toil, society spurned, and the company of females particularly avoided, there is strong reason to suspect the . . . excessive and destructive loss of semen."[47] Although spermatozza was widely believed to have dire consequences, many of these Victorians held that disease and decline ensued just as inevitably from sensual thoughts and acts. The latter disturbs and debilitates vital bodily and mental functions; it leads to a life of excess, perversion and ruin.

Insofar as the sexual instinct was deemed such a powerful force that it could bring ruin to the individual and to civilization, it had to be controlled. Its benevolent effects could only be realized if it was properly channeled. The sexual instinct had to be strictly regulated and a range of sexual feelings and acts vigorously censored.

The effort to evolve a sexual ethic that was guided by science and consistent with Christian dogma yielded a sexual hierarchy that amounted to a moral ordering of sexual desires and acts. Fundamental to this regime of sexuality was the belief in the naturalness and therefore the correctness of heterosexuality. Frequently, heterosexuality was explained in terms of a kind of magnetic or biological attraction, a natural complementarity between the male and female genital organs. "The sexual organs of men and women are wonderfully adopted to each other, and have a perfect power of attraction," observed James Ashton.[48] Or, "It has been suggested that this mutual attraction is a species of real *Animal Magnetism*, the male being *positive* and the female negative, so that they are drawn irresistibly together."[49] Heterosexuality was, at times, described as an elementary gender attraction rooted in biology. "Women," wrote Dr. Foote, "need the magnetism of men; it strengthens them; it supplies something their peculiar organizations are incapable of producing. . . . Man needs women's magnetism; without it his surplus masculine elements either petrify and make him intolerably coarse and boorish, or they drive him to solitary vice and ultimate decay of his masculine qualities."[50] It is important to observe that the term *heterosexuality* and what we today take as its natural antithesis, *homosexuality*, were absent from these discourses. Indeed, there is virtually no reference to same-sex intimacy and love in these popular medical texts. The absence of a discourse on homosexuality should alert us to the point that the relevant contrast to the Victorians was not between heterosexuality and homosexuality. Heterosexuality was contrasted to all sexual activity that did not occur between a man and a woman. This included sodomy, bestiary and, most importantly, masturbation.

Proper sex occurred as part of a relationship between a man and a woman in the service of a high purpose, e.g., reproduction, creating a family, or promoting health. Within this sexual order, masturbation was proscribed. As a solitary act aimed at sensual gratification, masturbation violated the norms of proper sex. Yet, in order to grasp the centrality of masturbation in the Victorian imagination we need to introduce a further consideration. The egoistic and pleasure-seeking features attributed to this act made masturbation an appropriate site in which to displace anxieties over the massive social changes that were taking place in the mid-nineteenth century. The release of young men and women from existing social controls evoked a deeply felt anticipation of disaster. Without the moral restraints of kin, church and community, the sexual desires felt by youth would surely succumb, it was thought, to the many temptations available in the cities they were migrating to. The association of individualism, sensuality and the ruin that was presumed to accompany modernization, surfaced in the Victorian discourse on masturbation.

Masturbation carried a powerful symbolic meaning in Victorian sex discourses. The anxieties stirred by masturbation are revealed in excerpts such as the following, which could be multiplied a hundredfold. Masturbation, wrote George Napheys, "produces bodily weakness, loss of memory, lower spirits, distressing nervousness, a capricious appetite, dislike of company and study, and, finally, paralysis, imbecility, or insanity."[51] This abhorrence of masturbation is not proof of Victorian prudishness or a sex-negative culture. Rather, masturbation anxieties symbolized the fears felt by many Victorians as social changes weakened the grip of external social controls over the individual. The presumed egoism and hedonism of masturbation stood as a symbol of the impending fate of humanity freed from the moral agencies of the church, family and the local community. Masturbation could not be viewed as a mere pleasure or even a minor normative infraction of the sexual order. Rather, it became a sign of a deeper character flaw or lack of moral development; it bore witness to the decline of moral order; it initiated the beginnings of a life of dissipation that would inevitably lead to decline, disorder and death.

Sexual expression was legitimate only as part of a social exchange between a man and a woman. Furthermore, only in one type of social configuration was sex permissible, namely, marriage. Sexual contacts outside marriage were condemned. To the Victorians, fornication exhibited the same egoistic and hedonistic qualities as in masturbation. Moreover, it had the additional risk of bringing disease and lust into the pure sphere of the family. Strict continence or complete abstinence from all sexual thoughts, feelings and acts was advised until marriage. This was considered neither difficult nor unhealthy, according to the standard advice text. Without the artificially induced stimulation produced in an unhealthy social environment, individuals, at least up to the age of thirteen, were thought to lack sexual desire. Graham held that "any use of genitals before 15 is unnatural."[52] In the years before marriage, abstinence would be neither difficult nor unhealthy. In marriage, sexual monogamy was prescribed. This was believed to be a necessary condition for maintaining the moral purity and solidarity of marriage. Adultery not only threatened to tear asunder the social bonds of marriage and the family but, given hereditarian beliefs, it threatened future generations by transmitting to them the disposition to sensuality and vice of their progenitors.

Exercising the sexual instinct properly meant, then, restricting sex to adults in a heterosexual marital relationship guided by a monogamous norm. Within marriage, sex was expected or considered obligatory. It was seen as an essential source of health and vigor. However, its legitimacy was enhanced to the extent that sex served the higher goal of producing a family and reproducing the species.

The moral function of sex was ensured not only by natural law but by the unique character of female sexuality. The female sexual instinct was thought of as basically spiritual in its motivation, i.e., it was defined as a passion for a husband, home and children to love. William Acton, for example, didn't deny that women had sexual feelings. Rather, he proposed that women's sexual desires are "very moderate compared to those of the male" and are motivated by the need "to please him [i.e. her husband] and "the desire for maternity."[53] The reformer Dio Lewis observed that "women are . . . to a certain degree passionless. [Their] pivotal passion . . . is the maternal."[54] Elizabeth Blackwell criticized the view of women as passionless, but insisted that their passion was spiritual, not carnal. "Those who deny sexual feelings to women . . . confound appetite [i.e., carnal desire] and passion; they quite lose sight of this immense spiritual force of attraction . . . which exists in so very large a proportion in the womanly nature."[55] In other words, women's sexual feelings are passionate but only in their spiritual dimension. This spiritualization of female sexuality was taken as a sign of women's elevated moral and spiritual state. "Woman are not like men in sexual matters. They . . . do not love lust for lust's sake. Passion must come to them accompanied . . . with the tender graces of kindness . . . and self-denial, or they are quickly disgusted. Women have more of the motherly nature than the conjugal about them."[56] Indeed, "the higher women rise in moral and intellectual culture, the more is the sensual refined away from her nature, and the more pure and perfect and predominant becomes her motherhood."[57] The Victorians did not deny that women had sexual feelings or were passionate in intimate affairs. Rather, they posited a unique female sexuality that defined women's sexual feelings as essentially spiritual, i.e., as an impulse to nurture and bond. This spiritualization of female sexuality not only served as a control upon male sexual desire, which was considered carnal, aggressive and promiscuous, but ensured the tie between sex and its moral social function.

Proper sex within marriage centered on the act of coitus. Noncoital sex is rarely mentioned by Victorian writers, and when it is, it is always accompanied by prohibitions. There is, for example, no mention in the popular medical texts I examined of foreplay or oral-genital sex. Erotic fantasy was explicitly proscribed as it was thought to stimulate sensuality. Sex meant coitus. Describing the sex act, William Acton spoke of three phases: penal erection, penal insertion, and ejaculation and penal withdrawal from the vagina.[58] Variation with regard to coital position was deemed unnatural. The bipolar gender order was thought to require that men assumed the controlling role while women prepared to receive them. "We would say," wrote William Ashton, "that the female should lie upon her back. . . . All other positions are unnatural and unhealthy."[59] The act of coitus was supposed to be brief. Acton described it as lasting a few minutes. Although there was a range of opinion regarding the proper frequency of coitus—from once or twice a week to once every few years—moderation was recommended. Sex should never become a controlling motivation. Coitus more than twice a week was suspected to be a sign of sensual motivation and excess. Finally, assuming a healthy constitutional endowment on the part of husband and wife, sex would be a part of marriage for a limited period. When they reached the age of 50, sex would assume a much diminished role. The sex drive was thought to be either absent by that age or enfeebled to a point where it would have little significance in the marriage. "As with childhood, old age is a period in which the reproductive functions are quiescent. . . . Sexual life begins [normally and naturally] in puberty and, in the female, ends at about the age of 45 years, at the period known as the menopause."[60] Men's sexual life extends, according to Kellogg, to about the age of fifty.

MARRIAGE, SEX AND LOVE
The Antinomy of Sensuality and Love

Middle-class Victorians seemed, in the main, to accept sex as a natural and positive part of human life. If properly exercised, the sex instinct brings health, mental vigor, ambition, creativity and social progress. The proper sphere of sex is marriage.

Victorian advice writers endorsed the importance of sex in marriage provided that it was moderate in its frequency and did not incite sensual desires. William Acton's comment would be typical in this regard: "The moderate gratification of the sex-passion in married life is generally followed by the happiest consequences to the individual."[61] Indeed, Acton held that sex can contribute to sustaining the marital bond. "Physical attraction, again, helps to tide over many of those little domestic differences which occur in married life."[62] Acton recommended "moderation in sexual indulgence" for the married.[63] He believed, moreover, that since sex is a "pleasurable sensation . . . of momentary duration," its place in marriage would normally be quite limited.[64] To elevate the role of sexual expression in marriage would degrade the husband and wife to "the level of an animal."[65] Advice authors typically grounded an ethic of sexual moderation in the principles of physiology. "Too frequent emission of the life-giving fluid, and too frequent sexual excitation of the nervous system is . . . in itself most destructive."[66] The issue for these Victorians was not the legitimacy of sex in marriage, but to determine its proper place and role.

Pursuing this theme further, it is instructive to consider the highly influential reformer Sylvester Graham. In his *A Lecture to Young Men on Chastity*, Graham acknowledged that sexual expression and its concomitant pleasures are natural and, indeed, beneficial. "Constituted as we are, our bodies must be sustained, for the good of our nobler powers; and with the performance of the voluntary and necessary functions of our bodies, God has connected enjoyment; so that while we perform functions for the physical good of our bodies, and of our species, . . . we fulfill the purposes of our bodily functions with pleasure."[67] Sex is necessary, argued Graham, to promote individual health and guarantee the reproduction of the species. To ensure that these ends are accomplished, sex is accompanied by sensual pleasure. These pleasures serve as a means by which the purposes of nature and God are realized. Graham was adamant, however, that eroticism should never function as an end in itself. Sex should never be valued simply for its expressive or sensually pleasurable qualities. "When we exercise our genital organs in the function of reproduction . . . we have great enjoyment and healthful results in the function; but when the pleasures of that function become a leading object of our pursuits . . . the instinctive propensity itself becomes exceedingly depraved . . . and terribly pernicious in its effects."[68] Elevating erotic pleasure to an autonomous value opens the way to the dominance of animal passions over reason in human affairs. Controlled by sensual urges, the individual loses self-control and social purpose. This inevitably leads to self-destruction, social chaos and decline. Accordingly, Graham advised moderation and warned of grave misfortunes—from impotence to organic disease, insanity and suicide—to individuals who indulged excessively or pursued sensual pleasure as an end in itself. Graham's text is less helpful in understanding how Victorians related sex to love.

This theme was addressed by the practical phrenologist and Grahamian Orson Fowler. *Love and Parentage* affirmed erotic pleasure as one legitimate purpose of sex. "The legitimate exercise of this [sexual] faculty is designed and calculated, in and of itself, to yield a great amount of pleasure, besides that experienced by its living products."[69] Indeed, Fowler believed that mutual sexual pleasure was a requirement of a happy marriage. "Matrimonial felicity can no more be had without reciprocity and mutual pleasure here."[70] Yet, in typical Victorian style he assailed "[sexual] indulgence sought for its own sake" because it reduced humans to "a kind of animal tool, a mere sexual thing."[71] In a supplement to *Love and Parentage*, Fowler reversed his earlier position by condemning the uncoupling of sexual expression from a procreative role. "The one ultimate end designed to be secured by this propensity is offspring. Hence, it should be exercised only by way of carrying out its legitimate destiny. To exercise it merely for its own sake . . . as a means of sensual gratification . . . is a violation of its laws."[72] This is a Grahamian theme: sexual pleasure is legitimate only as a unintended consequence of the procreative act.

The role of sex in marriage is further clarified when we consider Fowler's notion of love. Although Fowler at times viewed sex as a sign of love, he did not identify sex as a significant component of love. Sexual expression is described as a duty or obligation of marriage; it is not definitive of love. The latter is seen as a spiritual phenomenon. Moreover, Fowler believed that the highest form of marriage is one based upon love. The tension between a marriage based upon a spiritual notion of love and the expectation of sex in marriage is the theme of the remainder of this section.

Fowler spoke of sex in relation to what he called "amativeness." This concept refers to an organic function that governs the sexual instinct. Amativeness is, like hunger or sleep, subject to the laws of nature. Amativeness is a magnetic attraction emanating from the genitals of the male and female. Fowler posited a physiological law which assumed a magnetic pull between the genital organs of the two sexes. This magnetic energy prompts the reproductive act. The mixing of magnet energies in the male and female ensures individual health and the reproduction of the species.

Fowler contrasted amativeness with love. Whereas the former pertains to a physical or sexual event, the latter is strictly spiritual. Paralleling his description of amativeness as a magnetic attraction between the male and female genital organs, Fowler conceived of love as a magnetic attraction between the gender traits of the two sexes. Love is an attraction between the masculine principle embodied in males and the feminine principle incarnated in females. "True love . . . appertains mainly to . . . this cohabitation of soul with a soul. . . . It is this spiritual affinity of the mental masculine and feminine for each other."[73] In other words, there is a magnetic attraction between masculine and feminine gender traits. "The man, in his very work, look, and action, gives off his masculine fluid a mentality, which his loving consort imbibes, and incorporates with her own, and vice versa as to women."[74] As the union of spiritual qualities conceived in bipolar gender terms, love is "a holy union of their inner natures."[75] From the vantage point of this spiritualized view of love, sexual intercourse itself appears more as a mental than a sensual act. "Nor should that intercourse which multiplies our race, be more sexual than mental and spiritual. . . . Indeed, the latter alone sanctifies the former—alone is human. All else is vulgar, debasing . . . because consisting . . . in the sensual indulgence of a animal propensity."[76] Fowler proposed that a spiritual notion of love renders erotic longings a threat to love and marriage. "No man or woman thoroughly indoctrinated with this cardinal truth of the spirituality of love . . . can become or remain licentious. To know and feel that it alone [i.e., the spirituality of love] embodies even sexual pleasure in its most perfect function . . . will root out sensuality and substitute moral purity."[77] Spiritual love and sensuality were conceived of as antithetical principles: "In exact proportion as the love of any individual tends to sexual gratification as such, it is debasing and brutal; because unguided by intellect and unsanctified by moral purity. . . . Whereas love based on the higher faculties kills sensuality as such, and remains satisfied with that spiritual inter-communion."[78]

If true love is spiritual, how did Fowler reconcile a marriage based upon love with the expectation of sex in marriage? His solution was to urge the desensualization of sex in marriage. "Indeed, spiritual love quells animal desire as such, and remains content with that holy communion of soul."[79] Marriage, in essence, becomes synonymous with spiritual love. "This perfect oneness of feeling and confluence of soul; the complete solution of every feeling and faculty of each with every feeling and faculty of the other, and longing for its attendant spiritual communion, alone constitutes true marriage."[80] In true marriage, sexual expression is desensualized and the place of sex is greatly restricted. Coitus becomes infrequent and confined to a procreative function. Indeed, Fowler encouraged a nongenital sexuality as ideally appropriate to true marriage, as it alone purges sex of sensuality. "Enjoyment of a higher order [can be found] in folding its beloved object in the arms of tenderness, and bestowing and receiving mutual caresses and embraces of love without one carnal desire as such. The supposition that all sensual pleasure is embodied in this ultimate function is most egregious."[81] Within the framework of true marriage, sex is cleansed of all sensual desires and pleasures; it functions as a vehicle to express spiritual love.

A pressing issue is to ascertain whether Fowler's view of the relation between sex, love and marriage was typical, at least of popular medical advice texts. It is my contention that while his attempt to ground these ideas in phrenology may be peculiar, the theme of the spiritualization of love is not.

Henry Guernsey, physician and author of *Plain Talk on Avoided Subjects,* asserted in no uncertain terms that sexual expression should be accepted as a natural aspect of being human. "The generative organs . . . are a part of us. . . . We must . . . accept . . . our bodies . . . and passions as they are."[82] Marriage was, of course, the proper domain of sex. Guernsey held, accordingly, that sex should be a necessary part of a happy marriage. "Orderly and well-regulated sexual intercourse is necessary to the married."[83] Indeed, Guernsey made it clear that sex was considered obligatory. "No women should ever marry without a full knowledge of her duties to her husband, particularly in the sexual respect, for without granting this privilege to her husband in full and free accord, there cannot be maintained a happy married life."[84] At the same time, Guernsey insisted that procreation was its principal aim. Sex for carnal pleasure was unacceptable. "All sexuality is in the idea of creation and, coming from the Lord, serves for high and holy purposes. It was never intended to be mere carnal

pleasure."[85] The place and meaning of sex in marriage is further clarified when Guernsey relates it to love. Conjugal love means "a union
of mind and communion of souls that lifts one above sensualism."[86]
It follows that in an ideal marriage or one based upon love, sex would
be desensualized. It would be conceived of as an act of spiritual union.
"To secure a real marriage, there must be a spiritual conjunction of
minds; and the conjunction of bodies in wedlock is simply the . . .
manifestation of spiritual principles in marriage."[87] Sexual expression
is affirmed, but only after it has been transfigured into an act of
spiritual union.

In many advice texts we find a weaker version of the spiritualization
of love theme. Sex is conceptualized as a part of love but its place is
highly circumscribed. Sensuality continues to be proscribed. Eliza
Duffey's *The Relation of the Sexes* nicely illustrates this symbolic configuration. Duffey frankly admitted that sex "enters as an important
element in marriage, especially for men."[88] Yet, she echoed the typical
contrast between love and sensuality. "Is it not possible that there
may be a love strong enough and abiding enough, untinged by [erotic]
passion, to hold a husband and wife firm and fast in its bonds, and
leave them little to desire? I believe it; I know it."[89] In an ideal marriage, the desensualization of sex would be of little consequence. Indeed, Duffey felt that it would be indicative of its moral elevation. "I
believe men and women can be happily married and even truly married with scarcely an atom of it [erotic desire], and I furthermore
believe that as a man and a woman continue in the conjugal relation,
this passionate feeling should be refined away and die out by degrees."[90] Duffey's final judgment on the place of sex in marriage reflects her devaluation of its role. "I believe in marriage all through—
the soul, the mind, the heart, and the body, and I would make the last
the weakest and least indispensable tie."[91]

The popular medical adviser Henry Chevasse struggled with the
problem of legitimating sex in a marriage ideally founded upon a
spiritual notion of love. He affirmed, at least initially, the place of sex
in marriage and love. "Love is not friendship. . . . Love contemplates
the indulgence of a passion which nature has implanted in all."[92] Nor
did Chevasse hesitate to acknowledge the pleasures we receive from
sex. "There can be no doubt that man is permitted this gratification
as one of the few pleasures granted him among so many sorrows and
cares."[93] Yet Chevasse maintained that, fundamentally, "love is an
attraction, a mental affinity."[94] Predictably, the standard opposition
between love and sensuality surfaces. "But while we thus speak of
pure and passionate love, we may refer to the animal passion, which
in no way is akin to love. We may gratify the passions of the body . . .

but this is not love."[95] Love may have entailed sexual expression, but it should lack any trace of carnal desire to avoid its degradation. Ultimately, sex should serve as a vehicle to exhibit spiritual love. Love must be passionate in a marriage but when "passion is [sensual] gratification, love ceases in such cases."[96]

Victorian advice authors acknowledged sex and the pleasures accompanying it as a legitimate aspect of marriage. They simultaneously defined love as a spiritual relationship which is the essential meaning of marriage. This created a dilemma. Insofar as sexual feelings easily evoked sensual desires, the norm of sex in marriage threatened to undermine its spiritual basis. Victorians reacted by demanding the desensualization of sex. Love and eroticism were framed as antithetical. Sensual desire did not of course simply disappear. Rather, it was supposed to be sublimated into the quest for spiritual and social companionship between the husband and the wife. Sex itself was transfigured into a spiritual act.

By way of concluding this section, I wish to briefly comment upon the link between the spiritualization of love and an emerging ideal of marriage as a sphere of companionship and self-fulfillment. Contemporary historians have noted that the emphasis in advice literature on limiting sexual expression was at least in part intended to improve women's lives.[97] To the extent that sex carried significant dangers for women (e.g., unwanted pregnancy, disease, death, and the stigma of impurity or looseness), minimizing sex and giving women control over this activity expanded their autonomy. From this vantage point, we can interpret the movement to spiritualize love and marriage as part of women's struggle to improve the quality of their lives. By appealing to an ideology of spiritual love, women had available a cogent rationale for enforcing male self-control. This undoubtedly enhanced women's power in marriage. Beyond promoting female autonomy, the notion of the spirituality of love entailed a new ideal of marriage. A marriage based on spiritual love carried high expectations for personal happiness and companionship.

This new ideal of marriage was frequently contrasted by advice writers with two other concepts: first, a pragmatic notion that frames marriage as a mutually beneficial practical exchange. The wife provides a range of personal and domestic services in return for social security and a respectable social status. A second romantic ideal describes marriage as resting upon erotic passions. In place of these two concepts of marriage, advice writers, especially in the second half of the century, proposed a view of marriage as a domain of companionship and self-realization. Imbuing marriage with expectations of personal happiness found support among many women because it provided a rationale for birth control and a normative basis to expand their demands for autonomy. Eliza Duffey, for example, appealed to this marital ideal in order to legitimate women's aspirations for freedom. "Men and women were made for themselves. . . . It is man's imperative duty to make the very utmost of himself. Every faculty must be educated, and brought into use. . . . Let him subdue his passions and thoroughly master himself in all his instincts. . . . When he has done all this, let him have children if he dare."[98] In the ideal marriage, "man and woman will live for the present. . . . In marriage they will see greater opportunities for self-development and harmonized action."[99] In the advice literature of the late nineteenth century, marriage was frequently viewed as a vehicle to bring personal happiness. "God set man and woman in pairs, that they might perfect each other, and complete each other's happiness. The irresistible desire for companionship is what incites to marriage more than the intoxication of the senses. . . . A perfect marriage means perfect companionship, a blending of individual tastes, wishes and wills. . . . It makes a union of all that is manly and womanly in a perfect whole."[100]

Women were not alone in promoting this ideal of marriage. John Cowan's *The Science of a New Life* endorsed the same ideal. Assailing marriages based on pragmatic or utilitarian grounds, Cowan proposed that marriage is the "opportunity . . . to improve all domestic, social and higher faculties of the mind, and of guiding the man and woman to a higher . . . standard of life."[101] He argued that "the true end of marriage . . . is the perfection of existence."[102] In an ideal marriage the union of husband and wife is based on their complementary qualities. Such a marriage should contribute to self-realization while preserving the solidarity of the union. "Perfect sexual love comes only of a perfect union—a union of resemblance of mind, soul, and body."[103] A "perfect union" requires a perfect meshing of the personal character of husband and wife. "If the man has the social faculties fully developed, so should his wife. If the man possess well-developed perceptive, reasoning, and reflective power, so should the wife. . . . It is necessary to a perfect union that the man and wife be equally developed, or as nearly so as possible."[104] Toward the end of the century, Victorians promulgated a view of marriage that valued it for its opportunities for self-fulfillment and social solidarity apart from other social or moral functions.

ADVICE LITERATURE AND THE REALITY OF THE VICTORIAN CULTURE OF INTIMACY

My analysis of Victorian intimate culture has relied upon popular medical and advice texts. The question needs to be at least briefly considered whether these documents are reliable indicators of cultural reality. Is this literature, as some historians have argued, prescriptive? Does it reflect a reform movement opposed to existing conventions and norms of intimate life? If so, in what sense, if any, can these cultural constructs be interpreted as indicators of a dominant cultural configuration? I will argue that their popularity, their support by important social institutions, and the fact that their key ideas surface in other movements make it plausible to interpret these texts as important documents of mainstream, middle-class Victorian public culture.[105]

Any attempt to ascertain the status of these discourses must reckon with their popularity.[106] William Acton's *The Function and Disorder of the Reproductive Organs* appeared in 1857 and by 1894, twenty years after his death, an eighth edition was published. Carl Degler says of Acton's book that it "was undoubtedly one of the most widely quoted books on sexual problems and diseases in the English speaking world."[107] Orson Fowler's *Love and Parentage* went through thirteen editions between 1844 and 1850. Fowler authored numerous popular books and, like many other advice authors, lectured widely. William Alcott published dozens of advice texts. His *Young Man's Guide* went through twenty-one editions in the course of two decades. His *Physiology of Man*, which was originally published in 1855, sold 27,000 copies by 1866. By the 1830s a popular health movement promoting sexual reform ideas was sufficiently powerful to repeal, in state after state, medical licensing laws that were considered essential to creating a medical monopoly for "regular" physicians. Samuel Thomson's *New Guide to Health* sold over 100,000 copies by 1839. By the mid-nineteenth century the Thomsonian movement claimed four million followers.[108] Another reformer, Sylvester Graham, initiated a popular health movement that gained considerable support among the working class as well. Graham's writing, especially *A Lecture to Young Men on Chastity*, became highly influential among medical regulars as well as reformers.[109] It went through ten editions in fifteen years.

Not only were the medical reformers quite popular among ordinary people, but their ideas were adopted by institutions and organizations that carried public prestige and authority in the nineteenth century. Their ideas found support in the emerging medical establishment toward the end of the century. Dr. Henry Kellogg, whose *Plain Facts for Old and Young* sold over 300,000 copies by 1910, drew heavily on the writings of Graham. He carried reform themes into the medical profession. Dr. Russell Trall, whose *Sexual Physiology and Hygiene* went through twenty-eight editions between 1866 and 1881, joined Graham's hygiene movement. Alongside Kellogg's and Trall's popular works in the 1870s, Dr. John Cowan's *The Science of a New Life*, a text that incorporates the central reform themes, was a near bestseller.

Dr. Frederick Hollick's *The Marriage Guide* went through 300 editions between 1850 and 1875. Dr. Edward Bliss Foote's *Medical Common Sense* sold over 250,000 copies by 1900. The widely cited *Tokology* by Alice Stockham was reprinted forty-five times between 1883 and 1897. Dr. Joseph Howe, author of *Excessive Venery, Masturbation and Continence,* a text which draws heavily on reform themes, was a medical establishment figure. As a professor of clinical surgery in Bellevue Hospital Medical College, fellow of the New York Academy of Medicine, member of the New York County Medical and Surgical societies, visiting surgeon to Charity and St. Francis hospitals, and much more besides, Dr. Howe carried the growing authority of these prestigious institutions in his writings. Dr. Samuel Woodward, whose *Hints for the Young in Relation to the Health of Body and Mind* exhibits the chief reform themes, originally published this text in the *Boston Medical and Surgical Journal* for his colleagues in the medical profession. In short, the key ideas of advice texts acquired the institutional authority that was accruing to the medical profession by the late nineteenth century. Carroll Smith-Rosenberg observes that "[during the first half of the nineteenth century] the reformers constituted a group quite separate from, and self-consciously at war with, the medical establishment. . . . It was only with mid-century that the establishment began to adopt the reformers' ideology."[110]

The sexual ideas of the popular medical advisers were not socially marginal. Not only were their views incorporated into what was becoming a medical establishment, but they found support in various religious and reform groups that by mid-century assumed a prominent role in shaping social mores. The proliferation of moral reform societies has been well documented. From Lyman Beecher's "Society for the Suppression of Vice and the Promotion of Good Morals" (1812), to the "Magdalen Society" created in the 1830s to abolish prostitution, to the myriad moral educationalist, hygienic and temperance organizations, these evangelical-inspired reform groups carried the principal sexual ideas of the popular advisers to millions of Americans.[111]

Typical is the Female Moral Reform Society, which in the 1840s had more than four hundred chapters in the Northeast and mid-Atlantic states. Drawing on evangelical Christian themes, these women reformers were responding to the perceived erosion of traditional social controls as young men and women migrated to cities. The reformers underscored the dangers of the atomistic individualism associated with urban life. In particular, they pointed to the dangers tied to the expanded inducements and opportunities for sexual indulgence.

The Female Moral Reform Society sought to provide forms of moral regulation appropriate to an altered social milieu. Central to their agenda was the reform of standards of sexual morality. They aimed to abolish the double standard and place more responsibility for restraint upon the individual. In addition, they sought to purge the public sphere of sexual representations and to restrict sexual expression to heterosexual marriage. Women were to be assigned the chief responsibility in controlling sex. Commenting on the impulse to sexual reform in the Female Moral Reform Society, Mary Ryan says, "Female Moral Reformers would not tolerate . . . permissive attitudes and attempted to purge local culture of all suggestions of casual, lenient sexuality."[112]

Similar reform themes appear in another moral reform movement, the American Tract Society. Located initially in New York City, this association aimed to preserve individual virtue and moral order by educating the public through the mass distribution of religious pamphlets. Paul Boyer tells us that this literature promoted one abiding message. "The individual who breaks free of the web of moral restraint to pursue his personal interests and pleasures, or who indulges " 'sensual lusts' . . . in violation of the rules of sobriety and chastity, faces a grim fate."[113] Self-control through the internalization of evangelical Protestant moral percepts (e.g., sobriety, purity, domesticity) was recommended. Boyer notes that by 1850 over five million tracts were being published annually, a fact surely indicative of the broad social resonance of its message.

It would be wrong to assume that these reform groups found their support predominantly among the more conservative segment of the population. Indeed, it is a mistake to characterize these movements in terms of present ideological categories. The agenda of these reformers can be read as having a "progressive" dimension in their historical context. The demand to abolish prostitution and the double standard, to desexualize the public sphere, to place elaborate restraints and responsibilities around sexual expression, and to give women control over sex, enhanced women's autonomy and status. It is, then, hardly surprising to learn that feminists, in the main, endorsed the sexual themes of these social reform groups. Linda Gordon documents feminist opposition to contraception since it was perceived as threatening to uncouple sex and conception and therefore to separate sex from marriage. This was thought by many feminists to be against their self-interest since women's power and status was thought to lay in their claim to moral superiority associated with the roles of wife and mother. Feminists demanded only that women control the timing of sex; they did not dispute, says Gordon, the link of sex to motherhood. In this regard it is instructive that the first birth control movement, the "Voluntary Motherhood" movement of the 1870s, enjoined sexual abstinence, not contraceptive use. Gordon points to the kinship between feminists and reformers with regard to their sexual ethics. "Throughout every reform movement, feminist influence tended to coincide with an attack on 'expressiveness' in sex. But this did not mean that the authors of these attacks hated sex absolutely. Rather they were concerned to make women's risks (e.g., health, pregnancy, violence) calculated, to create some limitations on men's unilateral right to define every sexual encounter."[114]

The implications of the above are twofold. First, these remarks underscore the fact that there was a pre-existing cultural receptivity to the sexual ideas of the popular medical advisers. In other words, we can reasonably infer from the popularity of advice literature and the widespread support of reform groups that many middle-class Americans endorsed similar beliefs and norms regarding sex. Sex advisers may have been critical or opposed to certain sexual conventions and norms, but that in no way denies that their ideas were descriptive of common beliefs and sentiments about sex. There is no contradiction in holding these two propositions. Reformers, at least popular ones, are popular and effective only to the extent that they express or articulate widely held feelings and ideals. Second, we can infer from the popularity of sex advice literature that its sexual ideology became part of the sexual culture of the nineteenth century. This conclusion is made more compelling when we recall that by the late nineteenth century the ideas of the sex reformers had acquired the institutional authority of science, medicine, religion and the backing of the state. At a minimum, it is fair to say that the sexual ideas of the reformers assumed the status of one publically available and legitimate construction of sexuality and love. The public and authoritative status of this discourse rendered it descriptive of at least one credible set of sexual beliefs and norms of nineteenth-century Victorian America.

CONCLUSION

The Victorians, at least as represented in medical advice literature between 1830 and 1890, did not deny the centrality of sex in their lives. They did not shroud sex in a veil of silence. Nor did they wish to repress all sexual longing. Instead, they consistently, perhaps obsessively, acknowledged its presence and power. It was precisely because sex was elevated to a force of such consequential proportions that they felt compelled to detail its proper use and to describe the evils that accompany its misuse. The Victorians sought to discern the natural laws of sex in order to exploit its powers to benefit the individual and society.

To benefit humanity, moral boundaries had to be erected around the sex instinct. In particular, the Victorians hoped to harness the benevolent power of sex while not activating sensuality with its logic of excess and ruin. Their strategy involved compartmentalizing sex or cordoning it off from other spheres of life. Sex was to be restricted to heterosexual marriage and, within that domain, it was centered on coitus. Since sexual intercourse within marriage was no protection against sensuality, an ethic of self-control enjoining the individual to extinguish all carnal thoughts and desires became necessary. Ultimately, sexual desire had to be transfigured into a quest for spiritual love in order to render it a benevolent power. Proposing to make love the basis of marriage may have allowed Victorians to control sexual desire, but it also demanded the de-eroticization of sex. This imperative, however, conflicted with the legitimation of pleasure as a condition of realizing the hygienic and moral benefits of sex. This conflict intensified to the extent that Victorians interpreted the spiritualization of love as a mandate to elevate marriage by desexualizing it. This contradicted their abiding belief in the omnipresence and benevolent power of the sexual instinct.

In their quest to make sex a benevolent power, the Victorians produced an elaborate system of sexual order. Pivotal is a contrast between coitus within marriage practiced in moderation and joined to social and spiritual ends and sex that occurs outside marriage, and sex that is noncoital or carnal in motivation. Masturbation played such an important role in the Victorian imagination precisely because it sharply violated sexual norms. It was a solitary and pleasure-oriented act. Many advice writers placed masturbation under the more general category of onanism, a concept that referred to a wide range of proscribed sexual acts or desires. For Chevasse, onanism covered *coitus interruptus*, pederasty, the use of a condom, and any sex that was pleasure-oriented.[115] James Scott described "onanism as a term of comprehensive meaning, applicable in a broad sense to all forms of sexual stimulation employed by either sex, singly or mutually, to produce orgasm in unnatural ways—i.e., otherwise than by coitus. The onanistic acts are as follows: 'withdrawal,' . . . pederasty; bestiality; 'mutual masturbation,' self-pollution, etc. None of these acts have in view the perpetuation of the species, all are therefore perversions."[116] Within this sexual regime all sexual thoughts, feelings and acts which fall outside coitus in marriage motivated by hygienic or spiritual considerations are unnatural. Hence, all nonmarital, noncoital sex and all sensual thoughts, feelings and acts are deemed unacceptable. They are, ultimately, taken as a sign of a deep psychological and moral defect. In their quest to harness the power of sex as a force of progress, the Victorians invested sex with enormous importance. Sexual thoughts and feelings as well as discrete sexual acts assumed a heightened personal and social significance. Sexual expression served as a sign of the physical and moral health of the individual and society.

2

True Love, Victorian-Style

A Spiritual Longing

In white middle-class Victorian culture, the importance of sex was not denied. The proliferation of popular medical and advice texts detailing the nature of the sex instinct and its proper function bears witness to the Victorian willingness, even compulsion, to speak about sex. These Victorians made sex into a topic of urgent public and personal concern. Sex could not be ignored or suppressed because it was viewed as a dynamic force shaping the fate of humanity.

The Victorian discourses on sex did not, in the main, advocate a repressive sexual ethic. For example, the popular medical literature spoke of the positive, beneficial aspects of sex, including moderate sensual pleasures. These Victorians sought to create a sexual regime that preserved the beneficent powers of sex while avoiding its ruinous excesses. The dangers of sex revolved around the possibility of erotic motivations controlling behavior. The pursuit of sensual pleasure was thought to drive the individual down the path of excess and inevitable decline. For the sex instinct to be empowering and elevating, the place of eroticism had to be circumscribed. By the mid-nineteenth century, many middle-class men and women thought that the control over sexuality was passing from external agencies (e.g., the family and the church) to the institution of marriage and the internal control of individual conscience.[1]

Marriage was considered the only legitimate sphere of sex. The permanent mutual responsibilities between husband and wife ensured the control of the sex drive. Moreover, since marriage was a domain of spiritual love, there were norms of mutual respect and propriety that could be appealed to in order to limit sexual expression. The ideal of a marriage based upon love was thought to function as a brake upon the propensity of sexual feelings to incite carnal desire. Love elevated marriage above a mere sexual or social exchange by rendering it a spiritual union.

In the previous chapter I analyzed the complex ways that sex was related to love. We observed that many Victorians believed in the power and beneficial effects of sex. Yet, sexual expression simultaneously opened the way toward the sexualization of marriage which could threaten its spiritual essence. Victorians tried to maintain a delicate balance between the sexual and spiritual aspects of intimacy. Some Victorians sought to purge marriage not only of eroticism but of virtually all nonprocreative sexuality. One unintended consequence of this effort to de-eroticize intimacy was the emergence of a sexual underworld that threatened the purity of marriage. These contradictory tendencies are at the core of the Victorian culture of intimacy.

In this chapter I will further examine the meaning of the Victorian notion of love and its relation to sexual expression. I will expand upon my thesis that many Victorians represented love as a spiritual phenomenon. I have drawn on dozens of personal documents to probe further into the meaning of Victorian love. In the concluding section of this chapter, I will offer an account of the social sources of the Victorian spiritual ideal of love.

MAKING SEX SAFE
From Eroticism to Altruism

For Victorians, eroticism or the pursuit of sensual pleasure as an end in itself was considered dangerous. The moral disapproval Victorians attached to eroticism relates to their association of sensual desire with egoism and the loss of self-control, rather than from any aversion to the body. An individual controlled by sensual motivations was considered to be reduced to an animal level of existence. Such a person was thought to be self-centered, impulsive and amoral. To be fully legitimate, sex had to promote a social and moral end.

Marriage was, of course, the proper sphere for sexual expression. Sex was an expected and integral part of marriage. This follows from two assumptions that were widely shared. First, sex for mature adults is necessary for health reasons. Indeed, moderate sexual pleasures were thought to enhance mutual affection between husband and wife. Second, the permanence of the marriage bond and its responsibilities lessens the potentially serious risks of sex—e.g., disease, violence and unwanted pregnancy. Only in the context of a marriage as a social bond based on mutual trust, respect and affection could sex avoid the dangers of sensuality. Marriage was considered to have the capacity to render sex an uplifting moral force.

Sexual expression in marriage was, ultimately, valued as a spiritual and moral act. The moral significance of sex was related to the altruistic meanings that were attached to its generative power. Sex was the means by which the family as a principal moral sphere of society originated. By connecting sex to the creation and continuity of the family, Victorians gave to it an essentially moral and spiritual import. Living in a family entails, for both husband and wife, duties and responsibilities to the child and to each other. The self-sacrifice and moral responsibilities that obtain in a family make it the principal moral and spiritual formative force in society. In addition, since sex was the means by which women became mothers and men became fathers, it was imbued with meanings having to do with realizing true womanhood and manhood. For example, feminists may have challenged the coercive condition under which women became mothers, but they rarely doubted that for a woman motherhood was "the felt climax of her being."[2]

Sex made possible the continuation of civilization. Through sexual intercourse, society replenishes its population, creates a labor force, and a new generation to further the progress of society. The act of coitus was thought of as a moral act—a sacrifice of the interests of the self in the present for humanity in the future. The high moral significance attached to the procreative act is conveyed by the feminist Sarah Grimké. "In marriage is the origin of life. In the union of the sexes exists a creative energy which is found nowhere else. Human nature tends to the uses of all the faculties with which it is endowed. . . . Hence the creative (or generative organ) is stronger than any other faculty, birth being the great fact of our existence here, and its legitimate exercise is the most natural result of the purest and more unselfish love."[3] Equally revealing of the moral importance attached to coitus is the frank exchange between Lucy Stone and her kin. In response to Lucy's persisting reservations about sex in marriage, Luther Stone remarks: "In answer to your inquiry about sexual intercourse I shall say in brief that all the organs he [God] has given to man are to be used with reference to his glory. Our generative organs should never be used except for propagation."[4] Francis Stone reminded a nervous Lucy of the essentially moral meaning of sex. "Have them [children] as fast as you can if you can take care of them, and . . . obey the command given to our first parents to multiply and replenish the Earth. . . . Think of the multitudes that have lived and that will live who would never had an existence, had the generations past and the generations to come acted as you advise."[5] Sex, of course, implicated Victorians in physical acts and, indeed, hygienic and, to a lesser extent, hedonistic rationales legitimated sex apart from its procreative purpose. Yet, in the end, sex had for Victorians a deeply spiritual and moral meaning that was anchored in its generative function. Sex was viewed as a means to demonstrate a selfless spiritual love for humanity and God. Sex was a chief way to achieve moral elevation through demonstrating self-control and self-sacrifice for society.

Sex was not, however, a way to demonstrate and sustain love. Although some Victorians viewed sex as a sign of love, sex, especially as a medium of erotic pleasure, played little or no role in the way Victorians thought about love.[6] This was inevitable given the tight connection assumed between sexual feelings and eroticism. To link sex to love was to risk a marriage awash in lust. Indeed, the spiritualization of love was one way to control sex and especially to keep eroticism in its place in marriage.

Clarifying the meaning of love is the aim of the remainder of this chapter. I begin by singling out three documents that provide insight into the dynamics of heterosexual love.

LOVE AS SPIRITUAL

The letters of Byron Caldwell Smith to Katherine Stephens will serve as my first case study. These letters were composed between 1874 and 1876, while Byron, a young professor and journalist, was courting Katherine, who was completing an advanced college degree. Throughout the courtship the two lovers saw each other only occasionally and for brief periods. The intensity and openness of Byron's feelings and the extended period of courtship makes these letters exceptionally revealing of Victorian beliefs and norms about love.

Following what was apparently the custom among the middle class, Byron took the initiative in pursuing Katherine. He repeatedly pressed her to acknowledge her love for him. "Oh, write, write I am perishing to see on paper the words—I love you."[7] To elicit this declaration, Byron reassures Katherine of how much she means to him. "For me life has but one solution—it must be filled with Katherine."[8] Byron speaks of his love for Katherine as "a great passion that fills me."[9] Yet Byron is careful to communicate to Katherine that his "great passion" is not a "romantic" type of love. The latter is described as transient and superficial—"a golden vagary, a self-created illusion, a spring—dream full of the flutter of doves' wings."[10] Byron describes his love for Katherine not as romantic but as "true love." True love is permanent, constant and elementary, an affair of the heart and soul, not of the body and desire. Hoping to convince Katherine that his love is, indeed, true, he tells her: "I love that deep subtle . . . heart that loves me."[11] But Katherine initially withheld her love, apparently having some doubts about whether Byron's feelings were really true love. Byron writes Katherine feeling somewhat hurt and indignant. "You had fears of my constancy! Heavens!"[12] In order to assuage Katherine's anxieties, Byron had to assure her repeatedly of the constancy of his love. Toward that end, Byron emphasizes that his love is not incidental or superficial but involves the deepest, most elementary parts of himself. "How could I be false to a feeling I could not stifle in my despair!"[13] Trying to assure Katherine that his love is sincere, he describes what he means by true love. "It is to love with all one's soul what is pure, what is high, what is eternal."[14] Byron repeatedly characterizes his love for Katherine in spiritual terms. "To feel that overpowering, tender yearning in which all things blend that are high, ardent and pure."[15] In a letter written toward the end of his courtship, he reiterates this spiritual notion of love. "A tender true heart that loves unselfishly and seeks and understands a love which is not the mere surprise of the senses . . . but why should I go on to describe what I love to her I love?"[16] In short, true love is essentially spiritual and therefore constant and true. Because such a spiritual longing springs from the very core of an individual and involves one's whole being, it is a "great life-passion."

True love is ennobling. Because it is pure and ardent, it is morally elevating. Indeed, Byron appeals to the power of true love to reinvigorate his own waning ambitions. "Your love is the world to me, and in it I shall find everything again, the sweet face of nature, the pleasant want of work, ambitions long forgotten."[17] The power of love goes beyond such utilitarian benefits. Byron continually defines love as a religious experience. "Dear Heart, your letter breathes that aspiring sentiment which makes our love a true worship. To be constant, tender, passionate is not enough for it. My heart, at least, in the excess of these, the elements of love feels a new sense born, and I have no word for it but worship."[18] Elsewhere, Byron describes the love between a man and a woman as the way in which the "Holy power" is revealed. "I feel somehow that the Holy power which sustains and moves the ancient universe . . . reveals itself to me as love."[19] Love appears as a truly religious way of being. "To love you . . . and to sink my life in the Divine life through you, seem to me the supreme end of my existence."[20] If love is viewed within a Christian religious framework, its essential meaning can only be spiritual. "Love is a cult and our love shall be our religion. . . . To each other we shall reveal only the divine attributes of tenderness and patience."[21] Sadly, Byron and Katherine were never married. Initially, financial considerations kept them apart and later his illness and death separated them forever.

The attempt to reconcile the Christian moral duty to love God with conjugal love figured prominently in the correspondence between the abolitionist and minister Theodore Weld and Angelina Grimké, abolitionist and feminist. Unlike Byron Smith, for whom conjugal love itself became a form of religious worship, Angelina and Theodore were more reflective in considering the Christian duty to love God and the heightened expectations of romantic love. Angelina, in particular, feared that conjugal love was a type of idolatry. "Am I putting *thee* in the place of Jesus? I am alarmed and confounded by my feelings. . . . I feel at times as if I cannot live without thee. . . . Am I sinning or would the Lord our Father have it so?" Angelina quickly tried to assuage her own anxiety. "I think it is all his work yet I am afraid to say so."[22] Conjugal love acquired legitimacy for Angelina only if she could see it as a divinely motivated and sanctioned act. "From the moment you were assured that I loved you, we became one—our Father has enjoined us together, he has given us to each other. . . . I feel that we are two equal halves of our perfect whole, and that our Father in Heaven smiles down upon the holy union."[23] Yet, Angelina wanted reassurance from Theodore. He harbored no reservations. Conjugal love was the work of God and a Christian duty. "How many times have I felt my heart . . . reaching out in very agony after you, and *cleaving* to you, feeling that we are *no more* twain but *one* flesh. Do you ask, is not this idolatry? I answer I have never had a sweeter consciousness of Divine Approval."[24] Indeed, Theodore interprets his love for Angelina as bringing him closer to God. "Do I love my blessed Savior *less* because I love *you as* I do? My heart beareth me witness that my love for you has greatly quickened me in . . . a more near and tender communion with him who loved us and died for us."[25] For both Angelina and Theodore, living a full Christian life is not at odds with conjugal love. But, we need to ask, what kind of love is this that carries divine approval?

Angelina describes her love as an affair of the heart and soul. "Yes my heart continuously *cleaves* to you, the deep of my nature is moved to meet the reaching agonies of your soul after me."[26] Theodore speaks in the same idiom. "How many times have I felt my heart . . . reaching out in every agony after you and *cleaving* to you, feeling that we are no more twain but one flesh."[27] Love is not an affair of the body and its desires, but a matter of the heart and its spiritual longings. Love is imagined as an overpowering spiritual affinity, an intermingling of souls that makes two individuals spiritually one.

An interesting exchange between Angelina and Theodore in which they puzzle over the dynamics of heterosexual love reveals much about what love meant to them. Angelina wonders why she is not satisfied with her love for the women in her life. "Why does not the love of my own dear sister . . . satisfy. . . . Why do I feel in my inmost soul that you, you only, can fill up the deep void that is there?"[28] Anxious that this utterance may suggest to Theodore a sensual basis of love, Angelina immediately remarks, "Then again I think I can say with you, it is the spirit . . . a disembodied spirit, with none of the associations . . . of the physical nature which moves upon me with overcoming power."[29] Angelina is convinced that her love for Theodore is essentially spiritual, not physical or carnal in origin and essence.

In an elaborate reply to Angelina's curiosity about heterosexual love, Theodore endorses the proposition that only heterosexual love is truly fulfilling. This is not, however, because of any erotic attraction between the sexes but stems from a deep, mysterious spiritual affinity. It is the mental, moral and social affinities between the two genders that explain the origin and necessity of heterosexual love. Theodore believes that the two sexes represent two different yet naturally complementary human types whose physical differences are indicative of mental, moral and social differences. It is these spiritual complementarities that form the basis of love. In the passage excerpted below, Theodore declares that any physical attraction between the sexes is not only irrelevant to love but is antithetical to it. "That to the mind in the exercise of this [conjugal] love the [physical] differences of sex is not a matter of consciousness . . . that it [physical sex differences] is not only not the original exciting cause of it but is, when suggested to the mind . . . an unwelcome intruder, of which the mind instinctively and instantly rids itself, feeling it to be a disturbing force, a felt non conductor, intercepting the progress of the soul toward the spirit that draws it and a veil dimming its vision of the loved one. That love is produced by the perception and apprehension of qualities, moral, intellectual, spiritual, social, sympathetic, etc. combined."[30] For Theodore, the mere consciousness of a physical or erotic aspect to love is said to be a "disturbing force" which detracts and obstructs the way to true love. Ultimately, Theodore underscores the origin of heterosexual love in an innate spiritual longing for individual completeness or wholeness. "I suppose that persons of the *same* sex cannot so intensely be drawn toward each other . . . for being of the *same* sex than their love is *not* aided by the . . . united and simultaneous affinities of *all* the susceptibilities of the compound nature acting together."[31] Only in the opposite sex does each of us find those spiritual elements which alone will make us complete and fulfilled. We gravitate, as if compelled by an unconscious force, "toward and after the absent half of . . . [our] own very identity."[32]

True love is then described as spiritual. "True love," reflects Angelina, "is the seeking of the spirit after spiritual communion, . . . the union of *heart* and *mind* and *soul*."[33] Because true love is described as a quest for spiritual union, lovers must know each other in a full and deep spiritual way in order to judge their spiritual kinship. True love must never be based on a merely incidental attraction or a superficial acquaintance. Instead, only on the basis of a full self-disclosure requiring each individual to reveal all the relevant details about oneself is true love possible. Love may be spiritual, but it must be entered into in a deliberate way. Accordingly, mutual self-disclosure functions as a norm of Victorian love.

Once Angelina and Theodore confess their mutual love, both proceed, in page after page of detail, to tell everything about themselves. Theodore, in particular, insists that Angelina must be aware of all his character defects and singular habits so that her love is not based on any deception or falsely romantic idea about himself. He proceeds to record in detail his most basic and intimate emotions, behaviors, habits and aspirations. "Now my beloved, I have told you in all frankness the chief, as far as I know them, of my deficiencies, follies, weakness, repulsive habits, ignorance, shame, and guilt. . . . I pray you not to understand me as asserting that I have told you all my evil habits and tempers and practices—that would take volumes. But merely that there is nothing either in my heart or history which I do not desire you to know. Nothing however base, disgraceful or loathsome which I would not put you in possession of, because I feel that it is preeminently your right and my privilege to develop it to you—yes if my whole heart and history were a transparency, with every feeling, word, and deed a point of light, I could send it with this letter for you to study the whole. . . . I would hold it before you till you had read it all. . . . I will not marry you Angelina with a curtain round my heart or a false gloss on my character."[34] Angelina concurs with Theodore that true love must not be based upon romantic feelings, with the inevitable idealization and transitory desires, but on a thorough knowledge of each other's inner nature. "I thank you a thousandfold for telling me your faults. I believe that those who look forward as we do to a sacred union ought to know and *study* each others characters. . . . Love which is blind to each others faults must be transient in its existence and *fatal* in its effect."[35]

Angelina and Theodore assume that only true love should be the basis of marriage. A marriage based upon a calculation of security, status, property or sexual desire is, they thought, debased. As Angelina says, the kernel of marriage is true love. "In the sight of God we are married, even tho we should never see each other face to face; from the moment you were assured that I loved you, we became one—our Father has joined us together."[36] The marriage ceremony is but the external sign of an inward state of spiritual love or union. Yet,

Angelina and Theodore disagreed regarding the purpose of marriage.[37] Angelina spoke of the "perfection of our being" and "happiness" as "the great end" of marriage. Theodore believed that this view of marriage diminished its pure and elevated moral status. "Why Angelina you know I don't love and marry you in order to promote my happiness. . . . My determination to marry you, is no result of a *calculation* that it will make me happy. To love you, to marry you is a mightly END in itself. . . . I marry you because my own inmost being mingles with your being and is already married to it, both joined in one by God's own voice."[38]

For Theodore, any utilitarian or pragmatic rationale for marriage, including approaching marriage as a means to individual happiness, diminishes its elevated spiritual and moral meaning. Rejecting utilitarian reasons for marriage does not mean, however, that practical considerations do not have an important role to play in marriage. Pressed by Angelina and his own conscience, Theodore offers a final statement detailing the rational and practical considerations that should be taken into account in marriage. "Persons who contemplate uniting in that sacred union should study each other profoundly and know each other perfectly. . . . They should . . . converse together on *all* the responsibilities involved in the marriage relation. . . . They should fix upon plans of life, modes of employment, the system by which to regulate their household, its order, rules, mode of living, dress, equipage, furniture, diet, regimen, exercise, family habits, hours, times and seasons, etc." The seriousness of marriage is based not only upon the fact that it involves extensive moral responsibilities, but that marriage is "the nucleus and original constituent of the social state."[39]

The opposition between "romantic" and "true love" appeared prominently in middle class Victorian culture. We have observed it in the tireless efforts of Byron Smith to persuade Katherine Stephens that his love is true because it is spiritual, constant and altruistic, not sensual, short-lived and egoistic. This antithesis is even more evident in the correspondence between Angelina and Theodore. Theodore shows disdain for a conjugal love founded upon sensual motivations and pleasures. It reduces human love to the level of animal attraction. He rejects, as well, romance as a basis of marriage since it involves excessive idealization, false hopes and deception. Angelina is no less contemptuous of a love which is anything less than ardently spiritual. It is telling in this regard that Angelina and Theodore declared their mutual love *before* having seen each other. Moreover, having proclaimed their love for each other, they proceeded to "test" its sincerity through an ordeal of critical mutual self-disclosure. Only this ordeal could determine whether their love was true and founded upon elementary, constant and spiritual affinities, or merely romantic and therefore based on illusory hopes and transitory feelings. Although these two case studies reveal an opposition between an erotically charged romantic love and a spiritual concept of true love, there is little evidence of an internal conflict. The case of Isabella Maud Rittenhouse suggests that at least some middle-class Victorians experienced this opposition as an on-going inner conflict between two models of love. Maud's diary, which records the details of a rich premarital romantic life, affords us a glimpse of a Victorian for whom a more "modern" concept of romantic love may have been unconventional, but was not without some social credibility.[40]

Maud was the object of many suitors. Between 1882 and 1884, the period covered in her diary, I count at least five serious suitors. Yet, two men held a privileged place in Maud's quest for love. Her first love is Robert Witherspoon. He is described as handsome, charming, highly educated, cultivated and exciting. Her thoughts of him frequently turn to his physical attractiveness. Maud can hardly think of Robert without feeling swept away. Robert clearly represents a romantic love object for Maud.

Maud's other suitor is Elmer Comings. Elmer is described as a good man who is ambitious, hard-working, reliable, responsible and kind. We are led to believe that he is plain-looking, socially awkward, and unexceptional with regard to his talents, intelligence and social graces. The opposition between Robert and Elmer, her ambivalent feelings toward them, represents Maud's internal conflict between the ideals of romantic and true love. The way this conflict is resolved is instructive. Maud rejects Robert. Although the events surrounding this decision are not divulged, she offers one explicit rationale. Robert, she says, has "beauty of feature and charm of tongue with little regard for truth and high moral worth."[41] In other words, Robert was not a suitable object of love because his character was flawed. Robert's actions were too controlled by sensual and other morally dubious motivations. Elmer, on the contrary, "though not graceful . . . and handsome . . . [had an] inward nobility in him."[42] It was to Elmer that Maud gave her love. Moreover, because her love for Robert is described as tied to the senses and involving romantic longings, Maud tends to think of her love for Robert—and romantic love in general—as youthful and immature. Only her love for Elmer, a love based upon spiritual qualities and affinities, is a mature, true love. "Elmer is good and noble and pure and I love him—of course I love him, and he does understand me too."[43]

Despite Elmer's moral and spiritual goodness and purity of character, Maud continued to have reservations about him. "If I do marry [Elmer] it will be with a respectful affection and not with a passionate *lover* love."[44] Maud's love for Elmer lacked passion, and she continued to recall Robert for whom passion was not lacking. Maud contrasts her love for Robert with her love for Elmer. "If I love him [Elmer] it is not a love stimulating me mentally. When I loved Mr. Witherspoon [Robert] it was different. Then I wanted to study, to expand mind and heart. . . ."[45] Although Elmer tried, as Maud says, to be "an affinity" by reading and keeping up on artistic and intellectual trends, it was to no avail. "All the time I am planning to bring him up to a standard where I *can* love him."[46]

What is noteworthy is that the passion Maud says is lacking in her love for Elmer is not characterized as erotic but intellectual, cultural or spiritual. Maud fears that her marriage to Elmer will not be spiritually uplifting. Indeed, she fears a mediocrity in her life with Elmer that is terrifying. "But I don't want to marry; I only want to study art and to associate with intellectual and refined people who will make me think and develop into something beside a frivolous child."[47] Even her passion for Robert is characterized as intellectual or spiritual. Maud is unable to describe even a romantic type of love as other than spiritual. "And even if I had my ideal lover, a lover tall and graceful with tact and refinement, with deep violet eyes and tender mouth, with chestnut hair . . . with a voice rivaling the bird and with an intellect rivaling Webster's . . . you think I'd want to marry him? not much! I'd simply want to love him, and to know that he loved me, to study and develop under his tender guidance, to grow better every minute from association with his kindly heart, and to paint him and to know that the thought of him urged me to all honest struggles for improvement in everything I attempted."[48] Needless to say, love without marriage is, for Maud, chaste. Thus, even a passionate, romantic love could only be conceived by Maud as spiritual. In Maud's sublimated conception of love we find a familiar Christian motif: only a love that urges one to a spiritually elevated state is true and fully legitimate.

Elmer's relentless loyalty and devotion to Maud eventually won her over. But even after she acknowledged her love for him, she was courted by men who, like Robert, represented a more romantic style of love. Maud stuck by Elmer and one has the sense that her attachment followed as much from the anxiety elicited by the sensual aspects of these romantic longings as the moral goodness of Elmer. We can conjecture that it was precisely her ambivalence toward erotic passions evoked by some men that led Maud to repeatedly flirt with these men only to finally reassure herself of her love for Elmer. The courtship ended abruptly when certain suspicious business dealings tarnished Elmer's moral purity and goodness.

These three case studies reveal important features of Victorian images of romantic love. When Victorians described norms of conjugal love, erotic desires were either absent or marginal. Love was essentially conceived of as a spiritual phenomenon. It was imagined as a powerfully felt attraction between the mental, moral and spiritual character of two people. Love originated from deeply felt spiritual longings; it involved an urge toward spiritual union. Because love was a mutual attraction between the spiritual nature of two individuals, true love was thought to encompass passions that were elemental and constant. True love was contrasted to a certain concept of romantic love which is said to rest upon more superficial and transient feelings. Furthermore, whereas romantic love was seen as based upon illusory ideas and hopes, true love was thought to rest upon a solid bedrock of knowledge about intimate motives and the true self. True love, then, implied a norm of mutual self-disclosure. To avoid the self-deception of romantic love, to go beyond an attraction based on superficial feelings, lovers had to know each other as thoroughly as possible. It is an individual's spiritual and moral qualities that were considered important in assessing whether he or she is worthy to be loved and compatible. Finally, Victorians placed a high value upon companionship in love. One standard of a successful love was whether the spiritual complementarity of the couple produced a genuine companionship. In the Victorian context, companionship meant mutual emotional support anchored in shared spiritual-religious aspirations. Companionship did not typically extend to sharing a range of social interests and activities. The differentiation of gender identities and roles, especially the feminization of the domestic sphere and the masculinization of the public sphere, made a more comprehensive companionate ideal implausible.

In the main, Victorians seemed to believe that the spiritual complementarities of a man's and a woman's nature made "heterosexual" love natural and inevitable. This belief did not, however, preclude love between same sexed individuals or the complementarity of "heterosexual" and "homosexual" love. What, then, was the nature of same-sex love? And, what place did it have in middle-class Victorian culture?

IS LOVE GENDERLESS?
The Case of Women Loving Women

Carroll Smith-Rosenberg has made a compelling case for the claim that love between women was commonplace in nineteenth-century America.[49] Emotionally intense, open and enduring relationships of love between women existed alongside heterosexual love. Typical is the "romantic friendship" between Sarah Butler Wistar and Jeanne Field Murgrove. They met when Sarah was 14 and Jeanne 16. A friendship formed during the two years they spent together in a boarding school. Indicative of the romantic meaning of their relationship was that each assumed a nom de plume, Jeannie taking a female name, Sarah a male one. Sarah's marriage did not end the deep affection between the women. Even as Sarah became a mother, she could still write to Jeannie, "I can give you no idea how desperately I shall want you."[50] And Jeannie's longing for Sarah could hardly be restrained. "Dear darling Sarah, 'How I love you. . . . You are the joy of my life. . . . My darling how I long for the time when I shall see you."[51] As Jeannie herself approached marriage, Sarah's anxiety over losing Jeannie heightened. "Dearest darling—How incessantly have I thought of you these eight days—all today—the entire uncertainty, the distance, the long silence—are all new features in my separation from you. . . . Oh Jeannie, I have thought and thought and yearned over you these two days. Are you married I wonder? My dearest love to you wherever and whoever you are."[52] Although they lived far apart from one another, Sarah and Jeannie continued to be emotionally bonded for nearly fifty years.

Love between women was frequently as passionate and as full of emotional pathos and significance as heterosexual love. As Lillian Faderman has written in her study of female love relations, "Female autobiographies and memoirs throughout the [nineteenth] century suggest that . . . passionate love between women was not atypical."[53] Nor did these same-sex love affairs bear any trace of the twentieth-century association with deviance or abnormality. For example, when the young student Carey Thomas wrote her mother describing the joy and turmoil of her love affair with a Miss Hicks, she did so without any trace of shame, guilt or rebellion. When Ms. Thomas declared to her mother that she wished "it were possible for women to elect women as well as men for a life's love," she did so without any anticipation of reproach or disapproval.[54] It seems that, at least for white, middle-class Victorians, the heterosexual and homosexual worlds were often viewed as complementary.

Smith-Rosenberg explains the appearance of female love relations by referring to the "rigid gender-role differentiation" characteristic of Victorian culture. This led to the physical and emotional segregation of the two genders and, in the case of women, to the formation of a female-centered social world. Women's lives were typically embedded in a dense network of female ties revolving around household chores, childbirth and rearing and kin relations. "Most eighteenth- and nineteenth-century women lived within a world bounded by home, church and the institution of visiting—that endless trooping of women to one another's homes for social purposes. It was a world inhabited by children and by other women. Women helped one another with domestic chores and in times of sickness, sorrow or trouble. Entire days, even weeks, might be spent almost exclusively with other women. . . . When husbands traveled, wives routinely moved in with other women, invited women friends to teas and suppers, sat together sharing and comparing the letters they had received from other close women friends."[55] The centering of women's lives in female relations combined with the formality and emotional distance within heterosexual relationships made "devotion to and love of other women . . . a plausible and socially accepted form of human interaction."[56] Smith-Rosenberg's thesis needs to be qualified in light of recent research which suggests that heterosexual intimacies were frequently informal, emotionally dense and often involved genuine companionship.[57]

Lillian Faderman introduces an additional factor explaining what made love between women socially acceptable: the absence of sexuality stemming from the assumption of female passionlessness. "Since middle- and upper-class women were separated from men not only in their daily occupations, but in their spiritual and leisure interests as well, outside of the practical necessities of raising a family there was little that tied the sexes together. But with other females a woman inhabited the same sphere. . . . She could share sentiment, her heart . . . with another female. And regardless of the intensity of the feeling that might develop between them, they need not attribute it to the demon, sexuality, since women supposedly had none. They could safely see it [love] as an effusion of the spirit. The shield of passionlessness that a woman was trained to raise before a man could be lowered with another woman without fear of losing her chastity and reputation and health."[58]

Faderman suggests that, in part, it was the lack of sexual expression or the presumption of its absence in female love relations that made them acceptable. I disagree with Faderman only in that whereas she explains the desexualization of female love relations by the Victorian ideology of female passionlessness, I would underscore the ideal of the spirituality of love. In other words, the legitimacy of female same-sex love was enhanced by a spiritual conception of love. Nancy Sahli has made the same point. "By defining their love for other women as a spiritual force, women were . . . able to sublimate any sexual feelings they may have had and make the intensity of their relationships acceptable to society."[59] As long as love was spiritual, the gender identity of the lovers was less pertinent. Commenting on her relationship to another woman, the abolitionist Mary Grew made precisely this point. "To me it [her relationship to another women] seems to have been a closer union than that of most marriages. We know there have been other such [relationships] between two men and also between two women. And why should there not be. *Love is spiritual, only passion is sexual.*"[60] The absence of sensuality in particular was taken as a sign of the higher or purer status of female love relations in comparison to heterosexual marriage. The feminist Margaret Fuller wrote in her journal, "It is true that a woman may be in love with a woman, and a man with a man. . . . It is purely intellectual and spiritual, unprofaned by any mixture of lower instincts."[61]

Although female love relations were taken seriously, Victorians did not consider them to be the moral or social equivalent of heterosexual love. A woman could not, as Carey Thomas complained, legitimately choose another woman as a life-companion. "It *is* possible but if families would only regard it in that light!"[62] Middle-class women were expected to marry. They aspired, moreover, to be wives and mothers as a integral way to fulfill what they took to be their true feminine nature. Additionally, female love relations were accepted because they were not considered to be a genuine threat to heterosexual love. Women's social, economic and political dependence on men ensured that the norm of heterosexuality would not be seriously challenged. Female love relations may have been permitted as complementary to heterosexual love, but their status remained secondary. In fact, with the heterosexual norm firmly entrenched, female same-sex love may have been seen as a way to keep women pure until marriage.

Few Victorians questioned the primacy of heterosexual love. Men and women were thought to represent two different and perfectly complementary psychic, moral, intellectual and social beings. Between them there was a magnetic-like pull; their mutual attraction was viewed as a law of nature. Because each sex was understood as incomplete, or governed by either a masculine or feminine principle, each was drawn to the opposite sex. Love between a man and a woman was thought to be compelling because the complementarity of masculinity and femininity in the male and female heightened their spiritual affinities. Sarah Grimké observed: "Marriage is a necessity of our being, because of our halfness. Every man and woman feels profound want, which no father nor mother, no sister nor brother can fill. An indescribable longing for, and yearning after a perfect kindred spirit. The man who feels within himself the lack of the feminine element, the woman the lack of the masculine, each possessing enough of the other's nature to appreciate and seek its fullness, each in the other. Each has a deep awareness of incompleteness without the other

... and seeks that divinity in her and in him, ... This divinity is the only true basis of union, out of it alone, grow these holy affinities which bind soul to soul ... in an ethical marriage."[63] The norm of heterosexual love and marriage was not seriously challenged in nineteenth-century middle-class culture. Reform was directed to establishing love as the highest basis of marriage. Even Elizabeth Cady Stanton, feminist and wife in an unhappy marriage, could write: "A man's love brings into a woman's existence an inspiration, a completeness, a satisfaction that a mother's [love] cannot. A true conjugal union is the highest kind of human love."[64]

Carroll Smith-Rosenberg has suggested that the complementarity of heterosexual and homosexual love in the nineteenth century made it easier than today for individuals to move between heterosexual and homosexual feelings and involvements. Far from the nineteenth century being more repressive than contemporary society, at least in this respect. Smith-Rosenberg believes individuals had more freedom to express a wider range of intimate feelings and to achieve levels of closeness with both genders than is possible today. Peter Gay has pressed this argument to a more extreme conclusion. He contrasts Victorian tolerance toward discreet patterns of homosexuality with the public intolerance toward more public styles of homosexuality in our century. Gay refers to the case of the English educational reformer Dr. C. J. Vaughan, whose homosexuality was acknowledged but tolerated in exchange for keeping it private. "Vaugham had lived out the compromise that the bourgeois century imposed on sexual heretics. He was fenced in but not exposed.... He could even indulge his sexual tastes as long as he chose his objects circumspectly and observed the rule of discretion. Then, towards the end of the nineteenth century, as the matter of homosexuality hesitantly came out into the open, principally for men, the fate of deviates only became more poignant. Far from easing their lives, the tentative new freedom only complicated them. The new attention generated hostility. ... This is the irony: the shift away from the delicacy that had governed the discussion ... about the aberrations before the 1880s only increased public censure.... The defensive stratagem of repression had its virtues.... Many heterosexuals and homosexuals alike, did not think this an improvement."[65] Whereas Smith-Rosenberg underscores a certain fluidity in social conventions governing intimacy in the nineteenth century, Gay finds a model of public tolerance. His argument is, however, not convincing. For whatever tolerance obtained for same-sex intimacy in the nineteenth century, such involvements were desexualized or at least sex was proscribed; they were, as well, often temporary and considered secondary to heterosexual love. Homosexual love was not accepted as a genuine alternative to heterosexual love. Whatever public hostility homosexuals countenance today, at least there exists the possibility of a homosexual love that is permanent and primary.

EXPLAINING VICTORIAN LOVE
The Role of Gender, Religion and Class

Historians continue to debate the extent to which the "cult of true womanhood" or the construction of women as spiritually and morally elevated was imposed by men as a mode of social control or was a self-serving creation of women.[66] On one point there seems to be a consensus: Victorian women appealed to this gender construction in order to demand expanded autonomy within and outside the household. For example, the claim to moral and spiritual superiority legitimated women's roles as social critics and reformers. Invoking feminine virtue permitted them to assume the lead in social reform in the areas of abolition, prostitution, temperance, women's rights, education, religion, moral instruction and municipal reform. More pertinent for our discussion is that the appeal to feminine moral superiority legitimated women's demand for respect and autonomy within marriage. Claiming spiritual and moral virtue allowed women to regulate sexual expression in marriage. In a context in which sex for women was often associated with pain, disease and unwanted pregnancy, controlling sex meant expanded control over their lives.

Women were a principal force behind the spiritualization of love. It was in women's self-interest to promote an ideal of love as essentially spiritual. By making love the only legitimate basis of marriage and its highest aspiration, it allowed women to demand that men control their sexual desires and sublimate them into caring, respectful behavior.

For many middle-class women in the nineteenth century, marriage was anticipated with deep ambivalence. On the positive side, marriage conferred a respectable social status and provided women with economic security. Also, these Victorian women typically looked to marriage to find self-fulfillment as wives and mothers. Many women interpreted the prospect of establishing their own household as a sign of adult autonomy. Managing a household entailed such a wide range of skills and responsibilities that domestic activity often gave women a sense of themselves as competent, useful and powerful.

Yet, marriage was approached by many middle-class women with serious reservations and, not infrequently, with genuine horror. Marriage meant an almost complete change in women's lives and frequently one for the worse. Young, single, middle-class Victorian women frequently enjoyed considerable freedom and opportunities for self-development. Higher education, especially in the second half of the nineteenth century, was open to virtually all middle-class women. And while the sciences may have been more or less closed to women, they could pursue the arts and humanities seriously. Victorian women often traveled extensively both within the United States and in Europe. It was not uncommon for young women to spend extended time abroad either pursuing a course of study or simply traveling. Furthermore, despite twentieth-century stereotypes, single women had wide latitude in their personal affairs. It was, for example, quite common for single adult women to date rather freely. Indeed, unless a young woman was engaged, she was expected to have several suitors in order to avoid conveying the false impression that she was in a courting phase or otherwise unavailable. And, as Ellen Rothman has documented, dating was routinely informal and the couple were permitted a great deal of privacy and freedom.[67] Marriage typically meant the end of these forms of autonomy. Once a young woman married she rarely continued her higher education; work outside the home or a career was, in the main, incompatible with marriage; pursuing intellectual or cultural interests often conflicted with the expansive demands involved in running a household. For many women, the decision to marry was thought to entail a sacrifice of personal autonomy. Highlighting this ambivalence in a sharp way, Maud confesses to her diary: "I don't want to marry; I only want to study art and to associate with intellectual and refined people who will make me think and develop into something besides a frivolous child."[68]

Marriage evoked anxiety and ambivalent feelings for other reasons as well. It typically involved physical and emotional distance from one's kin network, friends and community. The lives of many women revolved around their parents, sisters and brothers, kin and friends. Getting married meant leaving home and separating from this emotionally dense social network. This was fraught with anxiety and deep regret. Again, Maud poignantly dramatizes a concern felt by many women: "Only today I sat wondering why I've always so abhorred the idea of marriage. First there'd be Mom and home, the boys and Papa to leave, severing all old ties, losing all my pleasant gentleman friends, most of my girl friends, having all my aims, my life in itself, confined on one spot, in pleasing one person."[69]

Getting married for women was a life choice; it essentially fixed a women's social fate. The feminist, but also wife and mother, Elizabeth Cady Stanton underscored how marriage bears on the two genders differently. "Marriage is not all of life to man. . . . He has the whole world for his home. His business, his politics, his clubs, his friendships with either sex, can help to fill the void made by an unfortunate union or separation. But to a woman, marriage is all and everything, her sole object in life. . . . In the present undeveloped condition of women, it is only through our fathers, brothers, husbands, sons that we feel the pulsations of the great outer world."[70] Because most women could not realistically expect to build a career or be economically self-sufficient, marriage was usually preferred to spinsterhood, with its insecurity and social stigma. Yet, the man a woman married determined more or less where she would live, for how long, and her standard of living or quality of life. The fate of a married woman was bound to that of her husband in a way that was not true of men.

Middle-class women grew up aware of the dark side of marriage. Despite the fulfillment and joys women anticipated and hoped for in marriage, they were all too aware that the reality often involved hardship, violence and degradation. Sarah Grimké pointedly expresses women's anxieties about the "fallen" state of many actual marriages: "How many women who have entered the marriage relation in all purity and innocence, expected to realize in it . . . the blending of their holiest instincts with those of a kindred spirit, have too soon discovered that they are unpaid housekeepers and nurses, and still worse, chattels personal to be used and abused at the will of a master. . . . O' the agony of realizing that personal and pecuniary independence are annihilated by [marriage]. . . . How many so called wives rise in the morning oppressed with a sense of degradation from the fact that their chastity has been violated."[71]

It was their deeply felt understanding of the dangers of marriage that compelled women to scrutinize their suitors to ascertain whether they would be responsible husbands. This same concern underlay women's insistence on the importance of mutual self-disclosure during courtship. A woman needed to know as much as possible about the character and habits of the man who would, in effect, determine her social fate. It was this profound ambivalence toward marriage that motivated women to reform it. Middle-class women were the principal agents in formulating an ideal of marriage founded upon a spiritual notion of love. As a norm of intimate behavior that emphasized mutual respect and autonomy for both the husband and wife, this ideal enhanced women's autonomy and improved the quality of their lives. This ideal could function as a standard to judge marital behavior. It could be invoked to criticize coercive, cruel or disrespectful male behavior. In the setting of nineteenth-century America, the ideal of a marriage based on spiritual love was looked upon as expanding women's autonomy.

From the vantage point of their social structural position, it was clearly in women's interest to promote norms that restricted men's power over them. Yet, to explain why women's response to their social structural situation took the form of a spiritual ideal of love and why it proved socially credible, we need to take into account the Christian cultural context.

From the end of the eighteenth century through the nineteenth century, successive waves of evangelical Protestantism swept across the nation. Evangelical Protestantism emphasized the need for spiritual revitalization and a more vigorous adherence to a life of moral virtue and spiritual purity. Historians have documented the impact of the evangelical revival on the making of gender identity and sexuality. Nancy Cott, for example, has connected the ideology of "passionlessness" to the evangelical conception of a woman as essentially a spiritual and moral being. "The evangelical view, by concentrating on women's spiritual nature, simultaneously elevated women as moral and intellectual beings and disavowed them of their sexual power. Passionlessness was the other side of the coin which paid, so to speak, for women's admission to moral equality."[72] The impact of evangelicalism on the Victorian construction of masculinity is less well known. Charles Rosenberg links evangelicalism to the ideal of a Christian gentlemen which was realized through a regime of self-restraint and sublimation. "The Christian gentlemen was an athlete of continence, not coitus, continuously testing his manliness in the fire of self denial. This paradigmatic figure eschewed excess in all things. . . . Continence implied strength, not weakness."[73] Evangelical Protestantism made a virtue of prudence, self-control and chastity or continence. Peter Gay comments on the impact of this religious movement on intimate life: "For nineteenth-century bourgeois the consequence of religious doctrines were all too plain: they subordinated concupiscence to affection in careful, lifelong marriage, and laid it down, once more, that erotic desire is permissible only as it is directed to the procreation of offspring. This Christian perspective remained for most bourgeois, a regulative . . . ideal."[74] Social norms formed under the impact of Christianity pressed for the sublimation of carnal desires into an ideal of spiritual elevation and social companionship. Conjugal love was to be a human manifestation of one's love of God. It should exhibit the same qualities as are revealed in loving God: moral constancy, devotion and spirituality.

I wish to allude to one point that is often neglected in these discussions. Victorian men were deeply influenced by the Christianization of American culture. Accordingly, we should not be too surprised to find some middle-class men struggling alongside women for conjugal reform. Henry Blackwell, businessman and abolitionist, wrote in perfect accord with his wife-to-be, the feminist Lucy Stone, "Any marriage not consecrated by love is monstrous—and the presence of love, makes dependence mutual."[75] Explaining his ideal of a marriage based on spiritual love and companionship, Joseph Lyman wrote to Laura Dickinson, "My ideas of married life are formed in the Bible that 'your twain shall be one flesh' and the more perfect and even mysteriously blended . . . the greater the happiness of both."[76] Dr. J. Marion Sims, the famous gynecologist, described his marriage in terms of an ideal of spiritual love and intimacy. "We have lived for each other. Mutual confidence and mutual love had made us as happy as it is possible for mortals to be."[77] Support among middle-class men for a reform ideology stressing a norm of spiritual love and companionship was not uncommon. It would, however, be misleading to explain this solely by referring to the cultural impact of evangelical ideas. Since at least Marx and Weber, we have often been persuaded to believe that ideas direct action only insofar as they are in accord with self-interest. The latter is a product of social class position or status group affiliation.

Briefly, I wish to propose a connection between social class and the Victorian ideology of conjugal love. An ideology that trumpeted the virtues of spiritual love, companionship, mutuality, moral constancy and spiritual elevation fit well with the needs of the middle class. The emphasis on self-control, sobriety, responsibility, and moral and mental fitness was congenial to an entrepreneurial class that had to daily countenance the insecurities and risks of a competitive market economy.[78] As a regulative ideal, these norms and values created a kind of mental toughness that was functional. The link between the middle class and an ideology of spiritual love is made clearer when we consider the materialization of a working class, the heightened social presence of African-Americans who migrated to the Northeast, and of the new European ethnics who were immigrating to the Northeast in large numbers. The new conjugal ideology fostered a consciousness of class difference and moral superiority. A life governed by self-control and spiritual goals was seen as higher than a life controlled by impulse and desire. To the extent that these "other" social groups were associated with sexual licentiousness, disease, carnality and excess, the ideology of spiritual love and companionate marriage stood as proof of the moral superiority of the middle class. By identifying their claims to moral superiority with their ideals of love and marriage, the middle class legitimated their claims to privilege and power. In other words, the middle class legitimated their class aspirations to political, social and cultural hegemony on the grounds of their intellectual and moral fitness to rule.[79] Renunciation of desire and its sublimation into an ethic of work and spiritual love served as proof of their superiority.

CONCLUSION

I have tried to make plausible the claim that at least one prominent middle-class Victorian construction of love defined it in spiritual terms. Love originated from the longing of the soul for spiritual elevation and completion through communion with a kindred spirit. The mutual attraction that Victorians described as love was basically a spiritual, mental and moral one. Love related to a condition in which the inner spiritual cores of two individuals were drawn together with the force of a magnetic pull. True love related to the most elementary kernel of the self below the surface layers of sensual appearance and desire. Accordingly, to determine whether an attraction was true love, the individual had to discover the essential spiritual self of the other. This was accomplished through a courting process that involved an ordeal of mutual self-disclosure. It was, accordingly, the prospect of spiritual and moral companionship and elevation that Victorians hoped for in marriage.

Ideally, love was to be the basis of marriage. Such a marriage was not intended to be chaste. Sex was too powerful a force to be denied. Under the proper conditions, sex was a beneficent power, potentially invigorating and uplifting. Marriage was the legitimate sphere of sex. Marriage functioned as a sphere of control over the sex instinct; it desensualized sex or at least limited eroticism and prevented its ruinous effects. Marriage channeled the sex instinct in ways that made it serve spiritual and moral ends. Only a marriage based on love could ensure the benevolent power of sex. Love checked the propensity of sexual feelings to elicit eroticism; it channeled egoistic, aggressive sex drives into an ethic of mutual respect and spiritual communion. The ideal of spiritual love as a basis of marriage was supported by many women for whom this ideology could be invoked to control male desire and limit conception. Moreover, middle-class men and women appealed to it in order to legitimate their claim to social power in the face of the rise of a laboring-class, African-American migration to the North and the influx of non-Protestant immigrants.

The Victorian sexual regime was not entirely successful. The sexual impulse that was to be controlled and sublimated into companionship, career or domesticity found an outlet outside marriage. A vast sexual underground emerged that centered around an elaborate system of prostitution and pornography.[80] In virtually every major city there appeared red-light districts. On the eve of the Civil War men could purchase guides telling them the addresses and relevant details of the available brothels. One such guide listed over one hundred houses of prostitution in New York City.[81] Further, the campaigns against masturbation and fornication that figured prominently in the Victorian century suggest that the effort to restrict eroticism to marriage and spiritually transfigure it were less effective in practice than in theory.

By the late nineteenth century there was a social reaction to the failure of the Victorian sexual order. Social movements were organized to abolish prostitution, outlaw abortion, censor obscene literature and representations, and eliminate the double standard that justified this sexual underground.[82] These social purity and reform movements had the effect of reconfiguring the relationship between sex, love and marriage. By the early decades of the twentieth century, there were demands to bring eroticism back into love and marriage. Discourses and representations conceived of love as anchored in and maintained by sex. Eroticism received legitimation as a means of demonstrating love. These discourses were reinforced by related social developments, including a more consumer-oriented society, changing gender roles, the rise of a new middle class, massive urban migration and ethnic immigration, and so on. In the course of the twentieth century, the antithesis between sex and love collapsed. Sex became a way to express, prove, maintain and revitalize love and marriage. Eroticism was legitimated because it now carried the moral sanction of proving love. This process of the sexualization of love and the eroticization of sex is the topic of Part Two.

Part Two

*Modern Times
(1890–1960)*

3

Remaking Intimacy

Sexualizing Love, Eroticizing Sex

Historians have long observed that beginning in the 1890s a far-reaching, perhaps unprecedented, public discussion about intimate life began.[1] What is unique about this discussion is not only the range of topics covered—prostitution, venereal disease, love, marriage, divorce, sex and homosexuality—but that it occurred across a wide range of media and included diverse participants. Sex was being talked about everywhere—in medical-scientific and religious texts, in sex education and hygiene tracts, in newspapers, magazines, journals, books, as well as in the movies, theater and art galleries. Contemporary commentators spoke of the "repeal of reticence" about everyday talk of sex.[2] Furthermore, the legitimate discussion of sex was no longer confined to either medical-scientific experts or religious guardians of the moral order. Everyone—from secular intellectuals, social scientists, psychologists, artists and writers to journalists, feminists, socialists, and ordinary citizens—claimed a right to speak about sex. Finally, although medical-scientific discourses were assuming a socially salient, if not dominant, position in contemporary sex talk, by World War I these discourses were becoming heterogeneous in their moral and political meaning. Psychoanalytical theories, for example, conveyed multiple messages for sexual ethics and politics. The writings of Edward Carpenter, Ellen Key, Havelock Ellis and important public intellectuals such as Max Eastman, Floyd Dell or Emma Goldman were quite liberal, even radical, in their approach to sex.[3]

Contemporary commentators may have been wrong to juxtapose Victorian silence and prudishness about sex to their own modern frankness and freedom. They were not mistaken, however, in believing that the current public discussion of sex was something new and that it pointed to changes in the conventions of intimate life. The changes that interest us are less related to the quantity of sex or sex talk than to alterations in norms and mores of intimate behavior. I chart a shift

65

in the way sex is related to love. This implies, as I argue, a change in the very meaning of sex and love. Sexual satisfaction now figures prominently as an important criterion for ascertaining and assessing love. It functions as a standard of a happy and successful marriage. As sex becomes a site for demonstrating and maintaining love, the erotic aspects of sex acquire legitimacy. The culture of romance in the early decades of twentieth-century America gave birth to a sexual culture that placed a high value upon the sensual and expressive qualities of sex. Before describing this cultural transformation, I wish to outline its social context.

THE CRISIS OF INTIMACY AND THE "MODERN" IDEAL OF HETEROSEXUAL LOVE

The sexualization of love and the development of a culture of eroticism in twentieth-century America occurred in the context of a perceived crisis in sexual morality and marriage. The years after World War I witnessed an outpouring of essays and books, research monographs and treatises, editorials and magazine pieces, scrutinizing every aspect of intimacy. This vast discursive production suggests that for many contemporaries the models of intimate life inherited from the Victorian era were viewed as inappropriate or in decline. There was a growing public perception in the early decades of the twentieth century that marital conventions were in a state of change and crisis.

Despite the fact that the institution of marriage had widespread public support and, in fact, more people were getting married than in previous generations, the concern of contemporaries about the state of marriage was not unfounded. A constellation of social developments pointed to a society whose axial institutions, including marriage, were in a state of transition. Robert Wiebe describes an epochal transformation that, beginning in the late nineteenth century, involved the breakdown of a "society of island communities" and the rise of a new social order.[4] Throughout most of the nineteenth century, the economy was dominated by small enterprises; social life was centered in relatively isolated small towns; social order was a product of a common Protestant culture enforced by the local agencies of the family, church, school and a ruling elite of white Protestant businessmen. By the 1880s these "island communities" were in crisis due to economic expansion, corporate build-up, the growth of commercial banking, the commercializing of farming, the rise of a national market, massive ethnic immigration and black migration to northern cities, labor unrest and so on. In the first two decades of the twentieth century a new order was evolving that was characterized by giant corporations oriented to national markets; an urban-centered, multi-ethnic and multi-religious, cosmopolitan population. Social coherence was a product of a bureaucratic apparatus administered by a new middle class who looked to the state for assistance in achieving economic growth and social order.

These social changes had significant bearing on intimate life. Consider, for example, the emergence of a corporate economic sector with its system of mass production and mass consumption. The latter is achieved, in part, by developing nonlocal markets, and also by expanding household consumption. Getting individuals to identify a range of their physical, psychological and social needs with commodities is integral to an economy of giant corporations. The evolving American corporate economy encouraged the rise of a consumer culture that connects self-fulfillment to hedonistic and expressive values. The sexualization of wants, desires and pleasures was integral to this consumer culture.[5] This social development conflicted with Victorian intimate conventions. Similarly, the massive population migration to cities that took place between the 1880s and the 1920s was a disturbing development from the standpoint of Victorian cultural ideals.[6] The rise of a more urban-centered society involved an expansion of individualism, including sexual freedom. The anonymity of the city, the diminished control over the individual by traditional local agencies (family, church, neighbors, school), the red-light districts that cropped up in all major cities and the emerging world of public entertainment (dance halls, cabarets, movies) made the city a place of expanded opportunities for sexual experimentation and innovation in the sphere of intimacy. This was seen as a threat by carriers of Victorian intimate norms and ideals.

These structural changes raised fears, especially among the older middle class, of a permissive, anomic intimate culture. The expanded opportunities for individual expression seemed to threaten to uncouple sex from marriage. In fact, surveys from the 1920s through the 1950s report a dramatic increase in nonmarital sex. This is not, moreover, a continuation of the nineteenth-century pattern of men frequenting prostitutes. At least since World War I, according to Kinsey, men visited prostitutes about one-half as often as in the prewar period.[7] Men were turning to "respectable" women for sex, and doing so before they were married. The research of the period shows a rise in premarital sex, especially among middle-class women. Comparing the generation of women born before 1900 with those born after 1900, Kinsey found that whereas 14 percent in the former group reported having premarital coitus, the figure increased to almost 40 percent in the younger generation.[8] The rise in premarital coitus was accompanied by the widespread use of contraceptives, despite legal prohibitions.[9] One researcher found that 92 percent of the men and 87 percent of the women surveyed admitted using contraceptives. These deviations from Victorian norms were, moreover, known to the public. For example, in a research report on marriage carried out in the 1920s, Robert Dickenson and Lura Beam declared that "compared with previous decades, in the last eight or ten years, there are fewer inhibitions and shocks; . . . General knowledge of control of contraception with its removal of fear of accidental pregnancy [and] . . . coital experimentation before marriage . . . [have] increased. There are more open liaisons, often enduring over long periods."[10] Many contemporaries were alarmed by public reports of the slippage between sex and marriage.

Anxiety over marriage and the perception of a crisis in intimate affairs were stimulated by changing gender roles. In the first half of the twentieth century, the rise of corporate and government bureaucracies, the growth of service sector jobs and the expansion of higher education resulted in a marked increase in the demand for low-level white-collar workers (secretaries, office workers, salespersons). Women were recruited for many of these jobs. Historians have documented that during this period more women, single and married, worked outside the home and were employed in a wider range of occupations than throughout the nineteenth century.[11] Although the overall percentage of women who worked for wages remained low, in comparative terms the proportion of women working between 1880 and 1920 jumped 50 percent.[12] The percentage of married white women who were employed increased 300 percent—from about 4 percent in 1900 to 12 percent in 1940.[13] By 1930 women comprised 50 percent of the professional work force.[14] The number of female professionals increased at the same rate as males in the 1920s. More than 400,000 women entered the professions in the 1920, although most were employed in gender typed occupations such as teachers.[15] Women were becoming a permanent visible part of the paid labor force.

The movement of women into the paid labor force, initially as domestic and factory workers and later as office workers, was part of a series of changes that pointed to women's growing independence. For example, the dramatic rise in female professionals in the 1920s was connected to the fact that more women were attending college than ever before. In 1870, 21 percent of all enrolled college students were women. By 1890 the figure increased to 35.9 percent and by 1920 the figure was 47.3 percent.[16] By 1920 women received one-third of all the graduate degrees awarded in the United States.[17] These facts point to more than the major inroads women were making in the world of higher education. College was a formative experience for middle-class women. It removed them from their home and from conventional female role definitions. At college, women competed on an equal footing with men. Women who attended coeducational institutions could mingle freely with men. Typically, these women looked to other women for social support and solidarity. Strong female ties were often formed which were sometimes imbued with a feminist awareness.[18]

It was these "new women," as Caroll Smith-Rosenberg calls them, who became career-oriented professionals and who assumed a vanguard role in social reform (e.g., in the settlement house or birth control movements) and in women's struggle for universal suffrage. This generation of white middle-class women who came of age after 1900 differed from their predecessors in one crucial way: they could realistically entertain the possibility of forging a female identity outside the ideology of true womanhood. They could, in other words, define themselves through their career or their public life as reformers or feminists. Moreover, with careers of their own and female-centered networks for social support, marriage could be approached as optional. Fueling the perception of a social crisis, many of these new women were, in fact, choosing not to marry. Smith-Rosenberg has noted a striking relation between college-educated women and marriage. "From the 1870s through the 1920s, between 40 and 60 percent of women college graduates did not marry, at a time when only 10 percent of all American women did not."[19] Many of these women were choosing to pursue a career or a public life of social reform and politics rather than to marry.[20]

These new women not only worked and socialized and organized together, but they often lived with each other. A popular social scientific textbook observed how common it was for educated women to live together. "In many cases women . . . are setting up true homes with the same interaction patterns as in the normal family home."[21] The appearance of a strata of women who pursued careers and often lived with each other raised the specter of women choosing a homosexual alternative to marriage. This fear was reinforced by the increased visibility of homosexuals, whose subcultures and lifestyles were frequently reported on in newspapers, scientific journals and popular literature. In fact, researchers observed a significant level of sexual activity in female intimate relationships. For example, G. V. Hamilton's study of white middle-class married couples found that 30 percent of the women said that, as adults, they had homosexual experiences involving mutual genital stimulation.[22] In her monumental 1929 study *Factors in the Sex Life of Twenty-two Hundred Women,* Katherine Davis found that over 50 percent of the more than 1000 married women she surveyed acknowledged that they had experienced an intense emotional relationship with another woman.[23] Over one-quarter of these women revealed that their involvement with women included sexual play beyond hugging and kissing.[24] Thirty-five percent of those women who disclosed having sexual feelings toward women reported that such same-sex feelings were natural and legitimate.[25] For many contemporary observers, the growing social, economic and political independence of women, especially highly educated professional and political women, was associated with the repudiation not only of Victorian gender codes but with the rejection of heterosexuality and marriage.[26]

Of course, many women did not attend college and most women did not pursue a career or choose to live with a woman. Middle-class women typically sought self-fulfillment in marriage. Yet, many women born in the early decades of the twentieth century demanded more freedom to define themselves than their parents and grandparents. They were less tied to Victorian feminine models and, for many contemporaries, that meant they were less committed to marriage. It is well known that by the early 1900s young women were choosing a more explicitly sexual and masculine style of self-presentation. Respectable women appeared in public with shorter dresses, low-cut blouses, short-cropped hair, and their faces made up in sexually provocative ways. Femininity was being redefined by these women to include the hitherto more exclusively masculine prerogative of claiming erotic desire. The "flapper" came to symbolize this phenomenon. She was young, assertive, independent, experimental, casual with men and a pleasure-seeker. The flapper embodied a free-wheeling sexual style. "Her speech, her interest in thrills and excitement, her dress and hair . . . [suggested] a more aggressive sexuality."[27]

This more sexually assertive self-identification was manifested in the entertainment women sought. Throughout the nineteenth century women's claim to moral elevation legitimated their public activity as spiritual leaders and reformers, but it simultaneously excluded respectable women from the public world of entertainment. This realm was associated with male lust and those "fallen women" whose uncontrollable passions drove them into this polluted state. Rebelling against the Victorian ideology which split off sensual feelings and pleasures from femininity, many respectable middle-class women were stepping out into the hitherto "impure" domain of dance halls, cabarets, movies, restaurants and bars. They smoked, drank and conversed with men. This new sphere of public leisure encouraged intimacy and sexually expressive behavior. "In the cabaret . . . men and women entered on a more equal level. . . . Men and women would stretch the night into hours of pleasure for themselves. . . . Out in public, removed from the restrictions surrounding work and home, they were free to explore the personal dimensions of their relationships."[28] Nowhere was the incorporation of a more free-wheeling sexuality into ideals of womanhood more visible than in popular dancing. In contrast to Victorian conventions in which dancing was a formal, group, and desexualized activity, the new dances—the horse trot, crab step, the snake, fox-trot, turkey trot and charleston—were expressive and couple-centered. Moreover, these dances involved a range of body movements—hip movements, swaying, touching, holding and finger snapping—that were saturated with erotic meaning.[29]

The new sexualized style young women evidenced in their dress, hair, make-up and leisure activities was not merely flirtatious. These young middle-class women were, in fact, more sexually active than their mothers and grandmothers. Petting and sex play without coitus was a legitimate aspect of their dating and courtship behavior.[30] Comparing the generation of women born before and after 1900, Kinsey found an increase in the incidence of premarital coitus, premarital petting and, in general, the younger generation experimented more with sex techniques and positions.[31] The "new woman" and the flapper were both claiming masculine privileges, and that included the right to express sexual feelings, to stay single or to marry but not have a family.[32] Women's expanded autonomy, especially in the context of a public discussion of marital instability and dissatisfaction, led many contemporaries to identify it as a precipitating factor in the current crisis of intimate life.

The perception of a change in women's social status did not, by itself, set off a public belief that marriage was in crisis. This change was part of a conjuncture of social events that included the rise of mass consumerism, urbanization, bureaucratization, the loosening of kin ties, the widespread acceptance and use of contraceptives, the visibility of homosexual subcultures and an increase in nonmarital sex. These developments were seen as threatening the social stability and moral credibility of marriage. The notion that marriage was in a state of turmoil was given empirical plausibility by the rise in the divorce rate. According to William O'Neill, in 1860 there were 1.2 divorces per 1000 marriages; the figure jumped to 7.7 divorces by 1920.[33] The influential social scientists Ernest Groves and William Ogburn reported to their contemporaries that "in the five years, 1922–1926, there was one divorce granted to about every seven marriages performed [which] indicates that divorce is very common. Moreover, the chances of a marriage entered into from 1922–1926 being broken by divorce may be nearer 1 to 5 or 6 perhaps than 1 to 7. The average annual divorces granted from 1922–1926 were about 15 or 16 times as numerous as in 1870, and yet the population is only about three times as large."[34] The rise in divorce rates, says O'Neill, was a public shock; it fed into the anxiety over the prospects of marriage. Contemporaries correctly perceived that current social developments were disturbing inherited middle-class intimate conventions. It was not unreasonable to speak of a crisis, if not in the institution of marriage, at least in its Victorian form.

The public response to this perceived crisis reveals a wide range of conflicting views contemporaries held about intimate life.[35] At one extreme were traditionalists who steadfastly defended the Victorian model. They traced the current crisis to a general demoralization process linked, for example, to a permissive urban environment, World War I, the women's movement or secularization. They advocated stricter divorce laws, opposed the legalization of birth control information and methods, assailed the intrusion of sexual representations into the public sphere (e.g., in movies, theater, dance halls, literature, art) and were against the liberalization of sexual morality. At the opposite end of the ideological spectrum were critics of marriage—a heterogeneous group covering socialists, free-love advocates and sex radicals. They interpreted the current crisis of marriage as proof of its psychological, moral and social bankruptcy. They drew from the ideas of Freud, European sex theorists like Edward Carpenter, Ellen Key or Havelock Ellis or from the exuberant expressive sexual ideology of literary romantics like Walt Whitman. They underscored the unhealthy aspects of marriage. These sex radicals proposed new models of intimate behavior that did not necessarily tie sex to marriage.

As we move toward the social and intellectual center, we find a range of positions that urge changes in the institution of marriage in order to adapt to the altered social circumstances. Conservatives rallied behind the sex education movement which, in the years immediately prior to and after World War I, achieved a position of social prominence.[36] Bringing together social purity and social hygiene groups, sex education advocates sought to preserve Victorian norms by shifting the primary agency of sexual regulation from the family to the school. The diminished control that parents had over the individual was thought to threaten to uncouple sex from marriage. The moral education of the individual could no longer be left to the parent in these altered social conditions. Sex education, it was argued, needed to become a public responsibility. The state had to be enlisted to educate young people in the public school on the morality, biology and hygienic aspects of sexuality. Yet, sex educationalists endorsed Victorian views regarding abstinence before marriage, sexual moderation in marriage, the primacy of the procreative function and the dangers of carnal motivations.

The counterpart to the sex education advocates were the liberal reformers. They included social scientists like Ernest Groves, Ernest Burgess, William Ogburn, E. A. Ross and Stuart Hall; sex researchers like G. V. Hamilton or Robert Dickinson; prominent public figures such as Judge Ben Lindsey and birth control advocates like Margaret Sanger. Liberal reformers viewed marriage as in a state of transition. The Victorian model, they thought, was losing social credibility. A new type of marriage was evolving that highlighted love and companionship as the principal conjugal bond. Furthermore, love was thought to be anchored in mutual sexual attraction and gratification.[37] Sex was not merely a sign of love but its origin, underpinning and essential ingredient.

It was, in my view, primarily for strategic political reasons that liberal reformers seized on sex as the vehicle to restore intimate life to a stable, healthy state. As representatives of the new middle class, they were in a struggle against Victorian elites. By claiming that the crisis of intimacy stemmed from restrictive Victorian intimate norms and prudish attitudes, these reformers could discredit Victorian elites as anachronistic and dysfunctional. By advocating the modernization of sexual attitudes and conventions as the way to revitalize intimate life, reformers could portray themselves as a force of social progress. It was a message that appealed to a younger generation for whom the language of self-fulfillment was often a medium to express their own generational identity and aspirations.

The liberal ideology emphasized the sexual and affectional basis of intimacy and carried heightened expectations for personal happiness and companionship in marriage. From our present vantage point, it seems clear that, at least among the white middle class, this companionate ideal has triumphed in the twentieth century. By at least the 1930s, even conservative critics acknowledged its social dominance.[38] Moreover, an impressive body of research has documented the widespread acceptance of this new code of intimacy among the middle class.[39] Its social success was not, though, an inevitable result of evolutionary social processes. For example, some contemporaries viewed the companionate ideal as a necessary product of the gradual loss of social functions by the family. Conjugal love was, in this view, an adaptive response by the family to processes of institutional differentiation and specialization. Long-term structural developments surely played a role in shaping an environment conducive to a companionate ideal. These social processes did not, however, create this model of intimacy, i.e. articulate its specific norms and conventions or provide the rationales that gave it legitimacy. This was the work of liberal reformers.

Among liberal reformers, none were more important in crusading for the companionate ideal than the writers of the hundreds of marriage manuals published between the 1890s and the 1950s. These advice texts are not only indicative of changing codes of intimacy; they were a key social force in making change. Liberal reformers saw themselves as simply describing the evolution of intimate codes. In fact, they were contributing to their very formation.

My focus in this chapter is on those publically available meanings which ordinary middle-class Americans in the early decades of the twentieth century drew from in order to define and regulate their intimate affairs. Marriage manuals are exceptionally well suited to get at these public meanings. They state clearly and in detail publically held beliefs and norms surrounding sex, love and marriage. Their credibility, as indicated, for example, by their popularity or high sales, lends plausibility to my claim that they articulate sentiments and beliefs shared by many middle-class Americans. The authors of these manuals were typically conventional figures, and frequently they had achieved considerable public authority. There is an additional advantage to using marriage manuals as evidence of at least one set of socially credible beliefs and norms. By comparing the ideology of the advice literature in the twentieth century with the advice literature analyzed in chapter 1, we can trace changes in public representations within the same literary genre.

FROM DANGER TO PLEASURE
The Sexual Underpinnings of Love and Marriage

Beginning in the 1890s, marital advice literature reveals a shift in its concerns. Nineteenth-century advice texts took for granted the social legitimacy of marriage. The aims of marriage and its norms were not seriously in dispute. Victorian advice writers sought to educate young men and women, single and married, on the physiology and morality of the sex instinct in order to harness its power for personal and social gain. They warned of the dangers to the individual and society of misusing the sex instinct. Their discourse was not prompted by a perception of the crisis of marriage.

Twentieth-century advice literature, at least through the 1950s, concentrates on defining and prescribing the very norms and conventions of marriage. These discourses were responding to the perceived collapse of clear marital norms. The social scientist and advice author Ernest Groves observed that "nothing in American life is attracting more attention than recent changes in marriage." He speaks of "new adjustments . . . forced upon it [marriage] and its attempt at adjustment suggests a revolution [in marriage]."[40] Marie Carmichael Stopes, the English author of a marriage manual that sold over 900,000 copies by 1940, dramatized the social significance of the current crisis of marriage. "The only secure basis for a present-day state is the welding of its units in marriage; but there is rottenness and danger at the foundations of the state [since] many marriages are unhappy."[41] As evidence of the present crisis, advice writers cited high divorce rates, the growing population of single adults, lower fertility rates and the increased visibility of homosexuals.

A variety of explanations were advanced for the current crisis. One popular account emphasized the loss of social functions by the family. This was said to destabilize marriage because the basis of the family narrows to highly unstable feelings and emotional ties between individuals. Another explanation pointed to the spread of individualism from the economic and political spheres to the domain of marriage and the family. Too much choice was thought to breed egoism and social instability. Many contemporaries believed that the widespread use of contraceptives, changes in gender roles or the loosening of sexual mores was the source of the present crisis of marriage. These "external" explanations, however, were overshadowed by accounts that focused on the "internal" dynamics of marriage. In particular, *sexual maladjustment and sexual unhappiness* were identified as the chief source of failed marriages. As early as 1896, Alice Stockham proposed in her marriage manual *Karezza* that "marital unhappiness is chiefly caused through ignorance [of] the sexual union."[42] Isabel Hutton, some three decades later, observed that "if the truth were known, the great majority of unhappy marriages are due to abnormality in sex life."[43] Rachelle Yarros, physician and feminist, stated what was believed by virtually all advice writers: "Much unhappiness among married people has been traced to sexual maladjustment."[44]

The crisis of marriage was seen as rooted in sexual discontents. Furthermore, advice writers were convinced that the factors responsible for sexual unhappiness were controllable by the individual, rather than rooted in the social structure or culture of society. A chief cause of sexual unhappiness was thought to be the lack of proper sexual knowledge and skills. "It is generally accepted that sexual incompatibility, often growing out of a lack of knowledge of modern sex technique, is one of the most common causes of divorce in America."[45] In his highly popular *Ideal Marriage*, Theodore Van de Velde highlighted the link between sexual ignorance and the troubled state of marriage. "Sex is the foundation of marriage. Yet most married people do not know the ABC of sex. My task here is to dispel this ignorance."[46] Equally destructive of a happy sex life were the fear and anxiety that surround sex. "Marriages built upon the shifting sands of [sexual] fear, shame and ignorance can never lead to happiness," declared the feminist Margaret Sanger.[47] Finally, it was fairly typical of advice writers, both female and male, to connect sexual dissatisfaction to "the sheer blind, isolating selfishness of the average husband."[48] Locating the source of marital discord in sexual maladjustment which, in turn, originates from ignorance, fear or male selfishness, implied that it was within the power of the individual to overcome marital discord. What was needed was expert advice, i.e., correct knowledge, proper skills and the right set of attitudes.

The aim of these marriage manuals was to make marriage more successful by reforming it. "My attempt is towards making marriage more of a success than it now is," declared Dr. Long.[49] Ven de Velde hoped not only to "improve [the] human prospects . . . of enduring happiness in marriage" but to "show you here the way to Ideal Marriage."[50] Central to this reform agenda is the proposition that the underlying sexual source of marital unhappiness has hitherto been unappreciated. A sex-negative Victorian culture was thought to have suppressed the awareness of the sexual underpinnings of marriage. Fear and ignorance about sex, a Victorian legacy, enfeebled its very foundations. With the end of the "conspiracy of silence," argued the modernizers of sex, the pivotal place of sex in marriage can now be fully acknowledged. At one level, the agenda of these liberal reformers was to bring sexual enlightenment—to abolish the reign of sexual fear and ignorance. Yet, they were bearers of a specific reform agenda. Its core message was simple: Only a marriage formed and maintained on the basis of mutual sexual attraction and gratification can be a happy and lasting one. "The basic marriage bond is sex attraction, the sex urge; and this being an inborn drive, its normal satisfaction becomes . . . a condition for sustained harmony and mutual satisfaction in all the other areas of the marital relationship. . . . Harmony and mutual satisfaction in the sexual sphere is likely to be the sustaining vital health of the marriage as a whole."[51] Few marriage manuals composed after 1900 and before 1960 would have disputed the statement by the widely respected Drs. Hannah and Abraham Stone that "a satisfying sex life is essential for a satisfying marital union."[52] Casting aside any doubt about the matter, Isabel Hutton insisted that "no matter how ideal the partnership is every other way, if there is want of sex life or abuse of it, marriage cannot be a success."[53]

In their crusade to remake marriage, these reformers altered the meaning of sex in relation to love. Sex assumed an exalted place in heterosexual love and marriage. Sex became "the highest form of communication between human beings, the most perfect way of showing love. . . . Sex can be the bond that unites, that exalts, that enshrines a marriage."[54] It is to the theme of the sexualization of love and marriage that I now turn.

IDEAL MARRIAGE
Companionship and Sexual Pleasure

Domestic advice writers, like liberal reformers in general, were adamant in their endorsement of the personal and social benefits of marriage. Van de Velde, for example, held that marriage provides "the strongest altruistic leaven to the primitive egotism of Nature's mightly urge—I, too, believe in marriage."[55] For the bestselling advice author Marie Stopes, the institution of marriage guarantees the prosperity and progress of the nation. Thurman Rice, in a pamphlet issued by the American Medical Association, opinioned that "marriage . . . now serves as the cement that binds society together."[56] These discourses propagated the belief that a happy marriage would confer physical health, a longer life, mental vigor and social success.[57] Marriage was, they thought, necessary for self-fulfillment. These rationales justified their effort to reform marriage.

Liberal reform ideals of marriage are revealed in the context of contrasts they made between an emerging "modern" type of marriage and its Victorian predecessor. Maxine Davis held that in the recent past marriages were held together "by law and custom, by the economic dependence of the wife, by a sense of duty in the average 'decent' husband . . . Today, marriage for love is a union of equals who choose to join their lives for companionship."[58] These moderns imagined Victorian marriages to be patriarchal and hierarchical; modern marriages were said to be a voluntary arrangement based on equality and respect. "True marriage is based upon the recognition of the individuality of both husband and wife which brings voluntary, not compelled, co-operation in all departments of family life."[59] Victorian marriages were thought to be maintained by external social pressures while mutual love sustained the modern marriage. "Essentially marriage is a personal relationship . . . a spiritual bond . . . a union of the two personalities."[60]

Victorian marriages were said to be arrangements that aimed at social and economic security; the goal of modern marriage was said to be to secure personal happiness and companionship. Indeed, although some advice texts continued to insist that the creation of the family is a chief purpose of marriage, the dominant view was that in an ideal marriage personal happiness is its chief rationale.[61] "[Marriage] has become a private world created by one man and one woman to share together as equals, to meet each other's deepest human needs and together to establish the atmosphere in which they and their children live and strive for fulfillment."[62] Like their Victorian predecessors, many liberal reformers believed in permanent marriage. "Marriage," wrote Van de Velde, "is the permanent form of monogamous erotic relationships."[63] Yet a concurrent, even if less prominent theme, makes permanence conditional on parenthood. "Permanence is essential to a union which contemplates or achieves parenthood."[64] To the extent that marriage was justified on the grounds of personal happiness, the legitimacy of more flexible divorce laws was seen as a logical consequence.

Liberal reformers exaggerated the extent to which their conception of ideal marriage was historically new. For example, the ideal of marriage as a voluntary relationship based upon mutual love and companionship was, as we have seen, proposed by many Victorians. To be sure, the norm of intimacy and companionship in marriage did not have the degree of social currency in Victorian culture that it achieved in the twentieth century. In one respect, however, moderns radically departed from Victorians, namely, regarding the meaning and role of sex in marriage.

Contrary to persisting popular stereotypes, middle-class Victorians did not typically expel sex from marriage. Sexual expression was considered an expected, even integral, aspect of a good marriage. However, its role in marriage was, ideally, to be quite restricted. Sex was legitimate for its hygienic and procreative functions. Sensual pleasure was accepted only in the very moderate levels necessary to ensure these higher functions. Sex was not expected to serve as an important unifying marital bond. Indeed, to the extent that sexual feelings easily stimulated sensual desires, it was believed to endanger marriage. It threatened to destroy the spiritual underpinnings of true marriage by reducing it to an exchange of carnal pleasure. For many Victorians, the essence of marriage lay in the spiritual unity achieved between the husband and wife; this love bond was embedded in a framework of social, economic and kinship ties and responsibilities that bound husband and wife forever.

In twentieth-century advice literature, we can observe a sea change with regard to the place and meaning of sex in marriage. Sex became a primary basis of marriage. Marriage was thought to originate from mutual sexual desire and attraction. "In early marriage, sexual love is dominant as summer's sun, at once the life force and the catalyst for merging two separate human beings."[65] Maxine Davis, author of *Sexual Responsibilities in Marriage*, believed that "first comes sex, then comes love."[66] Marriage not only arises from sexual impulses but sexual pleasures and longings are described as the very foundation and underlying reality of marriage. "Marriage consists . . . of many demands. . . . Like the radiating spokes of a wheel, most of these demands spring from and return to the hub of the marriage itself. *This hub is the sexual relationship. Attitudes, values, decision-making and most other aspects of marriage are colored by the climate of marital sex.*"[67] Put more succinctly, "Satisfying the cravings of sex, is the basis of marriage."[68] Accordingly, "good sex" or mutual sexual gratification was framed as an elementary condition of maintaining a happy marriage. "The basic marriage bond is sex attraction, the sex urge; and this being an inborn drive, its normal satisfaction becomes . . . a condition for sustained harmony and mutual satisfaction in all the other areas of the marital relationship. Frustration or maladjustment in the sexual sphere seriously jeopardizes the attaining of a vital, creative companionship. . . . Harmony and mutual satisfaction in the sexual sphere is likely to be the sustaining vital health of the marriage as a whole."[69]

The very success of marriage depended upon achieving sexual compatibility. Margaret Sanger made mutual sexual adjustment the key to a successful marriage. "In marriage, as distinct from every other human relationship, the bedrock of lasting happiness . . . in every respect, lies in a proper physical adjustment of the two persons, and a proper physical management of their mutual experiences of [sexual] union."[70] Marie Stopes regarded the success of coitus as the barometer of a successful marriage. "Where the acts of coitus are rightly performed, the pair can disagree, can hold opposite views about every conceivable subject . . . without any . . . desire to separate: they will enjoy each other's differences. Contrariwise, . . . if the sex act is not properly performed . . . all that harmony and suitability in other things will be of no avail."[71] Dr. Isabel Hutton concurred. "No matter how ideal the partnership in every other way, if there is want of sex life . . . marriage cannot be a success."[72] In some advice texts, sexual fulfillment was conceived of as a condition of marital growth. "If husbands and wives ever attain to the highest condition of married life, it can only be after they know and practice, what is right in all their sex relations."[73] Ultimately, mutual sexual gratification was said to justify the institution of marriage. "In these modern days when friendships, mutual occupations, businesses, almost every phase of our civilized life, bring men and women together in innumerable ways, the only justification of marriage is the mutual need for and the mutual enjoyment in sex union."[74]

The extent to which these texts promote the sexualization of marriage is further illustrated by referring to two advice authors who resisted this construction. Drs. Hannah and Abraham Stone were the authors of the enormously influential *A Marriage Manual.* The Stones believed that marriage is based upon a range of common interests and commitments, only one of which is sexual in nature. "I consider the main purposes of marriage to be companionship, sexual intimacy and the establishment of a family. . . . An ideal union is one that fulfills most effectively these several requirements."[75] In this formulation, sexual satisfaction is identified as just one bond of marriage, not more fundamental than companionship and the creation of a family. "Sex alone," the Stones declared, "does not make a marriage, and that no really lasting relationship can be based merely on sexual attraction. For a truly happy marriage, there must, of course, be present mutual love, . . . a community of ideas, of interests, of tastes, of standards, an adequate economic arrangement, and a satisfactory adjustment in personal, family, and social relationships."[76] Sexual adjustment is apparently but one factor determining marital happiness. Yet, the above excerpt is followed by this passage: "On the other hand, it is also true that a successful marriage can hardly be achieved where sexual attraction does not exist, or where the marital sex life is unsatisfactory and inadequate. . . . *The sex factor plays a leading role in marital satisfaction.*" The two physicians go on to assert that "the development of a harmonious sex life should constitute one of the aims and ideals of the marital union."[77]

A second text that promotes the sexualization of marriage apparently against its own intentions is Van de Velde's bestselling *Ideal Marriage.* In the introductory pages, Van de Velde proposed that a good marriage depends upon a range of factors. He underscored the importance of the emotional and social compatibility of the husband and wife. He urged the husband and wife to strive for intimacy by sharing interests and activities. In addition, he emphasized that the couple must arrive at an amicable agreement about whether or not to have children. A "vigorous and harmonious sexuality constitutes the fourth corner-stone of our temple."[78] Although he made sexual adjustment the fourth and last component of marriage, he proceeded to elevate its significance. "It [sexual adjustment] must be solidly and skillfully built, for it has to bear a main portion of the weight of the whole structure. But in many cases it is badly balanced . . . so can we wonder that the whole edifice collapses soon?" Whereas sexual satisfaction was initially just one component of marriage, it now assumes a primary role. "Sex is the foundation of marriage."[79] Van de Velde counsels that "sexual incongruence or incompatibility must be guarded against" for "as soon as sexual attraction is extinguished . . . enmity manifests itself."[80] *Ideal Marriage* is primarily a primer on erotic technique, a recipe book for achieving mutual sexual fulfillment in marriage.

BRINGING SEX BACK INTO LOVE

An ideal of marriage based upon love and companionship was a part of middle-class Victorian culture. Yet, the sharp social division of male and female gender roles, the norm of large families (five to seven children), and women's legal, social and economic subordination to men, blocked the realization of an ideal of marital companionship. In the first half of the twentieth century, the gap between the ideal and reality of companionate marriage diminished. Men and women went to college together and often shared the workplace as well as leisure pursuits. Companionship in marriage extended the intermingling of the two genders in other social spheres. Furthermore, while women were by no means the social equals of men, expanded opportunities in education and employment, coupled with women's more assertive social style, made them feel more men's equals. Finally, the commercialization of many household tasks (e.g., food preparation), along with the dramatic decrease in family size (two or three children were commonplace among the middle class), allowed wives to be more attentive to their own needs and to their marital relationship. In this social setting, the ideal of a companionate marriage was much more socially credible. Intimate companionship figured prominently as a standard of a happy and successful marriage. Paralleling this change was an alteration in the meaning of love, at least with respect to the role of sex. In the early decades of the twentieth century, a spiritual conception of love gave way to a sexualized view.

Heterogenous meanings cluster around the concept of sex in twentieth-century advice literature. Like their Victorian predecessors these authors believed in the omnipresence and power of sexual motivations. The sex instinct seemed to underpin individual behavior, social conventions and cultural innovations. "Not only is sex the very foundation of marriage, it provides the motive-power which drives all the machinery of life."[81] The fate of humanity seemed to these reformers to depend on the way the sex instinct is exercised and regulated. In this regard, the heirs to Victorianism depart from their predecessors not so much in imagining the power of sex, as in emphasizing its productive and beneficient power. Virtually absent from these discourses is a rhetoric of the dangers of sex. Sexual expression was seen as conducive to health, mental vigor, social success and, as we will see, a happy conjugal love.

In early twentieth-century advice texts, the Victorian norm that sex be primarily procreative is prominent. For example, Dr. Long held that the primary purpose of sex is the "reproduction of the race."[82] Typically, this reproductive rationale was joined to the equally Victorian notion that the family is the natural completion of a marriage. "The husband and wife need children to make a home complete and a complete home is the supreme attainment of human life."[83] Indeed, "childless couples (when fertile and sound) are a menace to civilization."[84] Childless marriages were thought to be inherently unstable. A successful marriage needed the emotional ties and social obligations of parenthood to give it the stability to withstand the inevitable internal disturbances. The family, in other words, was viewed as a safeguard against a failed marriage with all its manifold personal and social costs.

The procreative rationale diminished in importance as we move further into the twentieth century. As childless marriages and smaller families became more typical and acceptable, uncoupling sex from its procreative aim acquired widespread social support. Hygienic justifications for sex were often advanced. The proper exercise of the sex instinct was considered essential for the maintenance of sound physical and mental health. "The . . . sex impulses . . . have been considered as having one purpose only—procreation. True but their secondary purposes . . . are as valuable. . . . They sustain that vigor without which . . . all progress ceases."[85] By the 1920s the major justification for sex related to its connection to love and romantic bonding. "In marital sex relations . . . the [sex] act is the most intimate expression of . . . love. . . . Aside from any procreative purpose, that is its meaning and its justification in marriage."[86] Although love involved intellectual, moral and social bonds, it is the changed place of sex in relation to love that signals the most dramatic departure from Victorian ideals of intimacy.

Victorian advice texts, at times, endorsed the notion that sex can serve as an outward physical sign of an inward spiritual union. Yet, because sexual feelings were thought to easily elicit carnal desire which threatened to pollute the spiritual essence of marriage, Victorians urged the de-eroticization of sex and, at times, the desexualization of love and marriage. The urge to spiritualize marriage, however, conflicted with Victorian's belief in the naturalness and beneficent power of the sex instinct. This tension, as we have seen in the two previous chapters, pervades middle-class Victorian intimate culture.

By the turn of the century we can discern a momentous shift in the way sex is related to love. The Victorian antithesis between eroticism and love collapses. The popular advice writer William Robinson comments. "Some writers attempt to make a clear distinction between sensual and sentimental love; . . . The first is called animal love or lust; the second pure love or ideal love; the first variety of love is said to be selfish, egotistic, the other—self-sacrificing, altruistic. . . . *There is no distinct line of demarcation between the two varieties of love, and one merges imperceptibly into the other. . . . In other words, there are not two separate, distinct varieties of love."*[87] Robinson was challenging the Victorian antithesis between sensuality and love; sex and its sensual pleasures are, he insisted, an integral part of love. Similarly, the social scientist and popular writer Ernest Groves took issue with the Victorian dichotomy of sex and love when he remarked that "sex does not need to be elevated into something else after the fashion of those who advocate spiritualizing marriage. It is, rather, a legitimate part of love itself."[88] Liberal reformers went beyond viewing sex as a legitimate dimension of spiritual love. They often maintained that sex is the virtual foundation and essence of love. The success of conjugal love was thought to hinge on the quality of sex.

Whereas Victorian advice texts anchor love in spiritual affinities, their successors trace love to mutual erotic longings. "In early marriage, sexual love is dominant. . . .[It is] at once the life force and the catalyst for merging two separate human beings."[89] Maxine Davis leaves no doubt about the sequential relation between sex and love. "First comes sex, then comes love."[90] The mutual sexual attraction that motivates marriage is so compelling that "many a couple marry under the misapprehension that sexual attraction and satisfaction are all that is necessary for harmony."[91] Although Ms. Davis wished to disabuse her readers of this belief, she nevertheless insisted that "whether or not the marriage is successful depends on a number of factors . . . But sexual love is always significant. . . . Successful marriage and successful [sexual] adjustment tend to go together."[92] The fate of conjugal love, ultimately, turns on "the . . . physical, mental, and spiritual intimacy sexual love generates."[93]

Ms. Davis sounded a theme which was widely shared among liberal reformers: the sexual underpinnings of love. "The foundation of, the basis of all love is sexual attraction," remarked William Robinson in direct contradiction to Victorian beliefs.[94] To be sure, Robinson went on to make the point that "a foundation is not a whole structure. . . .

Many more factors . . . are needed before the wonderful structure called love is brought into existence."[95] In other advice texts, erotic motivations are more than the origin of love; they are the key to its vigor and growth. "Nothing in all their married fellowship can contribute more toward the growth of their love . . . than this beautiful and sacred contact [i.e., sexual union]."[96] Sustained mutual sexual gratification was thought to keep love vital. "The winning of love is but the first stage of a long adventure. Its maintenance calls for more thought and skill than its gaining. And all the means of stimulating [sexual] desire must be enlisted in the task."[97] Sexual maladjustment signals a crisis in love. "When sex deserts the bed, love flies out the window. With the breakdown in the sexual relationship comes a corresponding breakdown in every other aspect of love."[98] William Robinson was even more succinct. "Without sexual attraction . . . there can be no love."[99]

Sexual expression was not only viewed as a sign of love but it was the highest way of showing love. Sex "is the . . . most perfect way of showing love."[100] Maxine Davis believed that the "mutual enjoyment of sexual intercourse [is] the most intimate and exclusive way to express love."[101] The intermingling of sex and love is further revealed by the claim that love is a condition of good sex. "Only where love is can sexual pleasure be at its highest, the orgasm ecstatic."[102] Sexual joy functions, in Van de Velde's formulation, as a rationale for love.

The sexualization of love is in evidence in the confusion of the language of love with that of eroticism. For example, in her enormously successful *Married Love*, Marie Stopes located the source of unhappy marriage in the lack of competency in the "art of love." The latter is identified with strategies that promote "mutual joy in sex."[103] Similarly, Eustare Chesser underscored the point that "the whole art of love lies in giving pleasure." Leaving no doubt that pleasure refers to sexual pleasure, he remarks: "Rule one for success in marriage . . . is this: Learn how to make love! The [sexual] attraction which leads people to mate at the start must be maintained."[104] When Chesser refers to love, he speaks of "to make love," not, say, to build or develop love as an emotional or moral relationship. Underlying this conflation of sex and love was the belief that, in the end, the range of emotional and mental feelings that we describe as love arise from and remain anchored in mutual sexual longings. "All manner of emotions and mental processes have crystallized around the impulse or sexual approach; they form the complex, the abstract conception of love."[105] In other words, Van de Velde proposed that love is a product of and rooted in the sex drive. The fate of love and marriage hinged, accordingly, on sustaining a high level of mutual sexual attraction and satisfaction. Thus, Van de Velde could reasonably conclude that succeeding in love and marriage is ultimately a matter of rejuvenating marital sex through learning proper erotic techniques. "Sexual . . . incompatibility must be guarded against. . . . It is possible if . . . both parties . . . are attentive . . . to one another's needs; display initiative and ingenuity in stimulating and satisfying one another's needs; and [this is possible] by [learning] a culture of erotic technique."[106]

GOOD SEX
The Making of a New Norm of Sexual Fulfillment

Between 1890 and 1960 the relation between sex, love and marriage changed. The Victorians accepted sex as a part of marriage. They did not, however, conceive of sex as an essential romantic or marital bond. As sex became the site where love and marriage succeeded or failed, it acquired a heightened importance. Great expectations were attached to sex. In particular, the giving and receiving of erotic pleasure became a standard by which to judge love and marriage. Eroticism or the pursuit of sex for its sensually pleasurable and expressive qualities acquired legitimacy in a context of love and marriage. Accordingly, there developed the need to define sexual satisfaction and to describe the conditions conducive to it.

These discourses constructed a norm of mutual sexual satisfaction. Sex was supposed to be cooperative, mutually respectful and involve shared responsibilities. Sex was not supposed to be something men did to women for their pleasure but a mutually pleasurable experience. This presupposed an acknowledgment of women's sexual needs and desires.

These texts affirmed a view of women as equal sexual beings to men. Victorian images of female sexuality had by no means disappeared. Women's sexuality was often defined as "more coupled with feelings of tenderness and maternity."[107] Similarly, women's sexual feelings continued to be described as more dormant and less genitally centered. "The woman . . . is sexually more passive, her desires are aroused more slowly, and they express themselves at first in a rather diffuse urge for general bodily contact and sexual play."[108] Yet this discourse of gender difference was not joined to a Victorian framework which posits female sexuality as lacking or diminished in carnal desire. Sensuality was not viewed as antithetical to femininity. Hannah and Abraham Stone may have constructed female sexual nature as different from male, but they insisted on equality with respect to erotic desire. "It is rather generally assumed at present that the woman's erotic desires are just as strong as those of the male, although the manifestations of the sexual urge may vary considerably in the two sexes."[109] Similarly, while Maxine Davis assumed that female sexual nature is more romantic, she was equally adamant that "men and women are equally capable of sexual desire and each is physically fully provided with the means for gratifying that desire."[110] In fact, Davis held that women's natural endowments enhance their potential for sensual pleasure. "Nature has obviously been more generous with woman than with man for it has thus endowed her with many physical opportunities for sensual enjoyment."[111] Van de Velde agreed: A "woman has a range of permutations and variations in sexual pleasure which are not possible to the man."[112] Furthermore, although these authors believed that female sexual desire is less genitally localized than in men, the clitoris was characterized as the principal site of carnal desire. "The clitoris is perhaps the main seat of the women's sensuous feelings."[113] Or, "The clitoris . . . has more to do with arousing sexual feeling than any other structure."[114] In these discourses, female sexuality was typically described as similar to male sexuality at least with regard to the intensity of the sexual drive and erotic desire. This signals an important change in public representations. It marks the declining power of the Victorian notion that sexuality is gendered in a rigid, bipolar way. Sensuality was no longer seen as integral only to men. Women were viewed as both feminine and erotic.[115]

The fuller sexualization of femininity was related to a norm of mutual sexual gratification. Once women's sexual needs were accorded an equal status to those of men, the norm of companionship and mutuality in marriage inevitably extended into the domain of sex. Reciprocal sexual gratification became a norm in the companionate marriage ideal. Echoing the sentiments of virtually all liberal reformers, the Stones remarked: "The sexual embrace should become . . . the expression of mutual desire and passion. . . . In other words, the joy of sex is increased for both when it is mutual."[116]

The norm of sexual reciprocity accounts for the feminist cast of these discourses. Husbands are repeatedly criticized for being selfish and nonresponsive to their wives' sexual wants. In part, this is explained as a product of male ignorance. Men are said to not understand women's sexual needs nor how to sexually fulfill them. Men are criticized, in addition, for their selfishness. "Male ignorance and disregard of women's sexual capacities and needs is obviously a prime factor in the apparent coldness of women and the [sexual] maladjustments that grow out of the unequal sexual relationship."[117] Husbands were advised to be empathetic and responsive to their wives sexual wants. "By studying his wife's responses, the husband will eventually know exactly what stimuli will arouse her on each occasion."[118] Wives were encouraged to frankly express their sexual wishes and exercise sexual autonomy. "She should not fear to tell her husband which of these [erotic] procedures are delightful and which are unpleasing; and he should be governed accordingly. She should not only cooperate with him in his efforts to make her desire for intercourse imperious and irresistible, but . . . should . . . encourage him the while."[119] In order for women to achieve sexual fulfillment, they are encouraged to overcome whatever sexual inhibitions and fears they felt. A history of sexual repression had presumably made sex seem degrading or dangerous for many women. To achieve their own and their husbands' happiness, women were told they had to learn to approach sex as a domain of pleasure and self-fulfillment. Margaret Sanger advised women to "cleanse your mind of purience and shame. Never be ashamed of your passion. If you are strongly sexed . . . you possess the greatest and most valuable inheritance a human being can enjoy."[120]

Good sex, then, was conceived of as involving a norm of mutual pleasure and responsibility. This entailed that husbands and wives be empathetic and caring (men's problem) and overcome their sexual fears and inhibitions (women's problem). Nevertheless, no matter how empathetic, caring and uninhibited a husband and wife might be, without the proper sexual knowledge and skills, sexual fulfillment would still elude them. Ignorance of sex technique was singled out as a major source of unhappiness in marriage. Van de Velde stated this in no uncertain terms. "Sex is the foundation of marriage. Yet most married people do not know the ABC of sex."[121] He was especially critical of men who are ignorant of their wives sexual needs and inept in pleasing them. For those lacking sexual skills, sex becomes tedious and unfulfilling. Sexual attraction turns into "sexual repulsion" which threatens the marriage. "Sexual . . . incompatibility must . . . be guarded against. . . . It is possible if . . . both partners . . . display initiative and ingenuity in stimulating and satisfying one another's [sexual] needs."[122]

Van de Velde recommended that individuals master sex technique as a necessary condition of mutually satisfactory marital sex. Acquiring such expertise entails learning the complexities and sequential logic of sexual fulfillment. Van de Velde described good sex as a developmental process involving distinct phases, each of which must be skillfully mastered. In all phases of sex, "equal rights and equal joys in a sexual union" were considered essential.[123] In stage one, the "prelude," erotic desire is awakened. Sexual interest is displayed in words, looks and smell, not in touch or taste. The "prelude" is a kind of erotic conversation that prepares the couple for the second phase— "love-play." Here the center of the erotic drama shifts from verbal and visual to sensual play. Love-play begins with the mouth-to-mouth kiss but gradually extends to the "body kiss" and the "genital kiss."[124] The expert lover is said to know all the possible ways to produce pleasure from the kiss. In "love-play," the hands are said to function as a key instrument of sensual pleasure. Van de Velde described in detail the various erotic zones and how they may yield pleasure from a multitude of tactile strategies, e.g., pressing, gripping, stroking, caressing. As sexual excitation builds, the couple enters the third phase, "coitus." This is the sexual climax. It is "the consummation of sexual satisfaction which . . . concludes with the ejaculation—or emission—of semen into the vagina." The orgasm initiates the final phase, "after-glow" or "after-play." The couple lies together, "their souls meet and merge, even though their bodies are no longer linked."[125]

Throughout Van de Velde's description of good sex, he underscored the point that sexual expertise involves not only mutuality and specialized knowledge but a spirit of experimentation. The husband and wife were encouraged to explore ways to enhance their mutual sexual satisfaction. He implored his readers to experiment not only with sex acts and positions but with their voice, dress, body odor and social setting to augment sexual arousal and pleasure. Only "cruelty and the use of artificial means for producing voluptuous sensations" were explicitly proscribed in "normal sexual intercourse."[126] Other advice texts posited mutual consent as the only limiting condition of marital sex. "As a rule let the husband and wife do whatever their desire prompts or suggests, and [whatever] they would like to."[127] The Stones declared that "no form of sex play is wrong in itself, unless it gives rise to physical injury or to an undesirable emotional or aesthetic shock."[128] The libertarian ethical tone of these statements appears to have relieved eroticism of the moral weight of bearing danger and shame. Yet, an ambivalence toward eroticism is still apparent in these texts.

The legitimation of sex as a domain of sensual pleasure was accompanied by some important restrictions. Erotic pleasures were accepted only in a social context of heterosexual love and marriage. Like their Victorian predecessors, twentieth-century advice writers assumed that heterosexuality was natural. Unlike their predecessors, they posited homosexuality as its unnatural antithesis. Moreover, whereas in nineteenth-century advice texts same-sex behavior was classified with a miscellaneous group of prohibited sexual behaviors (e.g., masturbation, bestiality, carnality, fornication), popular advice writers of the early twentieth century singled out "homosexuality" as a distinct category of sexual deviance. Drawing on a medical discourse of homosexuality that was being popularized by contemporary sexologists and psychologists, advice authors defined homosexuality as an illness, a pathological symptom of an individual's failure to achieve a normal state of heterosexuality. For example, Hannah and Abraham Stone described homosexuality as a "sexual abberation" and an "inversion" of normal psychological development.[129] The physician and popular author Mary Calderone held that homosexuality "should be viewed as an illness."[130] Advice texts functioned as one vehicle for propagating a construction of "the homosexual" as a unique and flawed human type.[131]

These advice texts uniformly upheld a heterosexual norm. Indeed, by sexualizing love, they contributed to the weakening of the Victorian tradition that accepted some forms of same-sex love. Romantic friendships were transformed into a sign of a psychopathological condition: homosexuality. Thus, women who loved women were labeled lesbians—an abnormal human type.[132]

These discourses perpetuated the Victorian norm that restricted legitimate sexual activity to marriage. Sexual expression outside of marriage was proscribed, with the exception of masturbation. Virgin marriage was still the ideal.[133] Strict abstinence for single people was considered obligatory. Undoubtedly, the continued defense of the heterosexual marital norm in the context of reformers' efforts to reconceive sex as a sphere of sensual pleasure and self-fulfillment helps to explain their acceptance of masturbation, and their advocacy of more flexible divorce law.

Within a marital context, sex that did not culminate in coital orgasm was also proscribed. Noncoital forms of eroticism were defended, but only as preliminary and prepatory to coitus. They were not valued for their own pleasurable and expressive qualities. Coitus continued to represent the natural telos of the sex instinct. It served as a sign of psychological normality and adult maturity. This view was, of course, given an elaborate medical-scientific formulation by Sigmund Freud and his American disciples.

Coitus was, in addition, taken as a sign of spiritual union. It was interpreted not merely as a physical act but as the realization of a great merging of the spiritual essence of the husband and wife. Although these texts made eroticism integral to love and marriage, they often counseled against uncoupling sensual pleasures from their spiritual meaning. The pursuit of erotic pleasure, these reformers proposed, should never become the sole purpose of sex. "Sexual intercourse is not an end in itself. . . . Voluptuous pleasure alone . . . cannot bring real happiness."[134] Coitus, declared Van de Velde, is "a means of expression that makes them [the couple] one."[135] For Helena Wright, an author of a marriage manual that rivaled the popularity of Van de

Velde's *Ideal Marriage*, "pleasures of the body are nothing in themselves; if pursued for their own sake they can end only in emptiness. . . . Used as an instrument for expressing union of body, mind, and soul, the pleasures of the body are inexhaustible."[136] Margaret Sanger reminded her readers "that sex-communion should be considered as a true union of souls, not merely a physical function. . . . Unless the psychic and spiritual desire are fulfilled the relationship has been woefully deficient and the participants degraded and dissatisfied."[137] The sexualization of love and the legitimation of eroticism did not challenge a heterosexual, marital and romantic norm.

CONCLUSION

At the turn of the century, Americans engaged in a spirited public debate on the troubled state of intimate affairs. The claim that America was in the midst of a crisis of sexual morality was sounded in magazines, newspapers, journals and books. A dramatic rise in the divorce rate, the spread of venereal disease, a heightened public awareness of homosexuality and the movement of sexual representations into the public sphere were taken as signs of this crisis. A lively public discussion ensued around the malaise of marriage and strategies for its reform.

A major party to this debate were liberal reformers. Although they saw themselves as advocating change, they believed that their ideas articulated an emerging visible reality. In other words, reformers assumed that their ideology was widely accepted by most Americans but lacked full public recognition because they were opposed by a small but powerful minority of old-style Victorian elites. For example, in their enormously influential *The Companionate Marriage*, Judge Ben Lindsey and Wainwright Evans described the companionate ideal as if it were a social fact. "I believe I have enough evidence to justify the conclusion not that this change in our sexual mores [toward a companionate ideal] is going to take place at some time in the future, but that is has already taken place and is developing and crystallizing into a tacitly recognized and increasingly tolerated code. It is not that such practices are new . . . but that they have support from such a large segment of society."[138] Although this claim cannot be accepted at face value, neither can we assume that just because advice writers were reformers their ideas were at odds with existing social conventions. The popularity of their books and the fact that their sexual ideology surfaced in a variety of public forms suggest that their views had substantial social currency. Setting aside the behavioral impact of these discourses, they represented one socially significant construction of intimate ideals. At a minimum, they tell us something important about the public beliefs and norms of the white middle-class between the 1890s and the 1950s.

These advice texts stand as evidence of a change in public conceptions of intimate life in America between the mid-nineteenth and twentieth centuries. Central to this change is the altered place of sex in relation to love. Sex was reconceived as a medium to express, sustain and enhance love. Accordingly, sex was imbued with great personal and social significance as it now carried the burden of being responsible for personal and marital happiness. As the giving and receiving of sexual pleasure became a standard of love and a happy marriage, the production of erotic pleasures assumed a higher value. It was now legitimate to focus upon ways of enhancing sensual pleasures. An elaborate language of sex technique, sensual pleasure and expressiveness materialized. In short, making sex a proving ground for love and marriage contributed to the birth of a culture of eroticism.

This theme will be further explored in chapter 5. The development of a culture of eroticism is linked to efforts in the 1960s and 1970s to legitimate sex for its pleasurable and expressive qualities alone. Before I sketch this development, we need to press further into the concept of the sexualization of love, exploring its implications for men and women as well as for same-sex intimacies. In chapter 4, I will consult sex surveys, autobiographies and novels of the period to get closer to American intimate culture in the first half of the twentieth century.

4

Bringing Sex Back In

The Birth of a Culture of Eroticism

The Victorian era did not come to an abrupt end with the turn of the century. Between the twentieth century and its predecessor, there is as much continuity as discontinuity. Thus, despite very significant changes in gender meanings and roles, the masculine gender identification with the public sphere of work and politics and the feminization of the domestic sphere were virtually unchanged.[1] Middle-class women were more likely to have paid jobs or to step out into the public world of night entertainment, but feminine self-fulfillment was typically sought in the roles of wife and mother.[2] The roots of middle-class, nonimmigrant men and women who came of age between 1900 and the 1950s still lay in Victorian culture. Many of them were reared in the Victorian century; others matured in communities whose culture had a decidedly Victorian cast; still others were influenced by Victorian culture through their parents, kin, teachers, ministers, or friends.

Contemporaries frequently described themselves as living in two worlds. Raised in a Victorian setting, they lived as adults in a world that often highlighted different attitudes and roles. Many of these men and women felt anomic. Reflecting this socially dislocated status, the writer and radical fellow-traveler Hutchins Hapgood described himself as a "Victorian in the modern age."[3] Living between two eras—a passing Victorian one and an emerging "modern" era—the generation that came of age after World War I experienced heightened generational conflict and imbued it with a larger historical significance. Helen Bevington described the tensions between her mother and herself as symbolizing a historical conflict between two eras.

> It was simply part of my mother's persistent bad luck to have a daughter like me growing up in the 1920s. By then the revolt was not only my own. It was general, a time of rebellion and whooping it up

among the young. And if most of us in high school evaded our Victorian parents and kept silent about our activities, it was because we thought we had to. . . . How could one explain to an angry mother what a necking party was?[4]

Like many of her contemporaries, Bevington interprets this generational conflict as a historical confrontation between a fading Victorian era and a nascent liberal modern epoch. Although not all of her contemporaries believed that these changes were for the common good, they seemed to agree that living in a transitional period provided them with a privileged standpoint from which to describe these changes. Many men and women of this period believed that their lives, ordinary in almost every respect, documented this great transformation.[5]

In the many memoirs and autobiographies written during this period, contemporaries detailed changes in economic, political and educational institutions, in rural and urban life, in their relation to the natural environment and so forth.[6] They documented equally far-reaching alterations in intimate matters. In particular, contemporaries commented upon the changing place of sex in relation to love, marriage and self-fulfillment. "The modern youth are neither so emphatic about the simplicities of sex, nor so spiritual in its further meaning. This is because the sex act, to them, is more natural, so they are not obsessed as the Victorian was."[7] Interestingly, Hutchins Hapgood contrasted Victorians to "moderns" by featuring the higher value moderns place upon the sensual aspects of sex over its spiritual dimensions. "To us Victorians, sex did not need a skillful prolongation . . . [of its] ultimate possibilities of sensation. To us the merely animal act produced the spiritual emotion."[8] Unlike Hapgood, who seemed to adjust well to modern ways, the well-known essayist and author, Henry Seidel Canby did not. In his exquisitely detailed and nostalgic reflection *American Memoir*, he concurs with Hapgood regarding the altered place of sex in relation to love. "But sex, naked and unashamed, with no purpose but its own gratification, was kept in its place, which was not friendship, not even the state of falling in love."[9] Sex for Victorians, continued Canby, "had little part in our relationships."[10] Hardly disguising his disapproval of current sexual conventions, he contrasts the role of sex in Victorian marriage with its modern successor. "Marriage for us, though not a parlor or dining-room affair . . . was dramatized in our imaginations as a state in which sex was only incidental. Today our town would have been mildly astonished if it had been told that the success of marriage depended upon embracing [i.e., sex]."[11]

These somewhat reluctant moderns were commenting upon a profound cultural change: the sexualization of love and marriage and the legitimation of eroticism. I argue in this chapter that sexual expectations and meanings changed in at least one crucial respect between the 1890s and 1950s: sex took on a heightened meaning as a sphere where love is demonstrated and success in marriage is achieved. Sex functioned not only as a sign of love or its proof. Love and the very success of marriage had to be repeatedly proven through the sensual pleasures given and received in sex. One result is that the erotic aspects of sex acquired legitimation as carnal pleasures assumed a higher purpose. This theme was developed in a general way in the last chapter. Here I want to be more specific. I explore this theme in both a heterosexual and homosexual context and with some attention to the link between gender, sexuality and love.

SEX RESEARCH AND THE SEXUALIZATION OF INTIMACY
From Mosher to Kinsey

Between the 1890s and 1950s, several major surveys of sexual behavior and attitudes were undertaken. This research varies from the small-scale, in-depth interviews which formed the basis for G. V. Hamilton's *A Research in Marriage* to the Kinsey studies, which involved elaborate statistical computations based upon thousands of interviews. This research can be profitably used to explore the dynamics of intimate culture in this period.

Perhaps the first sex survey in the U.S. was done by Dr. Clelia Duel Mosher. Between 1890 and 1920 she surveyed forty-five married women on varied aspects of their intimate life, including their sexual behavior and attitudes. The survey, entitled *Statistical Study of the Marriage of Forty-Seven Women*, was never completed nor published by Ms. Mosher. Since its discovery by Carl Degler in 1973, and its publication in 1980, the Mosher survey has become an important document in the debate over Victorian and post-Victorian sexuality.[12]

Revisionist interpretations of Victorian sexuality have appealed to the Mosher survey to press their claim that the Victorians were decidedly more hedonistic than is acknowledged by the popular stereotype of the repressed Victorian.[13] These interpreters suggest that the Victorians were moderns when it came to integrating sex into their intimate affairs. They point out, for example, that most of the women Mosher interviewed reported that sex was necessary for men and women, that coitus was mostly agreeable and that sex should be pleasurable. The revisionist reading of the Mosher survey is somewhat weakened because the meaning of key terms such as "necessity," "agreeable" or "pleasurable" are nowhere clarified by Mosher or the respondents.

There is a more basic flaw in the revisionist interpretation of the Mosher survey.[14] These historians fail to take into account the fact that half of the completed interviews were done before 1900 and the remainder after 1900. Furthermore, the women interviewed before 1900 display significantly different attitudes toward sex than those interviewed after 1900. Consider the differences in their responses to the question about whether sexual intercourse is a necessity for both men and women. Among those women interviewed before 1900, three out of eighteen respondents whose interviews I could definitely date, or 17 percent of them, answered with an unequivocal yes. Six of these women (33 percent) said it was not a necessity, and another 33 percent reported that sexual intercourse was a necessity only or chiefly for men. Of the twenty women interviewed after 1900 whose interview dates I could establish, twelve (60 percent) reported that sexual intercourse was a necessity for both men and women. Only one woman indicated that sex was a necessity only for men. Even more revealing of the differences between these two groups of women is the way they relate sex to reproduction and to a spiritual meaning. Of the seventeen interviews conducted before 1900 for which I have established definite interview dates and obtained the relevant information, ten respondents (59 percent) reported that reproduction was the primary aim of sexual intercourse. The comparable figure for the group interviewed after 1900 is two, or just 12 percent. Furthermore, only four (23 percent) of the women interviewed before 1900 claimed spiritual justifications for sex (e.g., affection, love or mental union). Among women interviewed after 1900, twelve (70 percent) identified sex as having a spiritual meaning and justification.

These figures suggest different conclusions than those of the revisionists. Women interviewed before 1900 overwhelmingly reported that sex was less integral and less necessary, especially for women. Sex was joined to procreation as its primary function. Sexual intercourse was only marginally, if at all, associated with a spiritual meaning. Women interviewed after 1900 overwhelmingly asserted the necessity of sex for both men and women. They defined sex in relation to spiritual considerations, especially as an expression or sign of love. Procreation was viewed as a marginal reason for sexual intercourse. The coupling of sex and love appears, then, to be a twentieth-century development, or at least decidedly more prominent in our century.

The Mosher survey points to a generational difference regarding intimate culture between the women interviewed before and after 1900. There is some evidence to support this claim. Those women interviewed before 1900 were on the average born in 1859 whereas the average birth date of women interviewed after 1900 was 1870. The women in the latter group came of age at a historical juncture of significant social change. These women, many of whom were interviewed as late as 1920, were exposed to sexual discourses and representations as well as a consumer-oriented economy that was antithetical to key aspects of Victorian intimate culture. In a word, the Mosher survey documents the first signs of a shift to a post-Victorian culture that reconfigures the relation between sex, love and marriage.

Although the Mosher survey seems to document a change in intimate norms, it does not give us much access to these altered meanings. Moreover, the Mosher respondents are, at best, indicative of a transitional generation. These women, many of whom were born in the 1850s or before, matured in a solidly Victorian culture. We need to consult research that addresses a generation born after 1890. Fortunately, the era of sex research took off around the 1920s.

In *A Research in Marriage*, the psychiatrist Dr. G. V. Hamilton interviewed one hundred white, middle-class married men and women.[15] He was interested in the relationship between sexual behavior and marital satisfaction. In order to assess the importance of sex in marriage, he asked a series of questions relating to the role of sex. One key question asked was "What is there in your marriage that is especially unsatisfactory to you?"[16] Twenty-five percent of the men and 15 percent of the women underscored sexual maladjustment on the part of their spouse. Consistent with this response, Hamilton found that both men and women identified "sex maladjustments" as "the principal source of [marital] trouble."[17] In response to the question "What things in your married life annoy and dissatisfy you the most?" fifteen men mentioned "sex maladjustments due to wife's inadequacy," while thirteen women answered "their sex life is unsatisfactory to both spouses."[18] Based on this research, Hamilton concluded that an "unsatisfactory sex life is the major source of marital dissatisfaction."[19]

Hamilton's conclusion found support in the research of his contemporaries. In their survey of over 1000 married men and women, Robert Latou Dickinson and Lura Beam reported that sexual dissatisfaction was more significant in explaining marital troubles than disputes around work, money or children.[20] "If the data in this study reinforce any one concept it is that satisfactory sexual relations are necessary to a fully adjusted and successful union."[21] Summarizing the data of a study of twenty-two hundred women, Katherine Davis concluded: "In married life the sex relationship . . . indisputably plays the major part."[22] We need not necessarily accept at face value the claim of these researchers that their surveys document that the success of middle-

class marriage hinged on sexual satisfaction. Nonetheless, their findings as well as their conclusions amount to compelling evidence that
sexual satisfaction had become a principal norm of true love and a
happy marriage.

The Kinsey research provides additional documentation of the
heightened importance that sexual pleasure had assumed in marriage.
By comparing an older generation born before 1900 with one born
after 1900, the Kinsey research demonstrated that while the frequency
of marital coitus remained constant, virtually every other aspect of
marital sex changed.[23] The younger generation engaged in more and
longer foreplay; they were more accepting of oral-genital sex and
experimented with more coital positions; they were more likely to
engage in deep kissing and the manual stimulation of the genitals;
finally, they more often engaged in sex naked.[24] In short, it is not
simply that the younger generation were less repressed, but that erotic
pleasure mattered more. In other words, the giving and receiving of
sexual pleasure assumed a new and higher meaning: it functioned as
a chief indicator of the state of love and marriage.

These sex surveys are, in the end, of limited value. They either omit
or are unable to give us access to the multiple layers of meaning that
surrounded sex at this time. They do not, moreover, articulate very
well, if at all, the expectations relating sex to love. To explore this
theme further it is necessary to consult other documents.

SEXUAL PLEASURE AND COMPANIONSHIP
Ideals of Heterosexual Love

Enjoyment of Living, the first volume of the autobiography of the
writer, popular lecturer and political radical Max Eastman, is extraordinary in its descriptive richness of a man's intimate life.[25] Although
he was unconventional in his politics, Max's feelings and hopes with
respect to intimacy seem to fall on the liberal side of the mainstream
pattern. Born in 1883 and reared in a Victorian household, Max's life
dramatizes some of the cultural dynamics and tensions involved in
the transition to a post-Victorian order.

Max's first adult love affair was with Inez. He was initially attracted
by her "physical magnetism."[26] This proved, however, short-lived as
he discovered that his deepest feelings for her were not sensual. "I was
no more attracted to Inez physically than she was to me."[27] He loved
her noble and dynamic character. Their apparent "spiritual affinity"
made them, thought Max, ideal mates. This was, then, basically a
spiritual love that bears resemblance to the Victorian ideal of love.
"Inez and I remained virginal in this love adventure of ours."[28] How-

ever, their spiritual kinship proved temporary. "I found in her no companionship for my moods."[29]

Later, Max confided to himself that their love affair failed not only because of its flawed spiritual affinity but because it lacked a "physical affinity." Retrospectively, Max thought that it was naive for him and Inez "to go on believing we were lovers" without a sexual component to their involvement.[30] The fact that Max invokes this absence in their romance as an explanation for their failed love implies that sex had become an integral part of love. The meaning of sex and its relation to love is further clarified when we turn to his next romance.

Max was in love with Ruth, his youthful companion of many years. His descriptions of Ruth highlight her physical attributes. "Ruth was a sufficiently physical and lustful little girl."[31] Max's attraction to her was erotic; it was her "beautifully proportioned" figure, her "light, strong body" that incited his romantic longing.[32] If his love for Inez expressed something of a spiritual ideal of love, his love for Ruth represented a contemporary norm in which sexual passion served as a chief standard of love. Love was not only to involve a spiritual affinity but an erotic affinity. Because his affair with Inez lacked this erotic aspect, it was judged by Max to be a flawed love. Unfortunately, Max was forced to admit that his love for Ruth was also defective. There was, he confessed, "too much naked lust" and not enough companionship.[33] "Ruth was . . . not intellectual enough for me. Once the romance of yearning, once that delicious drink, the thirst of the unattained, was removed from between us, we would have little to talk about. . . . I wanted someone with whom I was moved miraculously to conversation."[34]

Love, Max's contemporaries thought, got its emotionally charged romantic power from erotic desire, but it was fully realized only if it evolved into a genuine companionship. The latter did not correspond to the Victorian ideal of spiritual affinity, which was imbued with a deeply Christian religious meaning. Moreover, the differentiation of feminine and masculine gender spheres and roles in Victorian culture centered the companionate ideal on a spiritual kinship. To be sure, this spiritual bond at times extended into a deeply emotional union. The twentieth-century companionate ideal anticipated a more encompassing romantic union. Lovers were expected to not only share social responsibilities and world views, to be sex partners and kin, but to be best friends. Lovers were expected to find in marriage a social unit that promoted individual growth while providing social integration. Modern companionate love was to make self-fulfillment possible within a framework of social and moral solidarity.

Max's disappointment with Inez and Ruth led him to doubt his likely success in the quest for love. He despaired over his "sense of failure with Inez [and his] knowledge that with Ruth I could never come down from passion to daily companionship."[35] Max longed for "the union of romantic exaltation with real companionship."[36] Then he met Ida. "The miracle had happened: I really loved to talk with a beautiful woman."[37] With Ida, Max felt he was able to combine erotic longing and friendship, the twin components of the modern ideal of love. Unfortunately, there was no happy ending to their affair. Max and Ida married, but estrangement quickly set in. Before long the affair was emptied of erotic passion and Max was forced to acknowledge, "I love Ida as a friend."[38] Estrangement led to infidelities and finally separation.

Undoubtedly, Max Eastman's difficulties in realizing a love that combined sensual passion and companionship relates to idiosyncratic psychological dynamics. Nevertheless, that he felt strongly that a satisfactory love must integrate these two components points to their prominence as cultural norms. In Eastman's love quest we can observe eroticism and companionship functioning as the chief standards of true love.

Dori Schaffer was a precocious young, white middle-class woman who kept a diary during the 1950s. She recorded the details of her intimate life. Her diary displays a romantic companionate ideal of love and the complexities involved in reconciling erotic longing and companionship.[39]

Dori's first love affair as a young adult was with Bert. As the affair seemed threatened, Dori wrote Bert: "I like you because you are intelligent, witty, and a good looking boy."[40] We don't know what Bert's physical appeal meant to her. Yet Dori made no mention that sexual attraction was important to her. She believed, however, that Bert's chief attraction to her was sexual and a matter of proving his masculinity. "To you, a girl means sex and someone to show off."[41] Dori acknowledged sex as legitimate only in marriage. "I can envision sex only in terms of marriage."[42] It appears that for Dori, sex had a different meaning or at least a different place in romance than for Bert. Sex for Bert, thought Dori, meant sensual pleasure and masculine power; Dori apparently thought of sex more as an expression of intimacy and fidelity.

Dori's next boyfriend was Bill. He was described as intelligent, sweet, gentle and, she thought, interested in her for reasons other than sex.[43] It was a tumultuous affair involving several separations and reconciliations. Dori longed to be married and tried to adjust to Bill. "I tried very hard to submit to his will in all things but sex."[44] Although Dori was sexually attracted to Bill, she seemed to link sex to intimacy.

"I want someone to have sex with legally and to sleep next to, in his arms. I want someone to talk to who will understand me. I want someone to make happy. . . . I am so lonely for a man to love."[45] For Dori, sex was integral to love, but mainly as a sign of intimacy and commitment and secondarily, if at all, as a sensual pleasure. Dori and Bill broke up. Interestingly, Dori concluded that Bill's love was not sincere. "I was merely a sex object."[46] Dori interpreted Bill's motivations in this one-dimensional way despite the fact that he had written Dori explaining that what he liked about her was not only "a beautiful face and figure [but] a lively intellect and broad interests, and warmth."[47]

Dori wanted to marry very badly. "I feel like I must get married very quickly. I'm afraid that I will either become a slut or else withdraw completely. . . . I want to love and be loved."[48] In this passage, Dori seems to be saying that she felt such powerful sensual desires that only marriage could save her from either becoming impure (a "slut") or remaining celibate and unhappy. The point, again, is not that she lacked erotic feelings but that such desires acquire legitimacy for her only in marriage or a relationship of love and intimacy. The place of eroticism in love, however, remains unclear.

Although Dori never did happily marry, she did find romance with Walter. After four weeks, Dori and Walter were having sex. Evidently, Dori now felt that it was acceptable to have sex in a romantic affair that was not necessarily oriented to marriage. Dori's affair with Walter reveals, moreover, the prominent place eroticism had assumed for her in the meaning of love. The sensual and expressive aspects of sex acquired a heightened importance. "Our sex is very satisfying because whenever I see him, he is affectionate and . . . gives me warmth and happiness. We are free and happy together, trying different positions."[49] Dori described how she is sexually uninhibited with Walter. "I am not shy or ashamed with him. . . . My breasts yearn to be kissed and caressed by him. A sweet intense feeling vibrates from my head to my genitals. I writhe and moan as he loves me. We explode together in sexual celebration."[50] When she now assesses her attraction to men, erotic considerations stand alongside nonsexual concerns. "Why do I love Walter? I delight in him physically and intellectually."[51] By the end of her diary, at the age of twenty-five, she has to struggle to avoid conflating love with eroticism. "I know that sexual love is . . . not enough. We must make some kind of contract, some good rules to coexist together."[52]

Sex was always a dimension of Dori's notion of love. Yet, as she moved through a series of relationships, the meaning of sex and its place in relation to love changed. Sex remained for Dori a way to express affection and achieve intimacy, but it gradually acquired a heightened hedonistic value. Sex was supposed to bring sensual pleasure; the giving and receiving of carnal pleasures became an important sign and standard of love. It is perhaps the very sexualization of love that explains Dori's willingness to have sex outside of marriage. It had become difficult, if not impossible, to be in love without demonstrating or expressing it through sex. Although Dori came to affirm and indeed celebrate the sensual pleasures of love, sex retained an edge of risk and danger. She feared that this symbol and medium of love was merely a pleasure or sign of masculine power for her male counterpart. And, as Dori came to learn, sex carried the risk of unwanted pregnancy and the terrible choice of a life-risking abortion or a life of diminished opportunities that, in addition, carried the stigma of an unwed mother. To be sure, sex carried multiple meanings for Max Eastman as well. Sex expressed love and intimacy; it was a carnal pleasure as well as an important way to confirm his masculinity. Max's sexual passion and successful performance with Ida "persuaded me that I was man."[53] There were risks as well for Max. Impotence or a failure to satisfy his partner evoked anxieties about his manhood or his ability to love. Without further pursuing the details of these two case studies, my observations suggest the gendered character of love. It is, perhaps, not sufficiently precise to speak of heterosexual love; we must be sensitive to possible historically conditioned variations in men's and women's styles of heterosexual love.

GENDER AND HETEROSEXUAL LOVE
Patterns of Love for Men and Women

Love does not have a fixed identity or essence. What it means and the practices it entails vary historically. Furthermore, within a specific society at a definite time, love may carry different meanings related to differences with regard to class, race or cultural status, or perhaps varying in relation to regional, ethnic, religious or age factors. Feminists have made a convincing case that gender must be acknowledged as an important social fact shaping identity, behavior and institutional dynamics. Like age or social class, moreover, gender is no less a social and historical category.[54] It relates to the ways in which appeals to biology are used to track "males" and "females" into different roles and identities. The gender construction of individual identity extends to the meaning of love. We would expect that, so long as the social position of men and women differ in highly general ways, this will be exhibited in their patterns of love.[55] For example, we have observed that sex had a somewhat different meaning for Dori Schaffer and her male lovers. These men, she reported, pressed her to have sex early in their involvement, whereas Dori resisted. Perhaps sex was less exclusively a sign of love or relational commitment for these men than for Dori. Similarly, sex seemed to have somewhat different risks for Max Eastman than for Dori. Whereas sex was a proving ground for Max's masculinity, the dangers of sex for Dori revolved around unwanted pregnancy, being deceived by men or being stigmatized as a "loose" woman.

Despite the limitations of the available documents, I'd like to tentatively explore some connections between gender and love. A very large reservation must first be registered. My research does not allow me to say to what extent the gender features of love I allude to are unique to segments of the white middle class or historically specific to the early twentieth-century U.S. Future research will need to analyze more carefully the changing and diverse gender styles of love.

I'd like to return, for the moment, to Max Eastman's struggle to combine erotic longing with a companionate ideal. We recall that the pattern of Max's love affairs was for sensual desire and emotional and social intimacy to split apart in spite of a stated wish for their union. Thus, it was with great relief that Max thought that he finally achieved an integrated love pattern with Ida. Unfortunately, soon after their marriage Max's erotic longings turned away from Ida. He had to admit that he loved her only as a friend. As his sensual passion for Ida disappeared, Max's romantic longings turned to younger women who stirred in him powerful carnal desires. Ruth began to occupy his thoughts. "I had never ceased yearning for Ruth's body, and now the yearning grew into an obsession."[56] Friendship or a deep spiritual companionship was not ultimately satisfying in a social setting where love was sexualized.

I will not try to fathom the complex psychological dynamics that may have been at work in Max's behavior. Yet, a theme that repeatedly surfaces in his intimate relationships with women is that of the loss of self. "Ida damped in me the creative verve and zest for being by which I live."[57] Max felt trapped with Ida; he was imprisoned in a relationship and he was losing his creativity and freedom. "Having thus surrendered my independence . . . I tried by altering the environment to get back a sense of being or possessing myself."[58] Max associated loving Ida with losing his erotic passion and his self. The intimate companionship he wished for seems antithetical to his wanting sensual and self-fulfillment. Max's sensual longing for Ruth may be interpreted as an effort to regain a feeling of being a separate and creative individual. Ida, it seems at least plausible to infer, like all women

Max felt intimate with, functioned as a powerful mother figure. Perhaps Max's love for Ida evoked feelings and wishes of the idealized love he felt for his mother.[59] Although the love between a son and his mother may make adult love possible, it may also induce a deeply felt and, at times, inhibiting ambivalence.[60] A son's love of his mother may carry potent feelings of resentment for being less important than his father; it may elicit erotic desires that must, ultimately, be repressed; it may entail a wish for freedom from maternal control in which the boy, at times, experiences himself as powerless. Max may have been unable to sustain erotic feelings for Ida because of his emotionally strong identification of Ida with his mother. Instead of pursuing this conjecture, I want to simply call attention to one point: the adult male experience of heterosexual love, at least in twentieth-century American society, relates back in crucial ways to the typically first male love relationship—a boy's love of his mother.

Ben Hecht, a minor literary figure of the time, was, by his own account, happily married for most of his adult life. Perhaps his hard-won marital fidelity and happiness made it possible for him to speak frankly of his intimate feelings. In his autobiography, *A Child of the Century*, Hecht reflects upon his experience of love and, in particular, how maternal love shaped his love of women as an adult.[61]

Although Ben's mother was "an enigma I could never know,"[62] he idealized her. "I saw my mother as perfect."[63] He recalls his happiness as a child merely being with his mother. "Whenever we were, happily, under the same roof, the house became animated for me. . . . She was always the most important person in the world for me."[64] As an adult, Ben was aware that it was an idealized maternal image that he valued most in women. "I grew up with a need to keep my mother's qualities alive in my world. Unfortunately, this need extended to finding these qualities in any woman who touched my fancy."[65] Ben admitted that he was so fixated on his mother that he was unable to see adult women as distinct individuals. "The moment a woman looked at me tenderly I imagined her, forthwith, to be the spiritual twin of my mother."[66] Ben acknowledged that he could only love a woman if she embodied maternal qualities. This sometimes led to deliberate efforts to fashion women in his mother's image. Ben demanded in women not only his mother's qualities but that their love exhibit strong maternal qualities. "Such was my happiness with my mother. In my . . . love affairs, I looked for a similar delight. In them I kept alive a concept of love I had fetched unchanged out of my boyhood. This was to be loved a bit madly and to owe no allegiance to one's love . . . to be the core of the loved one's existence and she never more than a generality in one's own life; to possess and never be possessed."[67] As Ben internalized the idealized love between himself and his mother as an integral aspect of adult heterosexual love, he looked for a woman's love to be unconditional, exclusive and unbounded.

The longing for a woman whose love is unbounded expresses one wish some men of this period brought to adult heterosexual love. Accordingly, some of these men felt, at times, that they were not loved enough. In his autobiographical novel *The Story of a Lover*, Hutchins Hapgood repeatedly laments his wife's insufficient need to love him. This was especially upsetting because Hutchins, in part, modeled adult love on the love of a mother for her son. Speaking of what he calls "maternal love," he wrote: "In this kind of love the deepest satisfaction lies. It is almost as if we were still enclosed in the womb. It tends to relieve him of all irritation, anxieties, and disappointed yearnings. It encloses him . . . and satisfies. This she likes to give as much as he to receive."[68] At other times, these men felt that "maternal" love was suffocating or imprisoning. The writer Edgar Lee Masters reflected on the ironic pleasures of being married. "We installed our cabinets, silver and rugs in these three large rooms, and I sat by at the great windows of the front room looking out . . . and trying to think along the path that had brought me to this prison. . . . I was sure that a new life had begun."[69] As if to reassure himself that relinquishing his independence had compensations, he reminds himself: "I would not be alone as formerly. I could settle down to long evenings of study. . . . Every night I went home [there would be] . . . someone who was waiting for me, and the little things of domestic management, like my laundry, need worry me no more."[70] Similarly, after one of Max's lovers moved in with him, he "was seized by the wish that she was not there. It was a wish to escape, to break away from a chain, to be free of a commitment, to be myself again in my own house."[71] It seems that one manifestation of Max's wish for separation and autonomy was a longing for erotic adventure. This pattern is in evidence for other men of this period. For example, despite his ostensibly happy and monogamous marriage, Hecht believed that for men "fulfillment does not remove desire, that finding a journey's end [i.e., true love or marriage] leaves untouched the impulse to travel."[72] Despite a happy marriage, men's desires, Hecht intimates, are never satisfied. Is this not, however, merely a symbolic way of expressing these men's longing for separation and autonomy?

Many white middle-class men of this period sought in women not only the qualities of their mother but a love that was maternal-like. Maternal love was, after all, typically their primary love experience. These men married, in part, to be loved as they were by their mothers. They wished and expected their wives to provide domestic order, assume the chief household and childrearing responsibilities, and to be nurturing. As Edgar Masters contemplated marriage, he describes his motivations: "I had decided never to marry; but there was the unending loneliness of having no one intimately in my life. I had to do everything for myself, such as to sew on buttons and to get my laundry gathered up and sent out. . . . I felt my talent for writing wasting away. . . . I fancied myself settled with a wife with my books around me during long peaceful evenings, when I could turn to write a poem. . . . And I longed inexpressibility to have one woman to put all this anxiety, all this hunting for satisfaction out of my life forever."[73] A wife was viewed, in part, as a motherly figure who established emotional, domestic and social order that would allow Masters to pursue self-fulfillment in his work. Yet, the situation was actually more complicated. Masters wished for companionship in marriage. Thus, he agonized over whether he and his wife-to-be could find in each other self-fulfillment and a satisfactory companion.[74] Many middle-class men in these decades struggled over the extent to which they wanted their wives to be genuine friends and companions. The latter implied for women a life apart from marriage and domestic concerns that made a wife much less of a maternal figure. Despite affirming an ideal of a companionate marriage, many men resisted its full implications; they sought to accommodate it to a Victorian gender order that identified womanhood with the domestic sphere.

Typically, men didn't need to resort to coercion or manipulation to get women to accede to their wishes in this regard. Women often aspired to a life centered in domesticity. In the dozens of autobiographies I consulted, white middle-class women frequently looked to marriage—to being a wife and mother and to a life that revolved around the domestic sphere—as the highest path to self-fulfillment.

As for their Victorian predecessors, marriage figured as the destiny of these women. For a woman who lacked economic independence and wished to avoid the insecurities and stigma of being single, marriage was the chief way to achieve economic security and social respectability.[75] Accordingly, despite the romantic fantasies many women imbibed in the romantic literature of the day, these women approached marriage in a very practical way. Love was sometimes a secondary consideration compared to economic concerns or the wish to be a wife and mother and to maintain a home.

Rose Talbott thought seriously about why she wanted to marry so soon after her first husband died. She concluded that she was unhappy living with her parents. "I came to a momentous decision. I would marry the first decent man who asked me! . . . Had I been happy at home, there would be no need to rush into a second marriage."[76] Rose did consider pursuing a career as an alternative to marriage. However, she believed that "dedicating myself to a career would not be enough for me. Possessing a woman's normal instincts, I wanted a home, a husband, and children. I longed not for love . . . but for . . . contentment. The man who would give me that would be the man I would marry!"[77] Rose valued marriage because it allowed her to realize her wish to be a wife, to manage a household and to achieve a measure of independence, security and social status. Rose was fortunate. She met and eventually married a man who, by her own admission, she didn't love but respected as a husband and family man. In her domestic life, Rose found fulfillment. "It was an exciting experience for me to furnish a home of my own, and I enjoyed every moment of it. . . . Between the children and the house, I was kept busy all day long, but I felt rewarded for my work. I knew peace of mind and contentment as never before."[78]

Many middle-class women in the early decades of the twentieth century felt as Rose did. They sought in marriage a way to escape their parents' home, to avoid economic insecurity or the stigma of being single or the fear of loneliness.[79] And while they hoped for love and companionship, practical considerations revolving around security and status and the wish to be wives and mothers managing a home of their own, frequently proved more compelling. Many women imbued domesticity with expectations and hopes of self-realization. Hortense Odlum begins her autobiography, *A Woman's Place*, by reflecting upon the meaning of marriage:

> I felt warm and protected and secure there in the family room with . . . the glowing fire in the hearth. I was so happy in this room, this house. It was mine and I had done my share in making it beautiful and peaceful. Everything that happened in it, that involved the people who lived in it, was my pleasant concern. The most gratifying and rewarding job that any woman could possibly have was mine— that of supervising the smooth functioning of a household for the happiness of husband and children. I was a woman who had found that rare and allusive thing—happiness.[80]

Creating a home was invested with higher meaning and value for Hortense. It meant building a shared life with her husband and family. Domesticity was surrounded with powerful meanings related to security, love, happiness and self-fulfillment.

> I loved caring for my baby and doing my housework. I had a constant sense of triumph because we were managing so well on so little. It gave me tremendous satisfaction to know that as my husband was

doing his job well, I was helping him by doing mine well. I felt that we were truly partners in our life together and I loved doing my end of the job. I knew that in its way it was just as important as his and my knowledge that this was so gave dishwashing and floor scrubbing dignity and meaning.[81]

For Hortense and many middle-class women, domestic tasks carried no less a dignity and value than their husband's work and responsibilities.

These same women felt, at times, deeply ambivalent about marriage. It was not simply that marriage more or less determined their fate. Marriage typically excluded the possibility of a life apart from the domestic sphere. Many women wanted marriage and a life independent of the home. "I wanted a big family but I also wanted to continue my life as an individual," remarked Agnes Meyer.[82] The "new women" of the period did not, in the main, repudiate marriage or domesticity but longed to "complete" themselves in nondomestic activities. Emma Goldman gives a feminist interpretation to this typically middle-class female predicament. "[Women today are] longing for fulfillment very few modern women find because most modern men too are rooted in the older traditions. They too want the woman more as wife and mother than as lover and friend. The modern women cannot be the wife and mother in the old sense, and the new medium has not yet been devised. I mean the way of being wife, mother, friend, and yet retain complete freedom."[83] Goldman did not repudiate or devalue marriage but only aspired to make it legitimate for women, as it was for men, to choose to pursue a life simultaneously outside the domestic sphere.

This conflict was not unique to twentieth-century women. Yet they experienced it in a far more intense way than their Victorian predecessors. The difference reflects women's altered social position in the twentieth century. These women were more educated and career-oriented than their immediate predecessors; smaller families combined with new labor-saving technology freed women from many household duties; the women's movement, as well as the reform ideal of a companionate marriage, legitimated women's demand for more personal autonomy. This social configuration made being a wife and mother more of a choice and less comprehensive as an ideal of self-fulfillment. Expanded opportunities and higher expectations for self-fulfillment heightened the ambivalent feelings women had about marriage.

Let's return to Dori Schaffer. Dori was a strong-willed, independent young woman. She was politically active, career-oriented and very

definite about her beliefs and values. Like many of her female companions, Dori wanted not only an independent life but marriage, family
and a home. In a moment of hope, Dori reflected on her dream of
marrying Bill. "Dear God, if you are, please let us marry and let me
be as he wants me to be. Let me make him happy and secure. . . . I
love him very much. I want to make him happy. I want to cook well
and keep a clean, pretty, happy house."[84] To get Bill to love and marry
her, Dori thought she had to renounce a life for herself. "I tried very
hard to submit to his will in all things but sex."[85] She was prepared
to sacrifice her own career aspirations for Bill. "If at all possible, I
will really get interested in real estate" [Bill's occupation].[86] Bill, like
other men, Dori thought, would not love and marry an independent
and highly educated woman. Marriage "demands that women be
sweet and quiet and unconcerned with worldly problems. This is the
type of person I must become for my own sake."[87] Dori believed she
had to suppress her hopes for an independent life as a condition of
securing heterosexual love and marriage.

The failure of her affair with Bill served as an object lesson. She
was now prepared to acknowledge that only a love that allowed her
to maintain her individuality was genuine. "I want to love and be
loved. . . . I want to help someone who feels the same toward me. . . .
I want to be married and have my own close friend and lover."[88] Dori's
subsequent affair with Walter was closer to her ideal. He respected
her individuality and career aspirations. Moreover, "I can tell him
what I'm thinking without first translating it into euphemistic half-
truths."[89] Dori thought she found in Walter a man whom she could
love without giving up her individuality. "I want him to be with me,
in me, of me, not in a devouring way but in a separate-but-together
manner."[90]

The conflict women felt between their desire for marriage and their
longing for a life apart from domesticity intensified when the issue of
pursuing a career was introduced. Consider the case of Fannie Hurst,
a popular writer in the middle decades of this century.

When Fannie was a young woman her aunt advised her in no uncertain terms, "Get married young. . . . The more you know, the less
desirable you become to men. They want a homemaker, not a superior
mind."[91] Fannie, however, had her mind set on becoming a writer and
valued her independence. Achieving success as a writer did not lessen
her desire for love, marriage and a home. She felt conflicted over how
she could combine love and a separate autonomous life. Her romance
with Jack seemed an ideal compromise. "The status quo I enjoyed
with Jack was what I wanted. . . . I was playing a more and more
important role in his way of life and thoughts. . . . Also, [I] was free

to carry on the long hours of writing and the many other interests that were accruing."[92] Illustrating the difficulty for a woman to be both married and career-oriented Fannie agreed to marry but only on the condition that it be kept secret. "We dined out, met when we so willed; or went our separate ways. . . . We were free, maintaining through the years our separate friends, seeing them separately, except when we felt like merging. There were few 'musts' between us. We accepted no engagements for one another. We were never 'dragged,' whether to a dinner party . . . or to see that dear old school friend."[93] Fannie was so convinced that pressures on a married woman to sacrifice her career were overriding that her marriage was not only kept secret for five years but Jack and she maintained separate homes.

FORBIDDEN LOVE
From Romantic Friendship to Lesbian Love

What love meant varied, in certain typical ways, between white middle-class men and women in the early decades of the twentieth century. We would expect, as well, differences between homosexual and heterosexual love. This divergence relates to different gender dynamics between same-sex and opposite-sex intimacies. It also stems from the socially marginal status of same-sex love in a society that upholds a heterosexual norm. In this section, I will analyze some changes in the meaning of female same-sex intimacy. In the first two decades of the twentieth century the tradition of romantic friendship between women began to be replaced by a notion of lesbian love.[94] Whereas in the former paradigm female intimacy is legitimate and valued, in the latter framework it is discredited and stigmatized.

The shift from a romantic friendship paradigm to that of lesbian love was made possible by the social prominence of a new discourse on sexuality that initially appeared in the second half of the nineteenth century. European sexologists such as Carl Westphal, Karl Ulrichs, Krafft-Ebing, Magnus Hirschfeld and Havelock Ellis developed a scientific-medical discourse on homosexuality.[95] Throughout the nineteenth century these discourses had little or no impact in the U.S. beyond very narrow medical and scientific circles. There was, for example, no reference to the term *homosexuality* in the marital advice literature, popular medical texts or personal documents I examined. If same-sex intimacy was mentioned it was classified under the general category of sodomy, which covered a heterogenous cluster of sex acts. By World War I, however, these scientific-medical discourses acquired intellectual prestige and assumed a prominent social role. European texts on homosexuality were translated and widely discussed; there was an outpouring of publications on homosexuality that appeared in scientific and medical journals; the basic concepts of these discourses surfaced regularly in newspapers, popular magazines, literature and plays.[96] In short, the scientific-medical discourse on homosexuality had achieved such a level of public authority that the everyday meaning of same-sex love began to reflect some of its basic concepts.[97]

The chief feature of these discourses can be readily identified: same-sex love was taken as indicative of an abnormal psychosexual condition. Whether this pathological state was explained as congenital or acquired, "homosexuality" was defined as a diseased psychological condition. Individuals who were attracted to persons of their own sex were now labeled as an abnormal human type. Although the terms describing this new human figure ranged from "invert," "uranian," and "homosexual" to "lesbian," the underlying point is that same-sex desires were interpreted as a sign of a deviant identity. "Homosexuals" had their own distinct physical, psychic and social nature.[98] They were neither men nor women but a new human type—a "third sex" or "intermediate type." Furthermore, homosexuals were defined as exhibiting a hyperactive sex drive. The homosexual was thought to be sexually aggressive, genital-centered, lustful, seductive and promiscuous. All same-sex love was thought to be, at least unconsciously, sexually driven and carnal in motivation. Within this framework, intimacy between women was viewed as a sign of lesbian love.

The change from a romantic friendship model of female intimacy to lesbian love is revealed in autobiographical and literary documents of the period. In a 1902 autobiography by Mary Maclane, we can observe a romantic friendship model. Love between women is open and, indeed, is idealized as morally and spiritually elevated. "Are there many things in this cool-hearted world so utterly exquisite as the pure love of one woman for another?"[99] Without the slightest trace of shame or self-consciousness, Mary openly admits that she loves her former teacher, Fannie Corbin, "with a peculiar and vivid intensity, and with all the sincerity and passion that is in me."[100] Mary longs to live with Fannie, to share a life together. "Often I think, if only I could have my anemone lady and go and live with her . . . for the rest of my life."[101] Mary's love for Fannie carried no implication that there was anything wrong, unnatural or perverse about it. Yet in a autobiographical memoir published fifteen years later, female intimacy bears these resonances.[102] Women who are intimate with other women are now characterized as a specific human type—"lesbian women."[103] Female intimacies are viewed as a tangle of perversity and pathology. Mary Maclane's description of "lesbians" reads as if they were excerpted from Krafft-Ebing's catalogue of sex perversions. "They are marvels of perverse barbaric energy. . . . To each other they are friends, lovers, victims, preyers, masters, slaves; the flawed fruits of one oblique sex-inheritance."[104]

In Wanda Fraiken's novel *Neff, We Sing Diana*, Nora observes how commonplace female intimacies are in her college. "Sometimes a girl had an older member of the faculty for her friend. She worshipped her, . . . studied to please her, sent her flowers."[105] Nora found herself the object of such a romantic interest. "Emily began to save a seat for her at meals; she made lengthy visits after dinner. . . . She asked for advice about clothes. . . . One evening Emily stayed longer than usual. Suddenly she threw her arms about Nora. 'You darling, you don't know how I love you, Nora.' "[106] Although Nora rebuffed these romantic advances, it was not because Emily's love for her was unnatural or wrong. Nora was frightened by any display of passion. She lacked similar feelings for Emily. Some years later Nora returned to the same college as a teacher. She observed that conversations were "full of psychological tags."[107] And "intimacies between two girls were watched with keen, distrustful eyes. Among one's classmates, one looked for the bisexual type, the masculine girl searching for a feminine counterpart, and one ridiculed their devotions."[108]

Charlotte Armstrong made the shift to a lesbian love framework the dramatic center of her novel *The Unsuspected*.[109] Ann and Elizabeth, two single, young working women, shared a room in a boarding house. Ann felt drawn to Elizabeth. "When in the evening, Elizabeth opened the door and smiled at her, she would jump up and throw both arms around . . . her friend."[110] Ann's fondness for Elizabeth was in the tradition of romantic friendships. Thus, Ann would say, entirely without feeling self-conscious or ashamed, "I love you, Elizabeth."[111] Gradually, Elizabeth developed similar feelings toward Ann. It became a routine, for example, for Elizabeth to kiss Ann before they went to bed. Yet, a new self-consciousness emerged regarding their mutual affection. Elizabeth explains to Ann that "some women can't love men" and that she was intimate with such a woman.[112] Judith, says Elizabeth, "loved me as a lover might."[113] Ann, however, seems to recognize that perhaps Elizabeth or herself may be this type of woman. She becomes deeply troubled and asks Elizabeth, "How was she [Judith] different from us?"[114] Aware that she is inciting disturbing feelings in Ann, Elizabeth responds defensively: "I shouldn't have told you this."[115] Struggling to repress the troubling thought that there is something wrong with themselves or their relationship, Ann responds somewhat desperately: "We are such close friends, Elizabeth, don't let anything spoil it!"[116] Ann and Elizabeth wished to forget this conversation, but it was too late.

Soon after that talk Elizabeth announced, as if to reassure Ann of their normality, that she had arranged a date for Ann. But on her date Ann could think only of Elizabeth. The story unfolds with Ann meeting Judith, the woman who loved Elizabeth. Judith acknowledges to Ann that she is different. She can only love women. Predictably, Ann is attracted to the older, subtly attractive and seductive Judith. "The thought of Judith has so changed her. . . . She was different from other people. She could love another woman."[117] Elizabeth implored Ann to resist Judith's considerable charms. "It's another world, Ann, [which] will be just misery, impotence, and some dreadful destruction!"[118] It was, however, too late. "There is," says Ann, "nothing else for me. I love her."[119]

In a remarkable text, *Diana: A Strange Autobiography*, we can observe the lesbian love paradigm becoming the dominant way to frame intimacy between women.[120] Female intimacy carries in this text a heightened self-consciousness that reflects its new psychological, social and moral seriousness. The longing for such intimacy is now self-revelatory. The lesbian steps forward as a new, discredited human figure.

Diana Frederics, a pseudonym, was as a young woman strongly attracted to another woman, Ruth. Following the pattern of romantic friendship, Ruth and Diana were inseparable. Their intimacy extended to freely exchanging hugs and kisses. Yet, Diana's attraction to Ruth carried a self-consciousness and aura of danger that was typically absent from romantic friendships. One evening as Diana and Ruth slept side by side, Diana became unexpectedly troubled by her feelings. "I had been surprised to feel curious sensations of longing the few times I had ever touched her, but I could never imagine the exquisite thrill of feeling her body close to mine. Then before I knew it, I realized I wanted to caress her. Then I became terrified by a nameless something that froze my impulse."[121] Afterwards, Diana's feelings toward Ruth evoked fear and danger. "Where I had been gay with Ruth, I now felt shy, self-conscious . . . and I began to brood about my growing desire to touch her, and the fear I felt at my impulse."[122] Although Diana was unable to clearly identify why her attraction to Ruth evoked danger, she relates this to the intensely sexual character of her feelings.

Self-clarification came soon enough. Accidently, as she tells us, Diana came upon a book on sexuality that included a chapter on homosexuality. It proved to be a self-revelation. "I was, then, a 'pervert,' 'uranian,' 'homosexual.' . . . I was subject to arrest! I was grotesque, alienated, unclean!"[123] Diana had discovered "the truth of my nature. . . . I belong to the third sex."[124] Nevertheless, Diana resolved to live a "normal" life. She withdrew from Ruth and generally avoided all intimate female relations. In a determined effort to prove her normality, she got engaged and ultimately married. Unfortunately, "normal love" proved intolerable. "I had hoped to the point of prayer that consummation would bring a change in my imperturbable emotions. Not once in eight months had physical intimacy meant anything to me but giving pleasure to Carl. . . . The words 'desire,' 'passion,' 'ecstasy,' were . . . symbols of unsounded experience."[125] The marriage ended with Diana finally and unequivocally acknowledging, "I am a lesbian."[126] At least she was consoled in knowing that "I discovered myself."[127]

Strong-willed and resolute, Diana was determined to live a life of self-respect and social value. "No one need know of my emotional inversion. If homosexual love ever came to me I would accept it."[128] At least intellectually, she came to accept her homosexuality as "a condition within the range of sexual variation."[129] Drawing on scientific and literary writings that contained affirmative images of homosexuality, Diana was able to conclude that "the homosexual was a fellow human being whose behavior was no better, or worse, than that of the heterosexual."[130] Diana would accept herself as a lesbian.

In the course of pursuing graduate studies, Diana began an affair. "Jane and I had a beautiful companionship, we loved each other. . . . We wanted a normal domestic life and we wanted our happiness together."[131] Unfortunately, social disapproval made this wish for a happy romance difficult. Diana knew that they would have to overcome enormous social obstacles to have a normal life. "Social intrusion began to tug at our consciousness. We were deviators from conventional morality. We had signed no papers from clergy or state; we were social outlaws. Our relationship must be clandestine; there could be no joy in sharing the knowledge with family or friends. . . . We must get used to hypocrisy and camouflage that degraded and humiliated."[132] To protect themselves against the "constant fear of self-betrayal," Diana and Jane withdrew from friends and conventional social involvements.[133] This, however, left Diana feeling painfully alone and unhappy.

The social stigma attached to lesbianism had psychological costs as well. Jane was less accepting of her homosexuality than Diana. Deeply ambivalent and torn over her intimate longings, Jane was sexually inhibited. The lack of sexual fulfillment left Diana miserable and resentful. "To be tantalized without achieving social fulfillment began to be a recurring disappointment."[134]

Although Jane came to accept herself as a lesbian and they had a satisfying love relationship, Diana was acutely aware that various social and psychological factors made lesbian love not only difficult but different. Intimacies between homosexuals, she thought, are short-lived, more informal and more intensely romantic. Typically lacking responsibilities attached to property and children, lesbian love leans heavily upon immediate feelings and needs. "So far as I could see, the odds against happiness in the lesbian relationship were double what I had first imagined them. No longer was it a simple question of enormous social pressure from without; but even more insidious, of mores from within. The lesbian liaison had not more strength than the weaker of its two partners."[135] Lacking social recognition and support by social conventions and laws, lesbian love often fell into a "callous casualness" that could only end in a "savage loneliness."[136]

From her initial awareness of being attracted to women, Diana imbued these longings with a sexual meaning. It was, we recall, the intensity of her sexual desire for Ruth that evoked a heightened self-consciousness. The wish for intimacy and love, in both heterosexual and homosexual contexts, was, by the post–World War I era, invested with sexual meaning. Sexual fulfillment had become a norm of successful and happy love. For example, despite the intimacy Diana and Jane shared, the lack of sexual fulfillment greatly disturbed Diana. After Jane had overcome her sexual inhibitions, Diana acknowledged that the presence of sexual satisfaction "marks the difference between frustration and fulfillment" in love.[137] Reflecting a late Victorian position, Diana typically described sex as important primarily as an "expression of love."[138] Yet, it is clear from her sexual frustration with Jane that she valued sex as well for its erotic qualities. Erotic fulfillment was an integral part of lesbian love. This point is made more explicit when Diana discusses the sexual aspects of her love affair with Leslie. "Leslie's joyous appetite soon led me to see how unsatisfying my sex relations with Jane had been. Now, in Leslie's passion, as hungry for my body as it was demanding of its own satisfaction, I knew a pleasure I had never known before. . . . I had never appreciated before what mutuality in the sex act could mean."[139]

The author of *Diana* was born around the turn of the century. Her roots extended deep into Victorian culture. For women born in the 1920s and 1930s and coming of age in the 1940s and 1950s, ties to Victorian culture were greatly attenuated. In the novels of important lesbian authors like Ann Bannon and Claire Morgan, we can observe the virtual disappearance of the romantic friendship model of female intimacy and the triumph of the lesbian love model. One indicator of this change is the extent to which love between women is sexualized in these novels. Sex functions not only as a sign of love but as a domain where love is demonstrated through erotic expression and fulfillment.

Consider the rich sensual character of lesbian love in Bannon's novels.[140] In *Odd Girl Out*, Laura and Beth share a room at college.[141] Bannon describes Beth's initial attraction to Laura as erotic. "She [Beth] thought how good it would be to skid her hands hard up Laura's thighs."[142] Laura felt similarly toward Beth. Her attraction to Beth is described as a "hot passion" or an "implacable desire." Beth incited in Laura an almost uncontrollable sensual desire. "When Beth was near her, her careful senses loosened, yearned, burst suddenly from the bonds of caution. Her mail-fisted moral code unclenched, and right and wrong rushed out and ran whooping into limbo."[143] Laura and Beth became lovers but it was not meant to last. Laura discovers that she is a lesbian; Beth, awakened to love by Laura, finds that her primary love is for men.

In *I Am a Woman*, Laura appears as a more or less self-accepting lesbian.[144] She has her first lesbian love affair. Beebo, the object of her affection, is a butch lesbian who is attracted to the younger, inexperienced and pretty Laura. Despite the fact that she is repulsed by Beebo's rough social style, Laura finds herself almost irresistibly drawn to her. "The thought of Beebo tortured her now . . . with her lithe little body."[145] Unable to restrain herself, Laura gives in to her passion. "Laura felt such a wave of passion come up in her that it almost smothered her. . . . She . . . clung to Beebo, half tearing her pajamas off her back, groaning wordlessly. . . . Her hands explored, caressed, felt Beebo all over while her own body responded with violent spasms."[146] Initially, Laura dismissed her passion for Beebo as little more than lust. But Jack, her homosexual friend, reminded her that "love has a body, Laura. Eyes and lips, legs and sex. We humans can't help that."[147] For Laura it was "a huge physical need . . . that drew her to Beebo."[148] Beebo knew that "this is love."[149]

Laura and Beebo lived together for two years before their affair unraveled. In *Women in the Shadows*, Bannon details its dissolution.[150] For Laura, "the fierce passion for Beebo that had boiled when they first knew each other flared up rarely now."[151] The waning of their love is identified with the disappearance of sensual desire. "She [Laura] could not be sure where she had gone wrong or when that lovely flush of desire had begun to wane in her."[152] Despairing over the fate of lesbian love, Laura entertains a marriage offer from Jack, who is convinced of the futility of homosexual love. They have the following exchange which reveals Laura's thoughts about the place of sex in love:

Jack darling [says Laura] I love you, but I don't love you with my body. If we married it would never be a physical union [says Jack]. If it wasn't a physical union, what would it be? Just small talk and community property and family plan fares?[153]

Bannon may have intended her story to serve as a moral tale warning lesbians against confusing eroticism with love. Yet, the lesbians in her novels are lustful, self-accepting and live lives of integrity.

By the 1950s the tradition of romantic friendship between women had virtually disappeared. Love between women became the exclusive domain of lesbians. Lesbian love appeared as a genuine alternative to heterosexual love. Although lesbian love was stigmatized in the public culture as diseased and deviant, it was at least possible for women to choose to love women as completely as loving men. In fact, many women of this period were able to resist public disapproval and evolve affirmative models of lesbian identity and love.[154]

To be sure, the stigma attached to lesbianism and lesbian love contributed to the general erosion of intimacy between women. The scientific-medical construction of "the lesbian" as an abnormal human type made women who sought intimacy with each other vulnerable to social disapproval and psychological distress. Feminist historians have documented a connection between the enhanced public authority of the scientific-medical discourse on homosexuality in the early twentieth century and the rising aspirations and opportunities women had to be independent.[155] Women's expanded career options, the suffrage movement, feminism and the search for new models of femininity challenged a gender order that underpinned a civic and moral order that privileged men. Labeling women who loved women lesbians or applying that label to women who pursued a career or who were political reformers was a defensive reaction to a changing gender order that threatened male privilege. The medical discourse on homosexuality was, as well, a reaction to the heightened public awareness of nascent "colonies" of homosexuals and lesbians. Social research, legal and medical commentaries, as well as newspaper stories in the early decades of the twentieth century made the public aware of homosexuals and their developing subcultures.[156] In a social setting where there was anxiety over the fate of marriage and the family as well as concern over the susceptibility of single young men and women succumbing to the temptations of the city, the disclosure of widespread homosexuality heightened fears of disorder and decline. Labeling women lesbians who were independent or who sought same-sex intimacies may have been a way for some men and women to ease their fears.

The lesbian label, however, simultaneously contributed to creating a lesbian identity and community. There is, as Michel Foucault has remarked, an irony in gay and lesbian history. The very construction of the lesbian as a primary personal identity helped create a common consciousness and solidarity among lesbians.[157] This, in turn, provided the basis, on the one hand, for the creation of a lesbian identity, and, on the other hand, for a lesbian politic of civil rights, social inclusion and social reform. I will pick up this theme in chapter 6.

CONCLUSION

Many white, middle-class men and women in the early twentieth century viewed their time as a transitional period. Raised in communities that had deep roots in Victorian culture but coming of age in the post–World War I period, they were living between two eras. Their socially dislocated status frequently gave them a unique vantage point from which to observe their times.

Changes in middle-class sexual culture were widely noted. Although contemporaries were mistaken to contrast Victorian repression with modern sexual freedom, some social controls were relaxed. For example, it was more acceptable than in the recent past to make sex a topic of public concern. There is, moreover, evidence suggesting that the regulation of nonmarital sex was relaxed. For example, more people born after 1900 were at least willing to report having premarital coitus than those born before 1900. Similarly, research suggests that sex in marriage involved more experimentation and concern with sexual satisfaction. The really significant change, however, was not that people were having more sex or talking about it more but that the conventions guiding sex and its very meaning were changing.

I have underscored a change in middle-class beliefs and norms relating sex to love between 1900 and 1960. Whereas middle-class Victorians accepted sex as a part of marriage, love was conceived of as spiritual. To function even as an appropriate vehicle of spiritual union, sex had to be purged of its erotic aspects. By the early twentieth century, sex became not only a principal sign of love but was viewed as one of its chief foundations. Sexual fulfillment had become a condition of true love. Moreover, the erotic aspects of sex acquired legitimacy. Sex became a sphere of sensual pleasure. Individuals expected sex to be sensually and expressively pleasurable. This heightened the moral and psychological significance of the erotic aspect of sex. It created a new focus upon erotic technique and skill. Erotic fulfillment appears as a new standard of successful love and marriage. In the last two chapters I have tried to document the thesis that the development of an erotic culture in twentieth-century America is intimately tied to the sexualization of love.

The sexualization of love is very likely related to the legitimation of premarital sex in the twentieth century. With sex becoming the site where true love and a successful marriage are demonstrated, there developed social and psychological pressure to determine sexual compatibility before marriage. The point is not that the sexualization of love caused a rise in premarital sex, but that it further prompted and justified this behavior.

Historians have documented that within middle-class youth culture from the 1920s on, sexual expression that was not necessarily tied to love or marriage achieved legitimacy.[158] Sex was accepted as an integral part of "dating." People dated, moreover, without any necessary expectation of marriage. In the early decades of this century, dating, unlike courting, was valued as a site of self-expression and play. Dating legitimated sexual expression so long as it did not include coitus. By the 1950s even this restriction began to erode. However, a movement to legitimate sex in middle-class youth culture for its pleasurable and expressive qualities apart from a context of love and marriage did not materialize in the U.S. until the 1960s and '70s. In this period there appeared discourses and representations that constructed sex as a domain of pleasure and self-expression valued apart from a context of love. Paradoxically, the erotic value that sex accrued as a vehicle of love now seemed to no longer require love to legitimate it. This theme forms the subject of the third section of this book.

Part Three

The Contemporary Period (1960–1980)

5

Eros Unbound

Constructing Sex as an
Autonomous Domain of Pleasure

I have charted a change from a Victorian culture that spiritualized love to modern efforts to sexualize love. The latter contributed, moreover, to the development of a culture of eroticism. Public discourses and representations in the 1960s and 70s legitimated approaching the body as a site of sensual pleasure and sex as a vehicle of self-expression and communication.

This chapter signals a shift in my focus. I will not further trace the modern trend toward the sexualization of love, since this is largely a matter of elaboration. Instead, I intend to analyze a third major shift in intimate culture, perhaps as momentous as the Victorian spiritualization of love and the modern sexualization of love. The post–World War II period witnessed a movement to uncouple sex from romance and love. Although sex continued to be valued in a context of romantic love—and indeed this has remained the dominant sexual norm— discourses and representations materialized in these years that legitimated sex for its pleasurable, expressive and communicative qualities apart from a romantic, intimate setting. The movement to uncouple eros from romance and its complex permutations among men and women, is the chief theme of this chapter. I begin by outlining the social context of this development.

RHETORICS OF REVOLUTION,
MOVEMENTS OF CHANGE

Between 1960 and 1980 social analysts often described the United States as undergoing a "sexual revolution." Of course, revolution was in the air. Third-world countries were in revolt against colonial powers and, on the domestic front, blacks, women, gays, students and segments of the younger generation were announcing a coming revolution. The revolutions abroad against imperial dictators were, according to these rebels, to be accompanied by domestic revolts against the tyranny of racism, sexism, heterosexism, puritanism and capitalism.

Retrospectively, we can see that the claim that America was experiencing a sexual revolution was more rhetoric than reality. The claim of a coming sexual revolution, like the idea of black or women's liberation, functioned as a powerful, emotionally charged symbol. The rhetorical intent may have been to imbue sex and sexual conflicts with a moral and political seriousness hitherto lacking. In any event, this rhetoric seemed to have had the effect of drawing sharp moral and political sides. Sexual rebels may have used this rhetoric to build solidarity while inciting fear in the opposition. Defenders of the established sexual regime may have applied the label in order to discredit all movements of sexual reform by exaggerating their danger to society. We must not confuse a rhetoric of sexual revolution with the real thing.[1]

Although a sexual revolution did not occur, important alterations in sexual and intimate patterns did transpire in the post–World War II period. At least three major developments stand out.

First, the "eroticization of female sexuality" which underpinned the decline of the double standard. The Victorian discourse that constructed male sexuality as carnal and female sexuality as romantic or maternal was gradually replaced by a concept of female sexuality that included erotic desire. Women, no less than men, were thought to be driven by carnal motivations. They could claim equal rights with regard to giving and receiving sensual pleasures. Researchers have documented the steady decline of differences between male and female sexual behavior and attitudes. For example, summarizing major surveys and studies of middle-class female premarital coital behavior in the postwar period, Paul Gebhard of the Kinsey Institute described a convergence of gender patterns. "The Kinsey data reveal that 8 percent of the females born before 1900 had premarital coitus by age 20 . . . and this percentage gradually rose until among women born between 1910 and 1919 some 23 percent had had premarital coitus by age 20. . . . Our own 1967 college study showed that at that date 33 percent of the unmarried college females were no longer virgins by age 20. The slightly later *Psychology Today* survey reported 78 percent of their female readers had had premarital coitus. Finally the *Playboy* survey in the early 1970s . . . found that . . . each younger cohort had had higher figures until their youngest group reported 81 percent. The *Redbook* survey gave somewhat higher percentages and again found the behavior most common among the younger generations. Figures for males are higher than those for females, but the differences are decreasing with each generation. Ultimately, we shall arrive at the point now reached in Sweden where roughly 95 percent of both males and females have experienced coitus before marriage."[2] Research through the 1970s confirms the same trend toward egalitarianism between the sexes with regard to initiating sex, demanding sexual satisfaction including orgasm, and patterns of marital, extramarital and postmarital sex.[3] This development appears to have accelerated in the postwar years, but it is continuous with a trend visible since the beginning of this century.

A second major change in sexual patterns relates to the rise of a homosexual identity and subculture.[4] Under the impact of a socially influential medical-scientific discourse, "the homosexual" stepped forward as a unique human figure imagined to possess his/her own distinctive psychic and social nature. Although documents indicate the existence of nascent homosexual networks as early as the 1880s, the heightened self-consciousness implied in the homosexual label greatly facilitated the formation of homosexual lifestyles and subcultures. By the 1940s and 1950s, homosexuality was a basis of individual identity and group life that was widely acknowledged in American culture. The 1960s and 1970s witnessed a great transformation of homosexual life.[5] Homosexuals, now reconfigured as gays and lesbians, forged a mass-based movement aimed at social inclusion and legitimation. This movement was anchored in an elaborated gay subculture which provided individuals with affirmative identities and lifestyles. This development was, in general, indicative of a trend towards a more sexually pluralistic society. Despite the resistance of many Americans, expanded tolerance toward homosexuality, the dramatic increase in cohabitation in the 1970s, greater acceptance of premarital and nonmarital sex, public receptivity to the "playboy" lifestyle and the proliferation of pornography, underscores the widening tolerance for the range of legitimate sexual lifestyle variation in the U.S. Although some of these changes—for example, the rise in cohabitation—are specific to the contemporary period, the overall trend toward sexual liberalism, including the transformation in the social role of homosexuals, extends back to the turn of the century.

A third shift in sexual culture concerns the "sexualization of the public realm." This refers to the infusion into public spaces of sexual representations and discourses. It also entails the appearance in the public sphere of commercial establishments that provide sexual aids (e.g., sex shops) as well as public places (e.g., theaters, gay bathhouses, heterosexual sex retreats, single and gay bars) that facilitate sexual liaisons. Spurred by capitalism's search for an expanded domestic market, and legitimated by hedonistic and expressive ideologies, sex was not only routinely used to sell commodities–from clothes and automobiles to magazines—but it created a new market: the sex industry.[6] From sex aids to sex manuals, pornography and erotic home videos, to heterosexual retreats and gay bathhouses, to personnel advertisement columns and dating services, the culture of eroticism offered rich commercial prospects which entrepreneurs predictably exploited. The sexualization of the public is a departure from the Victorian era, which ghettoized public sexual expressions—i.e., sex was cordoned off into illicit or stigmatized urban spaces. Aided by a series of Supreme Court decisions that substantially narrowed the legal definition of obscenity, sex not only went public but it pushed its way into the social center. "By the 1970s," writes Jeffrey Weeks, "explicit sexuality (or at least of a heterosexual sort) pervaded the social consciousness from newsstands to televisions, from private clubs to theaters and cinemas, from advertising billboards to street life. . . . Sex [was projected] into all corners of social life."[7] And as Weeks, among others, has noted, the origins of the movement of sexual images and behavior into the public sphere can be traced to the consumerist economic emphasis and cultural rebellion against Victorianism in the early decades of the twentieth century.[8]

These three developments mark a major departure from middle-class Victorian intimate culture. They did not, however, originate in the aftermath of World War II. These changes reflect long-term trends that extend back to the beginning of this century. Accordingly, if we still wish to speak of these three movements as part of a sexual revolution, it would be more accurate to view it as a century-long event.[9]

Yet, I wish to propose that there did occur one major change in the postwar period: the appearance of discourses and representations carrying public authority that legitimated sex as a domain of pleasure, self-expression and communication apart from a context of intimacy or love. As a medium of these secular values, sex was defined as acceptable in virtually any consensual adult context. Eros was, in effect, transfigured into a site of individuation and social bonding. This represents a transformation in the meaning of sex as momentous as its construction as a domain of love.

Any compelling explanation of this development would, in my view, have to be articulated at many levels. From a social structural point of view, I would emphasize the impact of consumer-oriented capitalism. Without rehearsing a well-known thesis, capitalism promotes the dissociation of eros from love in its pursuit of new markets (e.g., singles bars, pornography, gay bathhouses, erotic magazines).[10] In a culture that initially binds sex to love, however, the success of capitalism would depend on the existence of a social stratum responsive to its message. In fact, a younger generation that came of age in the 1960s and 1970s was quite receptive to approaching sex as a domain of pleasure and play.

An elaborate middle-class youth culture had already materialized in the 1920s and 1930s.[11] This youth culture innovated dating rituals which included sexual expression that was not necessarily oriented to love or marriage.[12] Yet coitus was strictly proscribed. Moreover, there were no authoritative discourses these youth could appeal to in order to legitimate their behavior. To be sure, bohemians and sex radicals advocated the uncoupling of sex from marriage but few endorsed the release of eros from bonds of romantic love.[13] Those that did carried little or no public authority.

The youth who matured in the late 1950s and after found themselves in a different milieu.[14] This was a middle-class generation witnessing unprecedented affluence. Moreover, in reaction to the wartime experience, this was a generation with a heightened focus on self-fulfillment. Whereas their parents might have pursued this through work and homemaking, the younger generation, encouraged by an expanding entertainment and leisure industry, looked more to personal avenues of self-fulfillment. This was a generation less influenced by a Protestant culture that connected the denial or restriction of sensual pleasures with autonomy and maturity. Indeed, these middle-class youth flourished in a culture that was decidedly more hedonistic, expressive and sexualized than those of their parents and grandparents. Thus, unlike their predecessors of the 1920s and 1930s, these youth not only accepted premarital coitus but could legitimate it by invoking discourses that were issuing forth from the very center of society. Bestselling fiction and advice texts, mass circulation magazines, popular music and art constructed sex as a sphere of pleasure and self-expression. An alliance was formed between segments of middle-class youth and powerful cultural elites. They formed a kind of vanguard in a movement to unleash eros from the culture of romance that gave birth to it.

There is, as I alluded to above, a more dialectical account of the release of eros from love that I would like to spell out briefly. The culture of eroticism that developed in the twentieth century was, in part, a product of the movement to sexualize love. As sex functioned as a medium to demonstrate, maintain and revitalize love, as the pleasurable, expressive and communicative aspects of sex were legitimate ways to show and be in love, the erotic aspects of sex were developed in a deliberate, energetic way. The result was the elaboration of a culture of eroticism. By this I mean a culture that placed a heightened focus on the body and on skills to augment sensual pleasures. This was a culture informed by an ethic of sexual experimentation. Sex was imbued with an aura of self-fulfillment. Although eroticism was originally embedded in a culture of romantic love, it came to gradually acquire its own moral rationale. In other words, the pleasurable, expressive and communicative qualities of sex assumed an independent value and justification; sexual expression no longer relied exclusively upon a romantic rationale. A movement to uncouple eros from love might not have developed had there not existed a culture that increasingly celebrated self-expression as a valued path to self-fulfillment. With a rising generation already focused on personal and expressive concerns and embroiled in a generational conflict, there materialized a social stratum motivated to spearhead a movement to unbound eros from love.

At the center of the contemporary period is a tension in its intimate culture. American society today exhibits a clash of sexual ideologies and ethics. The culture of romance with its norm binding sex to love remains solidly entrenched and dominant. A movement to uncouple sex from love—or, more correctly, to loosen this nexus and to invest sex with meanings related to authentic selfhood and communication—emerged in the 1960s to form a kind of sexual counterculture. Contemporary American culture constructs sex in highly ambiguous and contradictory ways that, in my view, are at the root of many of our sexual strains and conflicts.

This chapter attends to these discourses that form part of this sexual counterculture. My discussion begins with advice literature, which has played a pivotal role in shaping this countercultural sexual ideology. Discovering similar themes in popular men's magazines and the pornography of the period forces us to ask whether this trend is primarily male-directed. This is a leading interpretation of the "sexual revolution" advanced by some second-wave feminists. I will describe a feminist perspective that portrays American intimate culture as divided along gender lines. I will proceed to evaluate this "dual culture thesis" by analyzing the sexual ideology exhibited in popular women's culture. I will conclude the chapter by reconsidering the relation between gender and sexuality in contemporary middle-class America.

VALUING SEX AS A MEDIUM OF PLEASURE AND PLAY
The Libertarian Ideology of Sex Manuals

The appearance of sex manuals in the 1960s in contrast to marriage manuals is indicative of a change in American sexual ideology. Sex manuals construct sex as a sphere of erotic pleasure and self-expression needing no other rationale. "The aim of this book," writes the author of *The Joy of Sex*, "is pleasure."[15] *The Joy of Sex* intends to teach its readers how "to use sex as play."[16] David Reuben describes the motivation to write *Everything You Always Wanted to Know About Sex but Were Afraid to Ask* as follows: "The purpose of this book is to tell the reader . . . what he needs to know to achieve the greatest possible degree of sexual satisfaction."[17] Although sex carries various meanings in these discourses, the production of erotic pleasure is conceived of as an autonomous value. Dr. Reuben speaks of sex as having three purposes: reproduction, love and fun.[18] The rationale for "funsex" is "the sheer physical and emotional exhilaration of feeling all the good feelings that come from a complete sexual experience."[19] Recreational sex needs no higher end to justify it. "The goal of recreational sex is . . . to obtain the maximum of pleasure from sexual activity without doing damage to anyone."[20] *More Joy of Sex* proposes that sex "can be reproductive (producing babies), relational (expressing love and bonding adults together), or recreational (play and fun)."[21] Each sexual option is legitimate. "The adult of today has all three options— sex for parenthood, sex as total relationship, and sex for fun accompanied by no more than affection."[22]

The focus of these discourses is the sex act. It is abstracted from considerations of time and locale that are irrelevant to erotic play and pleasure. Individuals are typified in a one-dimensional way so that attention is focused on erotic body parts and behavior. Social interaction is emptied of its thick emotional content as it is narrowed to a bounded erotic exchange. The focus on intensifying erotic pleasure entails a heightened concern with the body and sex technique. Every conceivable organ and orifice is explored using every possible stimulant for the sole end of maximizing pleasures, exploring feelings and expanding communication. These discourses urge a rich, diffuse body eroticism. A preoccupation with genital sex, especially vaginal intercourse, is criticized. The authors of *The Joy of Sex* complain that sex today is "over-genital" and "too focused on vaginal intercourse."[23] They insist that "to have good sex . . . we need the total acceptance of our whole body as a source of pleasure."[24] Similarly, David Reuben advises his readers to utilize "all the available erotic pathways to reinforce and add to the 'cumulative gratification' of the sex experience."[25] "M" urges the Sensuous Man to use his hands and mouth, not his penis, as his primary sex organ and to make "his entire body an instrument of sexuality."[26] Exercises and sensitizing strategies are suggested to re-eroticize dulled body regions and to make one sexually adept at giving and receiving pleasure.

Sex can, in these discourses, legitimately be approached with an eye to pleasure and fun. The reader is encouraged to put aside all his or her inhibitions. Erotic fulfillment is said to require that one can be adventurous and experimental. Variety with regard to act, position, place, role and so on is encouraged to enhance erotic pleasure. Nor should we be deterred from erotic experimentation by anxiety over the normality of our behavior. David Reuben proposes that the very term "sexual perversion," which functions to stigmatize and inhibit harmless sexual pleasures, should be replaced by the morally neutral phrase "sexual variation."[27] These manuals aim to expand the range of legitimate sex acts to include all types of body rubbing, voyeuristic and fetishistic behavior, oral-genital sex and anal eroticism. "J" encourages the Sensuous Woman to use "dirty sex talk" to enhance sexual excitement. "Whispering 'I love you' to the average man doesn't have nearly the exciting effect on him that 'your cock makes me so hot I can hardly stand it' does."[28] *The Joy of Sex* recommends exploring aggressive feelings. Flagellation games and bondage are referred to as "harmless expressions of sexual aggression and a venerable human resource for increasing sexual feeling."[29] Eroticizing aggression and games of power pushes sexuality deeper into the realm of fantasy. These manuals encourage the reader not to resist since the sexual sphere represents an ideal setting for probing tabooed wishes and fears. "This [sex] is the place to experience things you can't possibly act out, and to learn your partner's fantasy needs. These fantasies can be heterosexual, incestuous, tender, wild or bloodthirsty—don't block and don't be afraid of your partner's fantasy; this is a dream you are in."[30] To put the reader at ease, he or she is assured that sexual behavior is not indicative of an individual's essential nature. Sexual preferences and behavior is not considered self-defining in any essential way.

One implication of valuing sex for its pleasurable and expressive qualities is that the range of relationships in which sex is acceptable expands. These discourses endorse a plurality of at least heterosexual lifestyle choices.

In *The Joy of Sex* and its sequel, *More Joy of Sex*, diverse models of heterosexuality are defended. It is noteworthy that these manuals, in contrast to former sex advice literature, are not written for people who are married or anticipating it. Rather, they are addressed to a "couple" whose relational status—married, cohabiting, long-term, short-term—is unknown and presumed irrelevant. The couple is instructed to enjoy sex as an adult form of play. They are advised that in a consensual, safe and respectful interpersonal setting, there is no compelling reason, other than individual taste, to refrain from having sex. For example, "we see no earthly reason why pairs of friends shouldn't make love together. . . . They would need either to be very good friends or total strangers."[31] Similarly, "there is no reason why sex should not be social if you wish."[32] The authors are suggesting that sex can legitimately function as a recreational or socializing activity. The value of sex would lie in its being a source of pleasure or social bonding. Although *Joy* defends sex in a variety of social exchanges, *More Joy* endorses "social polygamy" as a major alternative to the romantic monogamous pattern.[33] Conventional marriage—heterosexual, romantic and monogamous—is not denigrated. Indeed, it is recommended for couples with children or for people who value it as a source of security and intimacy. *More Joy* proposes that for a variety of reasons—the availability of safe and cheap birth control methods, longer lives, a more sex-positive culture—people are experimenting with different patterns. Individuals, it is argued, are today more willing to design their own intimate arrangements to suit their singular needs and values. In particular, social polygamy or combining one primary relationship with secondary, more sexually focused involvements, is, the authors think, on the rise. In this regard, they promote the concept of "open marriage," since it unites the social and emotional security of a monogamous relationship while allowing for sexual variety. This is viable, however, only if each partner can differentiate sex as an expression of love from sex as pleasure and play. The latter are supposed to be emotionally thin, sexually oriented liaisons which would not threaten the primary relationship.

These manuals promote a view of sex in which the range of individual choice with respect to sex act, meaning and type of relationship is expanded. Yet, moral limits are placed upon the range of permissible sexual expression. The sex ethic of these manuals may be described as "formal" and "minimalistic." By this I mean that it is not a substantive ethic. Particular sex acts carry no intrinsic moral significance. No sex act per se, be it voyeurism, fetishistic pleasures or anal intercourse, is deemed immoral or perverse. It is the interpersonal context of sex that determines its morality. Sex is viewed as part of a social interaction; its interpersonal dynamics provide the normative standard. Moreover, it is only the most abstract and therefore minimal features of the interpersonal context that function as norms. Specifically, sex is legitimate so long as it is consensual, reciprocal in its pleasures, and involves mutual respect and shared responsibility. To be sure, the ideal sexual relationship may include additional ingredients, for example, love or marriage, but these are not deemed essential. This sex ethic may be termed libertarian.

Only sex between consenting adults is considered legitimate. Sex between an adult and a child is not acceptable. "Never involve children in adult sexual activities," says *The Joy of Sex*.[34] As a sphere of reproduction, love or pleasure, sexual involvement should be voluntary. Any sex act that includes coercion or results from physical or psychological manipulation or is injurious to a participant is said to be unacceptable. Masters and Johnson succinctly state the guiding norm: "Our basic concept is that any sexual practice taking place in private between consenting adults is acceptable. . . . Mutual consent implies that the practice is mutually enhancing [and] mutually pleasurable."[35]

The imperative that sex be consensual implies a further moral condition: respect for individual needs. The integrity of each partner's desires must be acknowledged. "Each partner must accept the other as the final authority . . . of . . . his or her own feelings."[36] Each partner must, in addition, be in a position to communicate his or her erotic wants as a condition of participation. Both partners should make a reasonable effort to secure sexual fulfillment for the other. *The Joy of Sex* offers two rules for sex. "(1) Don't do anything dangerous or that is not enjoyable (2) Find out what your partner needs and satisfy them if you can."[37] "M" advises that "to be a Sensuous Man, you must respect your woman. You must consider her sexual pleasures as important as (or more so than) your own."[38] Accordingly, mutual sexual satisfaction achieved through communication and adjusting to each others needs is a guiding norm. "Really good sex comes when a man and woman . . . learn to work together for mutual satisfaction."[39] It follows that sex should be an exchange between equals. Responsibility for initiating and participating in sex and its consequences ought to be shared. "Sexual responsibility," say Masters and Johnson, "has a twofold implication in today's world. Primarily, we are responsible only for ourselves in our sexual commitments, for full communication of our sexual wants—subsequently, for physical expression of our sexual drives. Also, we are committed to remaining fully attuned to [our] partner's communication and to the cooperation necessary to enable one's partner to satisfy his or her sexual needs. Secondarily, our sexual responsibility extends not only to full obligation for pregnancy, but to adequate control of contraception."[40]

Although the discourse of these manuals legitimatize sex as an exchange of pleasure, the norm that sex be cooperative and involve mutual respect and responsibility is intended to preclude an instrumental and exploitative approach. The latter reduces individuals to egoistic pleasure-seekers who respond to each other as mere bodies or objects of gratification. Without a norm of respect and reciprocity, the individual's status as a moral person is suspect. Recognizing that their defense of sex as a domain of pleasure would provoke the charge of promoting the instrumentalization of sex, these manuals addressed this issue directly.

A focus on the body and techniques for augmenting pleasure is not considered dehumanizing insofar as the sexual exchange entails shared expectations and norms of mutual respect and responsibility. *The Joy of Sex* refers to the case of a woman who uses erotic dress to arouse her male partner. The authors contend that this should not necessarily be construed as degrading; she is not reduced to a sex object. Assuming a context of mutual consent and a norm of reciprocity, the woman's conduct may be interpreted as exhibiting respect for her partner's erotic wishes. She should feel pleasure in being able to please him. Furthermore, this behavior should not necessarily be taken as indicative of her status beyond the sexual sphere.[41] Indeed, the authors of *The Joy of Sex* maintain that one of the chief rationales for sex as pleasure is its genuinely *humanizing, anti-instrumentalist* character. "Sex is the one place where we today can learn to treat people as people. . . . If we really make it [sex] work it makes us more, not less, receptive to each other as people. This is the answer to anyone who thinks that the conscious effort to increase our sex range is 'mechanical' or a substitute for treating each other as people—we may start that way, but it is an excellent entry to learning that we are people."[42] *The Joy of Sex* is not exceptional in repudiating instrumentalist conceptions of sex. In *The Pleasure Bond*, Masters and Johnson assail the view of sex as a mere physical exchange of pleasure. "Preoccupation with manipulative technique turns people into objects; and touching is turned into the science of stimulation for the purpose of sensual gratification, which in turn is for the purpose of reaching a climax. . . . Sex then comes perilously close to being an exchange of impersonal services, which weakens the bond between a man and woman. Since neither one prizes the uniqueness of the other, all that each partner must do to find a replacement is to choose a person who can perform the necessary functions."[43] Masters and Johnson are not appealing to a conventional romantic ideology; they defend the view that sex should occur in an emotionally supportive setting, but this need not be a romantic one.

The shift from a substantive ethic centered on the sex act to an ethic attentive to the formal moral qualities of the social exchange implies a discourse promoting sexual diversity. Likewise, the construction of sex as a domain of pleasure suggests a tolerance for various nonprocreative sexualities that at the time were prohibited or marginalized. Yet, the actual position of these manuals is quite ambivalent and contradictory toward sexual variety. To the extent that such phenomena as transvestism or sado-masochism are mentioned, they are not considered simply as sex acts but are stigmatized as symptoms of a personality disorder. In other words, the residue of an older medicalizing discourse with its underlying Victorian morality persists and places limits on sexual diversity that are inconsistent with the libertarian ethic of these discourses.

This inconsistency can be nicely illustrated by considering the status of homosexuality in these discourses. Valuing sex as an act of pleasure and self-expression apart from its reproductive role opens the way toward accepting homosexuality. Indeed, a formal ethic centered on the moral qualities of the social exchange would seem to imply that homosexuality per se is morally neutral. If it is the moral qualities of the interpersonal exchange that serve as a normative standard, then the gender of the participants should be morally irrelevant. If what counts is the presence of mutual respect and responsibility or caring behavior, then it is difficult to see how the gender of the individuals should carry moral significance. This is not the case, however, insofar as homosexuality is viewed as a symptom of mental illness or social deviance. In other words, to judge sex acts by the gendered identity of its participants rather than the moral qualities of their behavior reflects a Victorian substantive ethic which these manuals have otherwise challenged.

These manuals are not, in fact, as consistent on the issue of homosexuality as the above might imply. To be sure, they do exhibit a clear heterosexist bias. Homosexuality is systematically excluded from these texts or is included as an aberration or problem. The underlying premise, at times stated directly, is that heterosexuality is natural and right. However, only David Reuben advances a strong anti-homosexual position. Without any awareness that he is subscribing to a type of sex discourse that he otherwise assails for its repressive character, Reuben perpetuates the myth of the male homosexual as a hyper-sexed, penis-centered, promiscuous and dangerous figure.[44] More typical is the ambivalent position of The Joy of Sex. In one of its few references to homosexuality, it declares that bisexuality is natural, while elsewhere it identifies homosexuality as a "major social problem."[45] It is noteworthy that in More Joy homosexuality is deemed normal and the rights of homosexuals are defended.[46]

The contradiction between the heterosexism of these manuals and the moral logic of their sexual ideology which presses beyond a morality of the sex act and the gender of the sex partners is, in part, explained contextually. In the mid-fifties there had yet to appear a visible, energetic gay movement that reconceived homosexuality in an affirmative way. The discussion of homosexuality was dominated by the psychiatric discourses of figures like Irving Bieber.[47] The authors of these manuals were influenced by negative medical models. Perhaps their heterosexism is indicative of a retreat from the radical implications of their own discourse.[48] In any event, I want to underscore the point that the heterosexist bias of these discourses is at odds with their sexual ethic. The latter implies a greater degree of sexual individualism and pluralism than is acknowledged in some of their explicit statements. In fact, the decidedly libertarian ethic of these manuals could easily be turned against their heterosexism. Gay men and lesbians had only to extend the critique of the morality of the sex act to the gendered identity of the sex partners to legitimate homosexuality.

The point I wish to underscore in this section is that these popular advice and medical texts, in contrast to virtually all previous ones, legitimated sex for its pleasurable, expressive and communicative qualities even in nonromantic settings. These discourses were not alone in the American public culture of the time. As we will shortly see, a parallel movement is visible in the new men's magazines and in the movement of pornography into the mainstream that occurred in the 1960s and 1970s.

MEN'S MAGAZINES AND PORNOGRAPHY
Is there a Male Sexual Culture?

Beginning in the 1950s a series of new mass circulation men's magazines appeared. Unlike the older publications which focused on, say, sports, automobiles, finance, work or politics, these new magazines addressed concerns of personal lifestyle. Paralleling many women's magazines, men's publications focused on career but also dress, sex, love, marriage, divorce and dating. These were, as well, the first mass circulation magazines that regularly featured female nudes.

By far the most successful of these magazines was *Playboy*. Launched in December 1953, *Playboy* targeted a young, urban single male population. Despite its market concentration, by the early 1970s its circulation topped six million. *Playboy* came to be more than a magazine. It eventually included *Playboy* restaurants, nightclubs, clothes, cologne and much more. *Playboy* represented a lifestyle that included fine dining and cooking, conversation, travel, work attitudes and ideals of intimacy.

Barbara Ehrenreich has argued that *Playboy*, in part, expressed a male revolt against marriage and the breadwinner role.[49] *Playboy*'s message, she says, was that the good life could be had without marriage and its extended commitments and responsibilities. *Playboy* was, in addition, a response by a younger generation of single middle-class men maturing in a boom economy and in a culture that featured hedonistic and expressive values. For these middle-class men, conventional masculine roles, including marriage and the breadwinner role, were less automatic. *Playboy* advised that men could not only prosper in a career, but could also cook, entertain, decorate their own homes, and look to women for pleasure and good company.[50] *Playboy*'s aim was less to denigrate or repudiate marriage than to conceive of it as one option or, more correctly, as a desired state but one to be chosen for the right reasons—personal fulfillment—and only when one was ready. Furthermore, the message of *Playboy* was that being single can be as fulfilling as marriage. This meant endorsing a sexual ethic that accepted sex outside marriage.

In his "Playboy Philosophy" column, Hugh Hefner, the founder and guiding spirit of *Playboy*, detailed a sexual ideology. *Playboy*, he said, aims to challenge the moral seriousness and repressiveness of American sexual culture. "We do not consider sex . . . sacred."[51] Hefner is equally scornful of a sexual culture centered on sex technique and performance. "There is a good deal more to sex than just the . . . physical techniques. . . . Sex is often a profound emotional experience."[52] Hefner imbues sex with romantic meanings. "No dearer, more intimate, more personal act is possible between two human beings. Sex is, at its best, an expression of love and adoration."[53] This does not mean, though, that sex is only legitimate as a medium of love. "But this is not to say that sex is, or should be, limited to love alone. Love and sex are certainly not synonymous. . . . Sex can be one of the most profound rewarding elements in the adventure of living. . . . Sex exists—with and without love."[54] Legitimating sex as a domain of pleasure, self-expression or communication does not, says Hefner, entail encouraging promiscuity. Sex is preferable as a medium of love but it is legitimate as a medium of pleasure. "This is not an endorsement of promiscuity or an argument favoring loveless sex . . . [since] we favor our sex mixed with emotion. But we recognize that sex without love . . . is not, in itself, evil; and that it may sometimes serve a definitely worthwhile end."[55] In short, for Hefner and the *Playboy* sexual ethic, sex carried two distinct meanings—a medium of love and a medium of pleasure and self-expression. The latter is valued for its individuating and communicative qualities and is legitimate so long as sex is not selfish, instrumental or dangerous.

Playboy's success spawned a succession of men's magazines in its mold. Yet, magazines like *Penthouse, Gent, Chic* or *Hustler* either diminished or entirely dropped *Playboy*'s literary and cultural interests. The sexual focus of these magazines became much more explicit and dominant. The line between these magazines and hardcore pornography was blurred. By the late 1960s the proliferation of these new men's magazines and pornography had made *Playboy* seem rather conventional.

The emergence of a full-blown sex industry marketing hardcore pornography was made possible by the liberalization of laws pertaining to obscenity. The purity and moral reform movements of the Progressive era successfully limited the public display of sex. From the 1930s onward, however, the courts steadily narrowed the definition of obscenity. Despite the resistance of groups such as the Legion of Decency or the National Organization for a Decent Literature, the trend toward the sexualization of the public sphere continued. Indeed, by the 1960s virtually all the legal barriers to pornography were removed. "Between 1957 and 1967, the justices [of the Supreme Court] heard a series of obscenity cases. Though rarely achieving unanimity, the Warren Court progressively contracted the domain of obscenity, in large part by affirming the appropriateness of sex as a matter for public consumption."[56]

Alongside bestselling novels like Henry Miller's *Tropic of Cancer*, bestselling nonfiction like Kinsey's *Sexual Behavior in the Human Male and Sexual Behavior in the Human Female*, and popular sex manuals like the reissued *A Marriage Manual* by Hannah and Abraham Stone, pornography flourished. By the mid-1960s, the porn industry had become a big business spanning a range of media (film, magazines, books). So visible had porn become that even in the midst of a period of heightened sexual liberalization, public concern moved the government to establish a commission to study its extent and social implications. In 1970, after two years of study, the U.S. Commission on Obscenity and Pornography issued a massive report.[57] It confirmed the growth and diversification of a porn industry. Porn was readily available in mass circulation magazines, paperbacks, and films. The commission estimated that perhaps 85 percent of all American adult men and 70 percent of all American adult women had been exposed to porn.[58] The typical consumer of porn was a white, middle-class, middle-aged married man.[59] The report concluded, though not unanimously, that porn did not have serious deleterious effects on the public. The available evidence, the committee surmised, did not suggest a relation between porn and violence, crime or sexual deviance.[60] In fact, the commission proposed that porn has decidedly positive benefits. It encourages people to be more communicative about their sexual feelings. It provides entertainment as well as information that is otherwise often unavailable.[61] The commission argued that porn stimulates sexual feelings and fantasies but does not directly lead to nonconventional behavior. The commission recommended the repeal of all existing federal, state and local statutes and laws that prohibited the sale, exhibition and distribution of porn or obscene material.[62]

The commission's report defined porn as sexually explicit material intended to be sexually arousing. Notwithstanding certain radical feminist interpretations which, at times, conflate sexual and gender dynamics, there is little disagreement among students of porn with the commission's definition. For example, in a recent study, Alan Soble, a Marxist, argues that porn "is consumed in order to experience sexual arousal, to gratify sexual curiosity, to generate sexual fantasy or otherwise to satisfy sexual desires with or without masturbation. Pornography is designed and produced with these purposes in mind."[63] Soble characterizes the sex that is represented in most porn as "affectionless sex."[64] That is, porn depicts sex as a sphere of pleasure and self-expression. It abstracts sex from the life of the whole person and from its emotionally dense interpersonal context. Porn "exalts sexual activity and bodily parts."[65] To the extent that porn separates sex from a procreative or romantic function, this underscores the point that at least one source of porn's appeal is its representation of the erotic aspect of sex. Porn offers a construction of sex as legitimate for its pleasurable and expressive qualities alone.

Playboy and its imitators prospered at least through the 1970s. Their female counterparts like *Playgirl* or *Viva* never succeeded. They were overshadowed by the more conventional women's magazines like *Redbook* or *Cosmopolitan*. Through the 1970s, porn flourished but its consumers remained overwhelmingly men. Its female counterpart, romance fiction, has prospered, especially in the 1970s. Yet, this romance literature typically embeds sex in a drama of love. Although sex is often depicted as sensual in these texts, it is rarely divorced from love. "In these romantic love stories, sex on a woman's terms is romanticized sex," comments Ann Snitow.[66] The question arises: Is it only a middle-class male culture that promotes an intimate culture that uncouples sex from love? Is the movement in the postwar years to legitimate sex apart from love predominantly male-directed? Must we talk of contemporary American society as composed of a male and female sexual culture?

FEMINISM AND THE CULTURE OF EROTICISM
The Dual Sexual Culture Thesis

The second wave of feminism occurred simultaneously with the emergence of movements advocating sexual liberation. Many in the women's movement were also supportive of the sexual rebellions in the counterculture or the gay movement. It was inevitable that feminists would consider the relation between the women's movement and these sexual liberation movements. Moreover, the complex implications of the ideology of sexual liberation for women led some feminists to analyze it with a seriousness typically absent among rebelling men. Their judgment was quite ambivalent and often decidedly negative. Many feminists criticized sexual liberation movements as reflecting men's interests and goals. Some radical feminists, in particular, grounded their critique of the American culture of eroticism in a concept of a woman-centered sexual culture and ethic.

In *The Feminine Mystique*, Betty Friedan interpreted the recent behavioral and ideological changes in U.S. sexual culture as promoting the uncoupling of sex from social bonds of intimacy and commitment.[67] Friedan described the legitimation of sex as a sphere of pleasure and play as entailing the "depersonalization of sex" which she thought was symptomatic of a "diseased and perverted state."[68] Movements to dissociate sex from its spiritual and social meaning were not, she argued, indicative of human liberation but of social pathology. The ideology that associated sexual liberation with release from social constraints was said to be promoted by commercial interests. Friedan believed that women were especially susceptible to looking to sex for self-fulfillment. Under the influence of the feminine mystique, many women succumbed to this false idol. Prevented from pursuing a career and often trapped in barren domestic lives, women invested sex with higher hopes for freedom, pleasure and fulfillment. Women turned to sex for personal happiness in a male-dominated society that denied them avenues of genuine autonomy. This displacement of the pursuit of self-fulfillment from a public world of work and politics onto sex not only proves unsuccessful but makes it "increasingly difficult for women . . . and men . . . to enjoy human sexual love."[69] Friedan concludes that the culture of eroticism has not delivered sexual freedom but has created the malaise of the "restless, immature sex-seeking of . . . young women [and] . . . homosexuality [that] is spreading like a murky smog over the American scene."[70]

Friedan's critique of the culture of eroticism was typical of an older generation of feminists. It reflects, as well, the conventional lifestyle values of many liberal feminists. As we turn to younger radical feminists, we find a different, though still quite ambivalent and critical standpoint. Many radical feminists endorsed trends that affirmed sexual choice, pleasure and pluralism. "A sexual revolution would require," declared Kate Millet, "an end of traditional sexual inhibitions and taboos, particularly those that most threaten patriarchal monogamous marriage: homosexuality, 'illegitimacy,' adolescent, pre- and extra-marital sexuality. The negative aura with which sexual activities has generally been surrounded would necessarily be eliminated, together with the double standard and prostitution. The goal of revolution would be a permissive single standard of sexual freedom."[71] Shulamith Firestone, in her radical feminist manifesto *The Dialectic of Sex*, offered a vision of a liberated polymorphous sexuality. Sex would cease to be a separate function; instead it would be infused in all interpersonal relations as a diffuse, life-affirming eros.[72] Many radical feminists struggled to legitimate women's right to define sex as a domain of pleasure. Thus, *Our Bodies, Ourselves* celebrated the female body and sexuality as a medium of pleasure; self expression and communication. "It [sex] is a vital physical expression of attachments to other human beings. It is communication that is fun and playful, serious and passionate."[73] This hymn to erotic pleasure and sexual diversity distinguished radical feminists from conservative critics. It also set them apart from many liberal feminists, for whom sex should be exclusively embedded in a heterosexual romantic framework. Yet, the radical feminist critique of the American culture of eroticism was, in many respects, severe and challenging.

How could radical feminists endorse a sexual ethic that affirmed pleasure, autonomy and variation, yet criticize a culture that expanded sexual choice, pleasure and pluralism? The answer lies in grasping a chief insight of radical feminism: sex was said to be no less gendered than work, leisure or domestic tasks. Radical feminists framed sex as a site of gender politics. What is defined as sex, who does what to whom, how and when, is said to reflect primarily gender power relations. From this standpoint, the changes in sexual conventions, especially the construction of sex as a domain of pleasure and play, was viewed as exhibiting the social and sexual interests of men.

Many radical feminists interpreted the evolving culture of eroticism as an effort by men to impose upon society a basically male sexual ideology that would deny or greatly limit women's sexual and social autonomy. In her brilliant explication of male literary representations of sexuality, Kate Millet sought to show that these depictions of heterosexuality revealed a politic of male dominance.[74] She contended that the way sexual expression is framed in these texts not only defines female sexuality according to male wishes but dramatizes male contempt toward women. Similarly, the radical feminist critique of the norm of vaginal orgasm was meant to show that this was an ideological, not biologically based, norm. The centering of sexual expression on vaginal orgasm was said to be promoted by men to advance their own interests. The claim that there is only one orgasmic experience for males and females that is biologically based provided a warrant for a genitally centered, heterosexual ethic. With the popularization of the centrality of clitoral orgasm by Masters and Johnson and others, the norm of vaginal orgasm was construed by radical feminists as a political strategy by men to control women through defining their sexuality.[75] Indeed, the very norm of heterosexual coitus was viewed by some radical feminists as little more than a political tactic of men to control women through controlling their bodies and sexuality. Writing in *Ms.*, Andrea Dworkin makes this point in her typically stark manner. "Fucking is the means by which the male colonizes the female . . . Fucking . . . in or out of marriage . . . is . . . an act of possession. The possessor is the one with a phallus."[76] The influential theorist of early radical feminism Ti-Grace Atkinson makes the critique of heterosexual coitus the cornerstone of feminist politics. "The institution of sexual intercourse is anti-feminist, first, because the source of women's arousal and pleasure is in the clitoris, not in the vagina. And, second, it is anti-feminist, because sexual intercourse is the link between the wife and the mother roles."[77]

As some radical feminists interpreted concepts like vaginal orgasm and coitus as products of a male sexual culture, it was a short step to viewing all sexual desire and expression as gendered. Thus, Dana Densmore interpreted the construction of sex as a medium of sensual pleasure as reflecting men's sexual values.

> Intercourse, in the sense of the physical act . . . is not necessarily the thing we [women] are really longing for. . . . Physically, there is a certain objective tension and release, at least for a man, when excitation proceeds to orgasm. With a woman even this physical issue is much less clear. . . . I think we might all agree *that* isn't why we go to bed with a man. . . . The release we feel . . . therefore is psychological. . . . We then enjoy the pleasures of closeness.[78]

Densmore connected female sexual values with intimacy, not sensual pleasure and play. "Without denying that sex can be pleasurable, I suggest that the real thing we [women] seek is closeness, merging, perhaps a kind of oblivion of self that dissolves the terrible isolation of individualism."[79]

Radical feminists proposed the thesis that men's and women's sexuality are different. Male sexuality is described as genital and body-centered, objectifying, instrumental and promiscuous; sex for men is said to be oriented to sensual pleasure and control. "The emphasis on genital sexuality, objectification, promiscuity, emotional noninvolvement . . . was the male style, and . . . we, as women placed greater trust in love, sensuality, humor, tenderness, commitment," declared Robin Morgan.[80] Women are thought to be more person-centered, holistic, less genitally focused; pleasures are diffused throughout the female body and women are motivated by affection and intimacy. Accordingly, the creation of an erotic culture that values sex solely for its sensually pleasurable qualities was seen by some radical feminists as reflecting men's sexual nature and interests. Men's sexual values do not necessarily promote women's freedom. "I would argue," reasoned Firestone, "that any changes [in sexual conventions in the sixties] were as a result of male interests and not female—any benefits for women only incidental. A relaxing of the mores concerning female sexual behavior was to his advantage; it increased the sexual supply and lowered the cost."[81] Far from liberating women, the trend toward sexualizing pleasure and loosening the tie between sex and love was seen by these critics as dangerous to women. Women are reduced to sex objects; they are made more sexually available for men; women find it harder to refuse sex; the dangers of unwanted pregnancy, disease and violence against them escalate.

In contrast to "the fake sexual revolution of the sixties," genuine sexual freedom for women, according to many radical feminists, would not mean mere sexual release or reconfiguring sex as a sphere of pleasure and play.[82] Rather, in a male-dominated society, female sexual liberation would involve expanding the right of women to control and define their own bodies and sexuality. "As women, we want our own sexuality under our control."[83] This would include the right to refuse sex without suffering a stigma; the right to choose celibacy or a lesbian alternative; the right to control the consequences of sex (e.g., access to abortion and birth control information); the right to choose when to have sex, with whom and how. The aim of a female sexual revolution would be to "change from sexual objects to sexual subjects. . . . We must define our sexual experiences in our own terms. . . . We must be guided by our own feelings, and learn sensitivity to our own bodies. We must respect our own needs and desires."[84] By the mid-seventies, radical feminists had evolved the notion of a woman-centered sexuality. This served as a standard to assess broader trends and movements in American sexual culture. In the radical feminist critique of pornography we can observe this critical standpoint at work. It can be taken, as well, as indicative of at least some women's opposition to the uncoupling of sex from romantic, intimate meanings and relationships.

UNBOUNDED EROS AS DANGER
The Radical Feminist Critique of Porn

By the mid-1970s, at least one important current of radical feminism had developed an impressive critique of pornography. Unlike liberal critics who objected only to the excesses of porn or to the public's involuntary exposure to it, especially in the case of children and adolescents, some radical feminists disputed the liberal presumption that porn has an enlightening social role. These radical feminists saw little or no redeeming value in porn. However, they distinguished their critique from conservatives who objected to the sexually explicit character of porn regardless of its content and context. Radical feminists insisted that their critique of porn was not directed at its nudity or hedonism or even the public depiction of sexuality. They criticized the way porn portrays women and their sexuality.[85]

Radical feminists held that porn is not, in fact, primarily about sex. Sex is merely the medium for relating a message about gender norms and roles. Specifically, porn constructs a drama of male domination. "Pornography is primarily a medium for expressing norms about male power and domination, thereby functioning as a social control mechanism for keeping women in a subordinate status."[86] Porn both dramatizes male power and rationalizes it by fostering an ideology of contempt for women. "Pornography functions to perpetuate male supremacy and crimes of violence against women because it conditions, trains, educates, and inspires men to despise women, and men despise women in part because pornography exists."[87] In short, porn was thought to promote men's power over women.

According to many radical feminists, porn depicts women in a way that reflects men's wishes and fantasies. Porn reveals men's impulse to control and do violence to women. "The true subject of pornography is not sex or eros but objectification, which increasingly includes cruelty, violence against women."[88] Violence need not take the form of men inflicting physical pain upon women. Porn displays the symbolic violence that occurs by obliterating women as autonomous sexual and social agents. Pornographic images of women render them mere objects of desire. They exist to incite and satisfy male desire. Susan Brownmiller protests that porn projects women as "anonymous, panting . . . playthings, adult toys, dehumanized objects to be used, abused, broken and discarded."[89] Porn's reduction of women to sex objects denies their status as men's equal. This withdrawal of autonomy is revealed in pornographic representations of women as passively accepting the control of men. Women are never shown to initiate action or direct their own or men's behavior. They simply react to male directives and, indeed, take pleasure in being subject to male control. "Women are represented as passive and as slavishly dependent upon men. [Their] role . . is limited to the provision of sexual services to men. . . . Women's sexual pleasure . . . is subordinated to that of men and is never an end in itself. . . . What pleases women is the use of their bodies to satisfy male desires."[90] Men's contempt for

women is said to be built into the way the latter are sexually objectified. Women frequently do not appear as whole, intact persons. Pornography dismembers them; they exist in the male gaze as eroticized
body parts. "Pornography propagates a view of women as nothing but
'tits' and 'ass'—silly creatures who exist to be fucked, sexually used,
and forgotten."[91] In short, porn is said to withdraw from women their
status as autonomous subjects by depicting them as passive and by
implying that their primary value lies in the pleasure they give men.

Radical feminists pressed the additional claim that porn denies
women's autonomy by suppressing their unique sexual desires and
values. This criticism assumes that women's sexuality is different
from men's. "Men are turned on by what they see, remember, or
anticipate; sex has a more central place in the male psyche where
sexuality tends to be impersonal and abstract; sex is centered on the
genitals; and it is closely related to aggression. . . . All told, male
sexuality is performance-oriented. Women respond to diffuse touching; their sexuality is more personal, intimate, and emotional—unlike
the reified male style, women's sexuality, is imbued with nurturance,
women's sexual style is process-oriented."[92] Porn is claimed to disregard these gender differences by projecting women's sexuality in ways
that reflect how men wish them to be. Typically, women are shown
to be body-centered (not person-centered), genitally focused (not dif-
fusely erotic), oriented toward sexual intercourse (rather than clitoral
stimulation) and motivated by carnal pleasure (rather than affection
and intimacy). Porn constructs female sexuality as men want them to
be to satisfy their own sexual needs and fantasies. In short, porn
exhibits a male-centered sexuality and in the process denies women's
unique sexual needs and autonomy. Porn, writes Laura Lederer, "is
almost totally penis-centered, often devoid of foreplay, tenderness or
caring, to say nothing of love and romance."[93] Susan Lurie remarks
that in porn "the male fantasy . . . represses the true nature of female
sexuality."[94] Porn is said to document men's sexual nature. At times,
this is construed to disclose a virtually demonic male sexuality. Thus,
Andrea Dworkin sees in porn's depiction of male violence toward
women the deep truth of male sexuality. "Male desire is the stuff of
murder, not love. . . . Male eroticism . . . is sadistic. . . . The penis itself
. . . is a knife, a sword, a weapon."[95]

Central to the radical feminist critique of porn is their objection to
the value placed upon sex as a site of pleasure and play. This is
said to entail a level of sexual objectification, depersonalization and
instrumentalism that many radical feminists find morally objectionable. Thus, Kathleen Barry protested all attempts to separate sex from
intimate ties. "In my mind, where there is an attempt to separate the

sexual experience from the total person, that first act of objectification is perverse."[96] Barry endorsed a sexual ethic that values sex only as an expression of an intimate, loving bond. She holds, moreover, that this ethic is grounded in women's unique sexual values. "We are really going back to the values that women have always attached to sexuality, values that have been robbed from us [by a male-dominated culture]."[97] These female sexual values "are the values and needs that connect sex with warmth, affection, loving, caring."[98] Indeed, Barry views these female sexual values as representing the essential positive meaning of human sexuality itself. "Sexual experience involves the most personal, primitive, erotic, sensitive parts of our physical and psychic being—it is intimate in fact."[99] The implication is that male sexuality, especially to the extent that it celebrates merely erotic values, is unnatural and alienating. Accordingly, Barry urged a shift in our sexual culture from a male culture that idealizes "depersonalized sex" to the healthy female notion of "sexual intimacy as true sharing."[100]

The radical feminist critique of porn, as it was articulated in the mid-1970s, leans on a strong belief in the gender differences between male and female sexuality. Porn is, in this view, produced by and for men. It does not, says these critics, represent human sexuality in general. The image of sex in porn is impersonal, affectionless, body-centered and pleasure-oriented; it exhibits men's sexual desires and values. Hence, porn suppresses women's sexual feelings and values, which is indicative of the contempt toward women that radical feminists claim is its essential meaning.

Disregarding the issue of the validity of the radical feminist interpretation of porn, their critique serves as evidence that at least some women resisted the construction of sex as an autonomous domain of pleasure and self-expression. For many of these predominantly young, white, middle-class women, the reconfiguring of intimate patterns in a direction the sexualizes pleasure and legitimates sex as a domain of sensual pleasure was viewed as a movement by and for men. The question we need to address is this: Are these women expressing beliefs and values widely shared by middle-class women in this period? Do we find similar sexual meanings in what we might call popular women's culture?

HETEROSEXUAL INTIMACY IN
WOMEN'S POPULAR CULTURE

The second wave of feminism departed from previous strains in the women's movement that coupled the demands for women's empowerment with a notion of female purity or virtue. Contemporary feminism pressed for women's rights on the grounds that women's capabilities regarding work and public life are equal to those of men. Furthermore, the demand for sexual autonomy, including the right to erotic pleasure and expression, was advanced as an integral part of the feminist agenda. Feminists argued that women's capacities for pleasure are equivalent to those of men. Accordingly, feminists endorsed, in principle, an intimate culture that promoted sexual choice, pleasure, and diversity. Yet, at least one influential version of radical feminism criticized social trends for promoting men's sexual and social interests in the guise of advancing human sexual liberation. They argued that the focus on genital sex, sexual intercourse, vaginal orgasm and sex technique, along with the legitimation of sex as a sphere of pleasure and play, reflects men's interests. The so-called sexual revolution was said to be a movement by and for men. True female sexual liberation, according to some radical feminists, would involve expanding women's control over their body and creating a culture that values sex as an intimate expression to be confined to committed loving relationships.

As we turn to documents of the cultural mainstream, this radical feminist standpoint seems less socially credible. I have consulted a range of documents that challenge the radical feminist thesis of a dual sexual culture. Relevant surveys of sexual behavior and attitudes reinforce this critique.

A year before Betty Friedan's *The Feminine Mystique* appeared, Helen Gurley Brown published a bestseller, *Sex and the Single Girl*. Where Friedan assailed the ideological construction of women as destined to be wives and mothers, Brown was advising young women that their lives need not orbit around men or domesticity. Her message was that a woman can live a fulfilling life without a husband and family, although heterosexual love and marriage are preferable. "You may marry or you may not. Your decision and it doesn't determine your fate."[101] It is instructive that whereas Friedan condemned a hedonistic, expressive and more open sexual culture, Brown held that it expanded women's personal and sexual autonomy. "Theoretically, a 'nice' single woman has no sex life. What nonsense! She has a better sex life than most of her married friends. . . . [For the single woman] her choice of partners is endless and they seek her."[102] Young women today, Brown thought, can approach sex more casually. "A girl may 'surrender' any time between two hours after she's met a 'possible' to two years of going steady."[103] In today's world of expanding sexual options, says Brown, sex carries multiple meanings: Sex can be a way for a woman to get what she wants, an expression of love or it can "be unadulterated, cliffhanging sex."[104]

In 1972 the first issue of *Ms.* was published. Although the magazine displayed a variety of views on sex and intimacy, radical feminist themes were prominent through the seventies. For example, in "Love," Ingrid Bengis criticized efforts to dissociate sex from love by constructing sex as a realm of pleasure and play. Sex, she said, "created unpredictable bonds . . . and I didn't realize that intimacy, physical intimacy . . . created highly unprogressive . . . bursts of possessiveness and jealousy . . . [and] I didn't realize that sex deepened love."[105] Bengis's message is that sex should be an expression of love confined to intimate relationships. This theme is echoed in a very critical view of *The Joy of Sex*. The reviewer condemns its focus on pleasure and sex technique, describing it as a "very male oriented marriage manual."[106] Reacting to several books by women which apparently celebrated the hedonistic, playful aspects of sex, Barbara Grizzuti Harrison complains that "these books are pornographic."[107] They may aim to liberate female sexuality, but "I hear echoes of the sexual revolution battle cry all over again: let's free women sexually so that they'll be more available for fucking."[108] Towards the mid 1970s, radical feminist sexual themes are quite visible in *Ms.* In an autobiographical memoir, Robin Morgan details her escalating hostility toward porn, which is, she says, part of "the fake 'sexual revolution' of the sixties."[109] Andrea Dworkin declares that "fucking is the means by which the male colonizes the female."[110] Underpinning such views is the notion of a unique female sexuality. "We [women] seem to be more aroused by subjects involving romance; itself a metaphor for emotional contact, affection, passion, tenderness, in other words, relationships between persons, not mere organs."[111]

In July 1965, Helen Gurly Brown became the editor of *Cosmopolitan*. A noticeable shift occurred in its themes. More emphasis was placed on intimate lifestyle issues, in particular on sex and romance. Images of sexuality appeared that valued it as a site of pleasure and self-expression, even apart from a committed relationship.

In a provocative piece, Edna O'Brien offered "a defense of the brief encounter." She describes this as "one of my most shattering pleasures." The brief encounter is not meant, she says, to be a substitute for a love affair or marriage. Instead, it should be an occasional adventure valued for its erotic exuberance that women should not pass up. In the brief encounter, the individual "lives for the moment" and "has a beautiful sense of celebration. Her openness is touching, her appetite unconcealed."[112] Alma Birk debunks the myth that women only enjoy sex as an expression of intimacy or love. "The modern argument goes: a woman cannot enjoy a sexual relationship unless it is also deeply emotional. . . . Needless to say, more men than women utter these propositions."[113] This notion, she argues, disempowers women; it stigmatizes women who find pleasure in sex apart from love. Although Birk believes that "sex without love or friendship is a graceless experience . . . it can still be satisfying, releasing—and fun. In all this romantic talk, it is conveniently forgotten that sex is also an appetite that needs feeding."[114] Cosmo does not advocate pleasure-centered, "casual sex" as preferable to romantic, intimate sex. Yet, Cosmo did campaign to expand women's autonomy by giving them the opportunity to approach sex as a medium of pleasure and self-expression without being stigmatized. Gael Green criticizes a liberal sexual trend insofar as it promotes an instrumental sexual ethic. "For some girls . . . sex . . . has become calculated trading—bed for insurance of a date next weekend or a dinner."[115] She assails the anomic strains of American culture. "Far too many girls . . . find themselves drifting aimlessly . . . from bed to bed out of resignation, routine, habit, passive nonresistance. And all this joyless bedding about is accomplished under the guise of sensuality and free love."[116] Although Ms. Green prefers romantic sex, she accepts sex solely as a sphere of pleasure and self-expression as a legitimate option for women. "Don't get me wrong. I'm not about to suggest that sex outside marriage is doomed to despair, or that sex without love should be avoided. Of course, the grand passions are the greatest . . . and a lot of less-than-love affairs have a legitimate place in the sexual scheme of things. Sex is a form of expression. . . . Sex can bring instant intimacy. . . . Sex does starve off loneliness. A girl can have an absolutely fantastic evening in bed with a fascinating man whose name she might not necessarily know and whose face she might not see again."[117] The Cosmo ideal is to frame sex as a bond of intimacy in a heterosexual marital context. Yet, Cosmo defends sex as a site of pleasure and self-expression both within and outside of romantic intimate relationships. This is not, at least for Cosmo and perhaps some of its millions of readers, a male sexual value.

Contrary to the radical feminist thesis, key documents in the cultural mainstream produced by women construct their sexuality in a way that overlaps significantly with radical feminist images of male sexuality. These popular representations of women's intimate practices and norms often construct sex as a sphere of intimacy as well as pleasure and self-expression. Let's return, for the moment, to sex manuals.

We need to recall that The Joy of Sex and More Joy of Sex as well as The Pleasure Bond were coauthored by women. The female counterpart to The Sensuous Man was The Sensuous Woman by "J," a book that has sold over nine million copies. Although The Sensuous Woman advises women to use sex as a way to get and keep a man, "J" also urges women to approach sex as a sphere of pleasure. Women, she says, are "bursting with sexual appetite" and should rejoice in the pleasures the body can yield. In order for the body to bring pleasure, it must be sexually tuned and sensitized. "J" suggests "sensuality exercises" and has designed an elaborate sexual training program to reawaken women to their erotic potential. "J" asserts that while sex is best when there is love, erotic pleasure or play is a sufficient rationale. "You can enjoy yourself sexually without love . . . but only with love can you be fulfilled."[118] Sexual pleasure, moreover, can be legitimately pursued in a variety of social settings, from the solitary pleasures of masturbation to heterosexual intercourse to "an occasional or regular foray into the world of orgies."[119]

The Sensuous Woman was written in the late 1960s and bears the trace of an older gender ideology. Eva Margolies's *Sensual Pleasure: A Woman's Guide* was published in 1981 and is perhaps more indicative of normative trends in women's culture of the 1970s. *Sensual Pleasure* was intended to help women augment their erotic pleasures. "This book will show you the way to have orgasm with your partners, as well as how to improve your sexual encounters and sensual pleasure in general."[120] Women's sensual pleasure, Margolies argues, has been limited by Victorian gender norms which legitimate sex only as a sign of love for women. "We've . . . been made to believe that sex should be an expression of love. . . . We've been told that sex is dirty unless it's an act of love."[121] This has deterred women from approaching sex as a sphere of sensual satisfaction. Margolies insists that sex can be both a medium of love and pleasure. "Sexual pleasure, in and of itself, has little to do with love."[122] Sensual pleasure, moreover, is said to be sufficient grounds to value sex. "Sex may be accompanied by love, and perhaps is most satisfying when love is present, but love is not, and need not be, a prerequisite to enjoy sex."[123] For Margolies, expanding women's sexual autonomy includes the option of choosing a lifestyle that involves sex for no other purpose than pleasure. Thus, she says that while monogamy is ideal for those who desire security, it does place "restrictions on your freedom to enjoy sex with other people."[124] Although she thinks that most women prefer an emotionally involved relationship, "there are some women who are ardent advocates of the one-night stand. They claim that by being free of any emotional entanglements, they are more readily able to let themselves go sexually."[125] Her final advice: "Let experience be your guide in choosing lovers who will satisfy your needs, and enjoy!"[126] The feminist demand for personal autonomy is drawn upon to rationalize sex as a domain of pleasure and self-expression.

Popular sex advice books written by and for women are not exceptional in defending sex as an autonomous site of pleasure. In their brief for the liberalizing strains of American intimate culture, Barbara Ehrenreich, Elizabeth Hess and Gloria Jacobs note the changing sexual environment for women. "There has always been a sexual marketplace for men, offering pornography, prostitutes, strippers, go-go dancers, and more erotic possibilities for the connoisseur. The extension of the commercial sex industry to include women as consumers . . . is . . . long overdue."[127] These feminist authors observe—and welcome—the beginnings of a sex market for women. There are now female counterparts to *Playboy;* male strippers and go-go dancers; male pinup calendars. The making of porn for women has gone mainstream. "No longer is sexually explicit entertainment directed at men only. Increasingly, X-rated video cassettes are being produced and packaged for a new audience—women and couples. Many of these 'couple films' . . . are being produced, directed and written by women or couples."[128] One study found that women are now major consumers of X-rated videos. "According to a recent nationwide survey of 1000 stores that stock adult videos, women or couples rent 63 percent of such tapes."[129] Although the X-rated videos consumed by women often involve more elaborate plots, fuller characterization of its actors and thicker emotional settings than much male porn, the sex is aggressive, carnal, orgasmic and frequently valued for its pleasurable or expressive qualities alone.

The new prominence of women's erotica in the 1970s is evident in the popular writings of Nancy Friday and Lonnie Barbach. Friday's *My Secret Garden,* an anthology of female sexual fantasies, contains representations that legitimate sex as a sphere of pleasure, play or self-expression.[130] The images of female sexual desire in this collection are, in key respects, indistinguishable from popular concepts of male desire. Commenting on this book, the authors of *Re-making Love* write: "To the distress of many readers, the female libido was shown to be remarkably similar to that of the male; women were interested in adulterous affairs, incest, prostitution, voyeurism, S/M, rape—even sex with animals. By traditional standards, this was the landscape of male sexual lust."[131] A feminist counterpart to Nancy Friday, Lonnie Barbach has published popular sex advice texts as well as female erotica. *Yourself: The Fulfillment of Female Sexuality* falls squarely into the mainstream of contemporary American sexual culture. Female sexual fulfillment, she says, requires that women master sexual skills and techniques, cultivate sexual fantasy, and enjoy the carnal aspects of sex. Experiencing erotic pleasure and achieving regular orgasms is decreed essential to obtaining "greater satisfaction and enjoyment of our sex."[132] Barbach's central message is that sexual enjoyment has been men's privilege; women must sexually empower themselves. Female sexual liberation means, according to Barbach, expanding sexual choice. "Being sexually liberated means the freedom to choose—to choose the kind of stimulation that works for you; to choose the sexual activities that are pleasurable to you."[133] Sexual autonomy means being free to choose your own pleasure (e.g., premarital, extramarital sex, group sex, homosexuality, bisexuality) so long as it is consensual, reciprocal and safe. In a subsequent effort, Barbach produced a major anthology of women's erotica. *Pleasures* amounts to a celebration of sexuality in its multiple forms and meanings. The basic theme is that women's sexual autonomy hinges on the right to choose the social setting and meaning of sex. Thus, while there are stories embedding sex in intimate settings, there are also narratives of "forbidden sex"—centered on group sex and "anonymous sex."[134]

A clear sign of change in middle-class female culture is the appearance of mainstream women novelists who write seriously about sex. In a study of novels written by women in the 1970s, Ann Snitow has analyzed the complex meanings sex carried in these texts. Although Snitow intends to highlight differences in the way female and male novelists represent sex, her study underscores significant similarities. For example, she shows that "women too objectify their lovers," that they also approach sex in an instrumental way or that women novelists use sex as a symbol of self-rejuvenation.[135] In addition, many female novelists of the period focused on the sex act and explored its nonromantic sensual and expressive aspects. For example, the novels of Erica Jong treat sex as an experience to be valued for its pleasurable and expressive as well as its intimate aspects. In her novels, sex is often projected as a dense sensual and expressive experience valued for its individuating qualities. Her concept of the "zipless fuck" imagines sex as an autonomous domain of pleasure and adventure.

> Zipless . . . because the incident has all the swift compression of a dream and is seemingly free of all remorse and guilt; because there is no rationalizing; because there is no talk at *all*. The zipless fuck is absolutely pure. It is free of ulterior motives.[136]

Jong considers the zipless fuck an episodic event, a rare adventure that interrupts a life that otherwise embeds sex in a romantic setting. A life of nothing more than an endless procession of bodies and pleasures is "certainly no liberation."[137] Jong wishes women to be able to choose both the sheer sensual exuberance of the zipless fuck and the stability and intimacy of a "deep relationship with one person."[138]

Admittedly, the documents I've commented upon cannot be said to represent, in an unambiguous way, the beliefs and sentiments of ordinary middle-class women. This, in any event, is not my claim. My point is that they provide one public image of female sexuality that carries normative authority. In these documents, women are viewed as sexually assertive, sensually motivated, oriented to clitoral orgasm but taking pleasure in vaginal intercourse. Sex is imbued with multiple meanings; it exists as a medium of love and as a site of pleasure and self-expression.

My aim has been to dispute a particular radical feminist critique of American intimate culture which links a trend toward hedonistic sexual constructions with a hegemonic male culture. In the final section of this chapter, I wish to reconsider the thesis of the gendered nature of sexuality in postwar middle-class America.

GENDER AND SEXUALITY
Beyond an Ideology of Identity and Difference

I have previously alluded to research that underscores the narrowing of differences in men's and women's sexual behavior and attitudes among the postwar generation. Rates of premarital sex—from petting to coitus—equalized between the sexes in the 1960s and 1970s. In one study comparing college students' premarital sexual behavior between 1956, 1965 and 1975, the researchers found that "among males there was no change in the rate of premarital coitus between 1965 and 1970. . . . For females, the rate of premarital coitus increased 9.6 percent between 1965 and 1970, and nearly twice that amount . . . between 1970 and 1975. Rates of premarital coitus during the first half of the 1970's did not rise significantly for college males, but greatly accelerated for college females. . . . [Similarly] by 1975 the difference between male and female petting behavior had become almost indistinguishable, suggesting that the double behavioral standard is diminishing."[139] Equally telling is the convergence in sexual attitudes between the two genders. In 1965, these same researchers found that 33 percent of the men and 70 percent of the women felt that premarital coitus was immoral. By 1975 the figure dropped to 19.5 percent for men and 20.7 percent for women.[140] Surveys of marital, extramarital and postmarital sex relate a similar story of narrowing gender differences. This trend reflects principally changes in women's behavior and attitudes.

By the late 1970s the image of female sexuality conveyed in survey data is, in a number of important respects, virtually indistinguishable from the dominant public image of male sexuality. For example, in the *Redbook Report* on female sexuality, a nationwide survey of young middle-class women, about 70 percent reported satisfaction with the sexual aspect of their marriage.[141] In part, their satisfaction was connected to their sexually active role. Almost 90 percent of these women indicated that they played an active part in sex at least half the time and often always.[142] Indicative of their enhanced sexual autonomy, most of these women reported that they regularly initiated sex and communicated their needs to their partners.[143] Central to their reported sexual satisfaction, the *Redbook* women acknowledged that they routinely augmented sexual pleasures by dressing in erotic ways, experimenting with sex acts and positions and using sexual aids (vibrators, dildos, oils, pornography).[144] About 64 percent of these women reported regularly achieving orgasm.[145] Although the *Redbook Report* documents that many women of this period approached sex as a sphere of pleasure and play, it also shows continuities with previous middle-class intimate conventions. Thus, 50 percent of the women interviewed said they had premarital sex with only one man; another 34 percent reported between two and five premarital sex partners.[146] These women not only were committed to a monogamous norm but continued to connect sex to intimacy and love. In response to the question "Of all aspects of sexual activity, which one do you like the best?" the highest response rate was for "feeling of closeness with my partner."[147] The portrait of heterosexual women that emerges in these surveys is one of women who, like their male counterparts, take pleasure in sex, experiment with sex acts and techniques to enhance erotic pleasure, look to clitoral orgasm but value vaginal intercourse as a climactic experience. A question remains: Is sex for women connected to intimacy and love in a way that is less true for men?

In *Sexual Behavior in the 1970s*, the popular writer and sex researcher Morton Hunt detected a trend toward accepting sex apart from its role as symbolizing love or enhancing intimacy. Somewhat disconcertingly, he observed: "There is a surprising degree of tolerance of premarital sex in the general population, even when there is little or no emotional relationship between the partners."[148] Tolerance for premarital sex without strong affection was especially pronounced when sex was noncoital. For a "majority of young males and a substantial minority of younger females . . . petting is also seen as acceptable even when there is little or no emotional involvement but only such motives as the desire for experience, or for self-gratification, excitement."[149] Equally revealing of a trend toward women accepting nonromantic constructions of sex is the response women gave to the question "Is good sex possible without love?" Almost 75 percent of the women surveyed in the *Cosmo Report* answered in the affirmative, with no significant difference between single and married women.[150] A nationwide survey by the social scientists Philip Blumstein and Pepper Schwartz offers further relevant information. Over 50 percent of the husbands and 37 percent of the wives surveyed said they approved of "sex without love."[151] The percentages increased to 72 percent for men and 67 percent for women when the respondent was cohabitating at the time of the study. These surveys suggest a level of social acceptance by both men and women of sex outside a relationship of intimacy or love. This was the conclusion to which Morton Hunt grudgingly came. The "recreational attitude towards sex now coexists with the former [liberal-romantic] in our society, even if the latter remains 'the dominant ideal.' "[152]

If, as some public documents and survey data indicate, there is a trend in the postwar years legitimating nonromantic sexual meanings, it did not threaten the link between sex, romance and love. Middle-class American men and women continued to imbue sex with romantic expectations; they preferred to embed sex in a romantic social and moral framework. Thus, the *Redbook Report* found that about 70 percent of the men surveyed indicated that being in love was essential for enjoying sex.[153] In the *Hite Report*, Shere Hite found that for "the overwhelming majority of women . . . sex meant a great deal to them, and the reason almost always given was because it was a wonderful form of intimacy and closeness with another human being."[154]

Although an intimate culture that values sex for its hedonistic and expressive qualities had the support of both genders, the evidence suggests that men were decidedly more approving of this trend. Research in the 1960s and 1970s documents that men endorsed "nonromantic sex"—pleasure-centered sex within and outside an intimate bond—with considerably less ambivalence than women; they held more accepting attitudes toward sexual variety; they were more tolerant of nonmonogamy, especially if the "secondary" sex was casual. For example, Morton Hunt found that whereas 71 percent of the men between eighteen and twenty-four approved of premarital coitus for men "where no strong affection exists," the figure dropped to 47 percent for women.[155] Indeed, twice as many men accepted premarital coitus for women as did women. Again, Hunt found that whereas 68 percent of the men surveyed approved of petting for males "where no strong affection exists," the figure for women was 30 percent.[156] Interestingly, a similar discrepancy, even if less significant, surfaced when comparing the attitudes of young men and women toward premarital coitus "where strong affection exists." Whereas 90 percent of the men under 25 approved of premarital coitus for men, the figure for women was 80 percent. And where 80 percent of the men indicated approval of premarital coitus for women "where strong affection exists," only 60 percent of the women approved.[157] The evidence strongly suggests that, between 1960 and 1980 men approve of separating sex from intimacy more than women and, even in intimate settings, men seemed to place more significance on sexual expression than their female counterparts.

My point is that while the postwar years witnessed a trend toward sexual equalization between the two genders, and while middle-class men and women occupied, by and large, the same universe of sexual meanings and conventions, a difference—perhaps more quantitative than qualitative—persists. To explain this gender difference we do not need to invoke the concept of a dichotomous female and male sexual nature or culture. Indeed, this account, as we have seen, greatly exaggerates the divergence between men's and women's sexuality in this period and ignores differences among these men and among women.

To explain the greater ambivalence toward sexual expression of some women during these years, I would emphasize that these women were more likely to imbue sex, especially nonromantic sex, with danger than men. This relates to the vulnerability many contemporary women felt toward sexually-related abuse and violence. For example, over one-quarter of the women surveyed in the *Cosmo Report* stated that they had been either raped or sexually molested.[158] It also reflects the fact that these women had to be much more concerned about unplanned pregnancy than men since they were assigned the primary responsibility for children. Conception, especially if it occurred outside an intimate, committed arrangement, implied a social fatefulness for women that it lacked for men. A single unwed mother suffered not only diminished social and economic opportunities but the stigma of illegitimacy and rejection.

There is an additional factor that accounts for the ways women in this period were more cautious than men in approaching sex. Although contemporary culture constructed femininity to include sexual and erotic longings, strains of a Victorian gender order persisted. It highlighted the spiritual and moral qualities of femininity. For example, women in this period were still expected to be responsible for controlling sexual expression; there were still lingering hopes, if not expectations, that brides would be virgins, or at least not be too sexually experienced. This Victorian strain is evident in the continued social resonance during the 1970s of the concept of the "good girl." A good girl exemplifies feminine virtues. She is pleasant, considerate and modest. A good girl controls and conceals her sexual interests.

She restricts sexual expression to a sign of love. Good girls are not sexually assertive or lustful. Observing the centrality of the good girl representation in middle-class female life, Paula Webster comments:

> As women, we have been brought up in a society where to be sexual in an active or 'promiscuous' fashion is to transgress the rules of femininity. Not just the rules set up by men but the rules set and enforced by other women. We learned that men were princes/beasts and we their expectant princesses/martyrs, waiting to be aroused by a kiss, leading to love and marriage and the protection of our vulnerable sexuality. The pursuit of sex threatens to make good girls bad, so we usually accept the cultural standard of sexual minimalism . . . few partners, fewer positions, less pleasure, and no changing of preference. Nice girls don't talk about desiring sex. . . . Being forward, pushy, seeking sex are not acceptable.[159]

Women who internalized good-girl standards of femininity may have imbued their own desires for erotic pleasure with feelings of shame and danger.[160]

Women in the contemporary period (1960–1980) differed somewhat from men in their intimate culture. This was due, in part, to certain unique dangers sex has for them. Sex for these women evoked the risk of abuse, violence, unwanted pregnancy, disease and stigma. In addition, although both men and women shared a romantic approach to sex and intimacy, for women at least in this period, romantic expectations were much more tied to gender identity than was true for men. In other words, sexual romanticism and femininity were much more mutually reinforcing than was sexual romanticism and masculinity. Indeed, for men of this period, approaching sex and intimacy as a sphere of pleasure, adventure and self-assertion affirms their masculine gender identity, whereas approaching sex as a sphere of emotional and spiritual union and self-surrender may have been in tension with a consistent masculine experience of self. Accordingly, while men and women of this generation may have approached sex as both a sphere of love and a sphere of pleasure and individualism, they experienced the ambiguities, strains and pleasures of this culture slightly differently. To simplify, men leaned on the individualizing, pleasure-oriented aspects of sex, while women emphasized its communicative, bonding, romantic aspects.

CONCLUSION

Sex outside a context of love and marriage is not, of course, new to the contemporary period. There is ample evidence documenting autoerotic behavior outside marriage, fornication, prostitution and homosexual behavior in the nineteenth and twentieth centuries. Yet, is was only in the postwar years that this behavior acquired some legitimation. In the 1960s and '70s, discourses and representations materialized that constructed sex as a domain of pleasure, self-expression and communication. These qualities were valued for their individuating or socially bonding capacities apart from any higher purpose, e.g., procreation, love or marital stability. Thus, by the mid-1970s there crystallized in the United States an intimate culture that constructed sex simultaneously as a site of love and romance and as a medium of pleasure and self-expression.

The social sources of this intimate culture are complex. I've highlighted the importance of the rise of a middle-class youth culture in a period of unprecedented prosperity and heightened expectations for self-fulfillment. The site of self-fulfillment was shifting, moreover, from work to leisure, in particular to happiness in intimate affairs. Given the preexisting emphasis on sexual fulfillment as integral to success in love and personal happiness, sex was inevitably imbued with hopes of self-realization. It was only left to this postwar generation to loosen the tie between sex and love or to uncouple the pleasurable, expressive and communicative aspects of sex from its romantic aspects.

The movement to legitimate eroticism apart from its role in maintaining romantic love appears to have had some support among both men and women. The radical feminist claim that this development was a self-serving movement by and for men, an argument that implies a dual sexual culture thesis, lacks empirical support. Indeed, I have introduced a range of evidence from popular women's culture—from sex manuals and women's erotica to women's magazines and novels—testifying to cultural constructions of a female sexual desire that differs little from that of men. I have supplemented this impressionistic evidence with data provided by sex researchers. The thesis of a dual sexual culture does not find corroboration in the broader cultural mainstream. Yet, insofar as our society privileges and empowers men, insofar as men exercise dominance through force or by sexual stereotyping or assigning women primary responsibility for children, sex, especially nonromantic sex, will carry risks that are unique to women. Social inequalities between men and women have created a strain toward gender difference.

Intimate cultures are shaped by broader social relations of domination and oppression. Thus, women's sexuality exhibits certain unique traits that reflect the peculiar ways women are socially disempowered. The role of power relations is even more crucial as we shift from heterosexual to homosexual intimate cultures. The ways in which homosexual patterns of sex and love diverge from heterosexual ones reflect, in part, their social disempowerment in a society that upholds a heterosexual intimate norm. In the next chapter, I will focus on contemporary changes in the meaning of homosexuality. I will examine the ways in which homosexuals are similar to and different from heterosexuals in their patterns of intimate life, focusing especially on the tensions between romantic and nonromantic sexual meanings.

6

Between Pleasure and Community

Eros and Romance in the Gay Subculture

Cultures of intimacy vary as the social characteristics of populations differ. Thus, I would expect differences in intimate conventions between, say, the working class and the middle class.[1] We have focused exclusively on the white middle class. Yet, even within this group we have observed some divergences between men and women. We would anticipate, moreover, variation in intimate patterns as sexual orientation varies. Although we have analyzed some changes in the meaning of same-sex intimacy from the late nineteenth century to the mid-twentieth century, the question of the difference between heterosexual and homosexual patterns has not been seriously addressed. In part, this reflects matters of evidence. Additionally, sexual orientation was not a category of identity through the Victorian period and the early decades of the twentieth century. It was not until the 1950s and 1960s that a homosexual identity and subculture materialized producing its own conventions of intimate life. As we turn to contemporary urban gay cultures, we find not only affirmative homosexual identities and models of intimacy but an abundance of evidence documenting a historically unique culture of intimacy. This chapter analyzes patterns of intimate culture among contemporary gay and lesbian people. I focus on the gay and lesbian subculture which is predominantly white and middle-class.

Underlying my discussion is a theme that I will elaborate upon briefly. Homosexuals, like heterosexuals of the period approached sex as a sphere of love and as a domain of pleasure. Homosexuals, no less than heterosexuals, sought in sex both intimacy and love as well as pleasure and adventure. They shared the same broad intimate culture as heterosexuals. Yet, their unique social position shaped their lives in distinctive ways. I refer to the fact that they were a population oppressed by discriminatory laws, public stereotypes and their social marginality. In part, homosexual intimate life was a response to the unique ways they were disempowered. Ironically, their marginality freed them from many of the social controls placed upon heterosexuals. Their situation, especially in the 1960s and 1970s, was comparable, in this regard, to bohemians, artists or musicians. In other words, homosexual intimate patterns, especially as we describe those of urban gay subcultures, are not simply a product of social oppression. Their social marginality permitted homosexuals wide latitude to forge their own intimate lifestyles. Homosexual intimate patterns exhibit strains that relate to their oppression and strains that reflect the wide latitude they had to innovate their own social conventions.

THE TRANSFORMATION OF SAME-SEX
DESIRE INTO A GAY IDENTITY

In chapter 4 I described a great transformation in the meaning of same-sex intimacy. The nineteenth-century tradition of romantic friendship declined under the impact of a medical discourse on homosexuality. Same-sex desire was transfigured into a pathological and dangerous condition. In the early decades of the twentieth century, "the homosexual" stepped into the public eye as a menacing figure subject to a range of punitive sanctions. There is ample evidence that individuals were labeled homosexuals and suffered the psychological and social costs of a stigmatized identity. Yet, even prior to the civil rights and liberation movements of the 1970s, at least some individuals managed to resist the medical model or reconfigure its moral meaning.

In 1930 Mary Casal wrote her autobiography, *The Stone Wall*. Born in 1864, Mary witnessed the shift from a romantic friendship model to a medical model. Yet she was able to affirm her longings by preserving the romantic friendship paradigm.

Mary realized as a young woman that she was attracted to women. In typical romantic friendship style, she speaks of her "absorbing friendship" with a female companion.[2] "We spent many nights together, always in loving embrace, repeating all the little love sayings, and sleeping in each other's arms, perfectly happy."[3] Mary relates stories of her youthful infatuations with female companions which lack any trace of shame or wrong doing. In high school, however, she learned of the homosexual label. Women were expected to date and marry men. This was taken as a sign of normality and maturity. Women who desired women were "homosexuals," a term indicating a deviant, inferior status. Her attraction to women now evoked shame and had to be carefully managed. The need to conceal her desire for women continued throughout her life, but not the self-doubt. "I now believe that urge [for women] to be just as normal for some as the contrary for others."[4] Mary resisted the stigma attached to same-sex longings by rejecting the lesbian label. Eventually, she took a woman as a lover. Far from disparaging same sex love as deviant or perverse, Mary believed that "it was the purest and most ideal union."[5] She felt no shame for her romantic longings. "It all seemed so natural and right to me."[6]

Diana Frederics, author of *Diana: A Strange Autobiography*, came of age in the early twentieth century. We might recall from chapter 3 that Diana eventually "discovered" that her romantic longings for women made her a lesbian. "I was, then, a 'homosexual' . . . I was subject to arrest! I was grotesque, alienated, unclean."[7] Although Diana continued to define herself as a lesbian, she purged the concept of its negative connotations. She drew on the writings of Edward Carpenter, Havelock Ellis, Freud and André Gide to evolve a morally neutral concept. "I no longer thought of homosexuality as a moral issue, but merely a condition within the range of sexual variation."[8] She came to view "the homosexual as a fellow human being whose behavior was no better or worse, than that of the heterosexual."[9] In other words, Diana repudiated the lesbian label to the extent that it defined her as a different and inferior human type. "I was determined to respect myself for what I was. . . . First, I was an individual; second, a lesbian."[10] Diana reconceived lesbianism as indicating a morally neutral category of sexuality, not identity.

In the correspondence carried on between 1924 and 1950 by the literary historian F. O. Mattheissen and the artist Russell Cheney, we can observe a positive transvaluation of the concept of homosexuality. Drawing on Edward Carpenter's "The Intermediate Sex," Mattheissen reconfigured homosexuality into a spiritually elevated condition. "The idea [is] that what we have is one of the divine gifts; that such as you and I are the advance guard of any hope for a spirit of brotherhood."[11] Mattheissen described the love between Cheney and him in positive, indeed idealized spiritual terms. "Marriage! What a strange word to be applied to two men! Can't you hear the hell-hounds of society baying in full pursuit behind us. But that's just the point. We are beyond society. We've said thank you very much, and stepped outside and closed the door. . . . In the eyes of the knowing world we would be . . . outlaws, degenerates. . . . [Yet] we have a marriage that . . . does not limit the affection of the two parties. . . . It has no ring, and . . . and no children but merely the serene joy of companionship. . . . Its bonds indeed form the service that is perfect freedom."[12] Although Cheney, twenty years Mattheissen's elder, remained deeply troubled by his same-sex longings, Mattheissen came to accept his homosexuality. "We are born as we are. I am no longer the least ashamed of it.

... Tell it? Well that's different ... for ... the world as a whole does not understand. ... But to your friends: by all means, just as I have ... and as I will continue to do throughout my life ... If you and I know that our love is the richest and purest and most sacred thing imaginable, if it strengthens and develops us as characters, if it gives each other ... the sense of completion that enables us to give our very best to our world and our friends, why should we not embrace it fully?"[13]

Decades before gay liberation, at least some individuals accepted same-sex longings. Yet, as the twentieth century progressed, the medical model achieved enhanced social authority and many individuals succumbed to it. Even those who managed to resist the stigma implied in the homosexual label were unable to fully elude its disapproving judgment. Thus, Mary Casal defended same-sex love, but only in its romantic friendship version. She refused to identify herself as a lesbian and thought of herself "on a much higher plane than those ... real inverts."[14] Similarly, Diana Frederics may have accepted her homosexuality as natural, but she confesses her dislike for "active lesbians" and refers to lesbianism as an "abnormality."[15] The capacity of these individuals and their contemporaries to elude the stigma implied in the homosexual label was greatly limited to the extent that homosexuality was viewed as an individual problem. Many individuals of the period who accepted a homosexual label approached self-acceptance as a matter of personal adjustment to a hostile society. The principal struggle was psychological: to achieve self-acceptance by accommodating to the homosexual label or by preserving a romantic friendship ideology. Few individuals viewed homosexuality as a problem of social prejudice. Few interpreted their discontents as social in origin and the alleviation of their suffering as political. In part, this relates to the absence or underdeveloped state of a homosexual subculture.[16] To be sure, homosexuals evolved networks, established some organizations and even marked out certain social spaces as safe, but these forms of shared life were extremely rudimentary, unstable, dangerous and involved a very small minority of individuals.[17] The medical model could be seriously challenged and same-sex longings transformed into a consistently self-affirmative desire only in the context of a homosexual community that could provide sustained social support. An affirmative self-conception presupposed the creation of a homosexual community.

There is a somewhat ironic relation between the homosexual identity shaped by the medical model and the evolving homosexual subculture that ultimately challenged this model. Although sanctions against same-sex sexuality in the nineteenth century and in the early twentieth century undoubtedly fostered a heightened self-awareness, the fact that sexual orientation did not function as a category of identity inhibited the rise of a homosexual subculture. By distinguishing the homosexual as a unique human type, the medical model facilitated a common consciousness which expedited community building around a homosexual identity.[18] Until at least the post–World War II years, however, such community-building efforts were limited. Typically, the social spaces homosexuals occupied were shared by other marginal groups (e.g., bohemians, petty criminals and hustlers) and imbued with an aura of danger and deviance. World War II and the 1950s were crucial years in the evolution of a homosexual community.[19] Nevertheless, the growing institutional prestige and power of the medical model, a conservative cultural climate stressing traditional gender roles and family values, and the accelerated harassment of homosexuals, obstructed the formation of a homosexual community.[20]

The breakthrough to an elaborated homosexual subculture occurred in the 1960s and '70s. The general trend toward social and political liberalization, the emergence of black and women's civil rights and liberation movements combined with the dense concentration of homosexuals in urban centers, provided a favorable context for the formation of a homosexual community.[21] In many cities across the country there cropped up exclusively homosexual bars, baths, bookstores, newspapers, social clubs, political organizations, health clinics and social centers. Commenting on the completeness of homosexual subcultures by the 1970s, the sociologist John Lee writes:

> Many heterosexuals and some homosexuals are unaware of the degree of institutional completeness of a typical gay community in the larger cities of North America. . . . A gay . . . can buy a home through a gay real estate agent familiar with the types of housing and neighborhoods most suitable to gay clients. He can close the deal through a gay lawyer, and insure with a gay insurance agent. If he is new to the community and cannot ask acquaintances for the names of these agents, he can consult the gay Yellow Pages, a listing of businesses and services which is available in many larger cities. Or he can approach a typical source of connection with the gay community, such as a gay bookstore, or he can consult a local gay newspaper or periodical. From any of these sources of information he will also learn where he can buy lumber and renovating supplies from a company catering to a gay clientele. He will find gay suppliers of furniture, houseplants, and interior decorating. He will find gay sources of skilled labour or gay cleaning services.
>
> Having moved in, our gay citizen can clothe himself at gay-oriented clothing stores, have his hair cut by a gay stylist, his spectacles made

by a gay optician. He can buy food at a gay bakery, records at a gay phonograph shop, and arrange his travel plans through gay travel agents. He can buy newspapers and books at a gay bookstore, worship in a gay church or synagogue, and eat at gay restaurants. Naturally he can drink at gay bars and dance at gay discotheques. He can obtain medical care from a gay physician or if he prefers, a gay chiropractor. If he wishes to remain entirely within the gay culture, he can seek work at many of these agencies and businesses, but he will have to bank his earnings at a nongay bank, though he may be able to deal with a gay credit union. He can contribute money to tax-deductible gay foundations, participate in gay political groups, and enjoy gay-produced programs on cable television. To keep him up to date on everything happening in his gay community he can telephone the Gay Line, which is updated weekly.[22]

Central to the formation of a homosexual subculture is the creation of an indigenous cultural apparatus. Although this includes art, music, theater and popular entertainment, its core is the homosexual press (publishers, newspapers, books, magazines and journals). Between the 1950s and 1980, a virtual explosion of discursive productivity by and for homosexuals transpired. Major literary figures like James Baldwin, Christopher Isherwood, Gore Vidal and Tennessee Williams addressed homosexual motifs in a complex and sympathetic way.[23] A new generation of homosexual-identified authors such as Larry Kramer, Edmund White, Andrew Holleran, Jane Rule, Adrienne Rich and Rita Mae Brown wrote from their own homosexual experience and in a self-affirming way.[24] In the 1950s and early 1960s major nonfiction works sympathetic to homosexuality were written by Edward Sagarin (alias Donald Webster Cory), Evelyn Hooker and Martin Hoffman.[25] These somewhat cautious defenses of homosexuality were followed by social and historical studies by Dennis Altman, Jonathan Katz, Lillian Faderman and Adrienne Rich that were major works of social criticism.[26] For the first time in the United States, mass circulation magazines and newspapers produced by and for homosexuals appeared. *One* was published in 1952, followed by the *Mattachine Review* and the *Ladder* in the late 1950s and by the *Furies*, the *Advocate*, *Gay Community News*, the *New York Native, Off Our Backs* and many more magazines and journals in the 1960s and 1970s.[27] The homosexual cultural apparatus reflected the changes of the period but was, as well, a key social force promoting change. It was pivotal in reconstructing the meaning of homosexuality as well as offering new models of lifestyle and community.

With the rise of a homosexual subculture, there appeared discourses that challenged the medical model and offered positive concepts of homosexuality. Homosexuality was reconceived as a natural sexual and human expression; as a positive identity and lifestyle; as the basis of a new minority group and as a political standpoint. Underlying these reconfigurations is the notion that homosexuality is an affirmative aspect of the individual and society.

Influenced by Kinsey's thesis that sexual desire is more a continuum than a fixed, exclusive orientation, and his purported findings of the pervasiveness of homosexual behavior, as well as by the research of Evelyn Hooker, who found no meaningful differences in social adjustment between homosexuals and heterosexuals, homosexuals in the 1950s and early 1960s began to redefine homosexuality as a normal variation in human sexuality.[28] The image of the homosexual as a different and abnormal human type, a "third" or "intermediate" sex, was challenged. Homosexuality was reconceived as one healthy expression of human sexual and emotional needs. An emphasis was placed on the common humanity of heterosexuals and homosexuals. Homosexuality may have been thought of as a social deviation or even a neurosis, but it did not rob the individual of his or her basic humanity. This view was especially prominent in the 1950s and early 1960s. For example, the major homosexual political organization of the time was the Mattachine Society. It advanced the view, already articulated by segments of the medical-scientific community, that the homosexual is different only in his or her sexual orientation. It is a social prejudice that forces the homosexual into a deviant and nonconventional lifestyle. "Broadly, the homosexual differs from no one else as a trustworthy and law abiding citizen . . . Once he does indulge in a homosexual act he becomes a criminal in the eyes of the law."[29] A key political strategy of Mattachine was to emphasize the common humanity of homosexuals and heterosexuals. "Society rejects the homosexual first and above all simply because he is homosexual. He is seen first and foremost as a homosexual and only secondarily, if at all, as anything else. The homosexual then becomes a victim of the same kind of thinking. . . . He presents himself to society as if that were the most important thing about himself. . . . Before change can be effected in others . . ., the homosexual must accept himself first as a man or woman more alike than different from other men and women."[30] Given that homosexual oppression was thought to be anchored in an ideology of difference and marginality, the Mattachine pursued a politic aimed at gaining social acceptance by featuring the shared humanity of homosexuals and heterosexuals. A frequent tactic involved soliciting expert testimony bearing witness to the normality of homosexuality. This political aim also explains Mattachine's insistence that homosexuals adopt a conventional public image, thereby communicating their common humanity.[31]

The Mattachine Society sought social acceptance by framing homosexuality as a secondary personality trait. Yet, so authoritative had the medical model become that the association of homosexuality with abnormality and inferiority continued to surface even among self-accepting homosexuals. Thus, Luther Allen, a regular contributor to the *Mattachine Review*, wrote in a review of Dr. Edmond Bergler's *Homosexuality: Disease or Way of Life?*: "Nobody would deny that homosexuals are more neurotic than heterosexuals, by and large. Many homosexuals are seriously sick, it's true. But I simply do not believe that homosexuality is the dread disease Dr. Bergler insists that it invariably is."[32]

In the altered circumstances of the late 1960s and 1970s, the meaning of homosexuality underwent further changes. Homosexuality was often viewed as an alternative lifestyle. The homosexual was affirmed precisely for his or her lifestyle differences. To view homosexuality as a lifestyle, a distinction was made between homosexuality and being gay. The former referred only to sexual orientation or to sexual behavior; the latter described an identity and way of life that included unique codes of language use, dress, sexual mores and ideals of self-fulfillment. In a keynote speech in 1970, Charles Thorp, a gay activist, drew the distinction between the homosexual and being gay in sharp terms. "Homosexual is a straight concept of us as sexual. . . . But the word gay has come to mean . . . a life style in which we are not just [a] sex machine. . . . We are whole entities. . . . Gay is a life style. It is how we live."[33]

The shift in the meaning of homosexuality to a lifestyle alternative is one change that separates the *Mattachine Review* from the *Advocate*. The latter was launched in September 1967 and by the early 1970s became the most successful homosexual magazine or newspaper in the United States. Even in its early years, when the *Advocate* sustained the liberal political agenda of the Mattachine Society, we can detect a new spirit of rebellion and pride. "The basic premise of the *Advocate*," wrote its first editor Dick Michaels, "is to publish a newspaper that . . . might help homosexuals realize that they are important human beings, that they should not be ashamed of their homosexuality, and that they have rights."[34] Departing somewhat from Mattachine and anticipating the centrality that "coming out" assumed in the gay liberation movement, Michaels declared: "We are here! We will be felt! We will be known! And we will overcome adversaries to become equals and visible human beings living our lives with just as many rights as every other law abiding citizen. . . . We are tired of hiding and we will be known."[35] With the editorial change from Michaels to David Goodstein in 1975, we can detect a shift in the emphasis of the *Advocate* to a focus on lifestyle concerns. Under Goodstein's editorial control, the *Advocate* served as a major social force redefining homosexuality as a lifestyle alternative, not simply a sexual orientation. "Being gay," announced Goodstein in a statement that could serve as the abiding message of the *Advocate* throughout the 1970s, "is more than just being attracted to members of the same sex. Being gay includes the affirmation and celebration of our varied lifestyles."[36] The construction of homosexuality as an alternative lifestyle implies an altered view of the relation between homosexuality, society and politics.

The representation of homosexuality as a distinctive lifestyle, not just a sexual need or behavior, brought its social character into prominence. The term *gay* was intended to indicate a personal and social identity that implicated the individual in a common social life. Indeed, the reconfiguration of homosexuality into a positive identity and lifestyle was made possible by the institutional elaboration of a homosexual subculture. As homosexuality was reconceived as a social condition, as involving shared institutions and cultural ideals, it seemed inevitable, especially given the nature of liberal politics in the United States, that homosexuals would politicize their identity along the lines of minority, interest-group politics. This development was facilitated by the appearance of sociological studies in the postwar years such as Donald Webster Cory's *The Homosexual in America*, Evelyn Hooker's "Male Homosexuals and Their Worlds," Martin Hoffman's *The Gay World*, and Del Martin and Phyllis Lyon's *Lesbian/Women*. They described the homosexual subculture as cohering around a network of institutions, dense interpersonal contacts, shared organizations and common experiences centered around "coming out" and the resistance to homophobia and discrimination. Like immigrant groups in the past, gays and lesbians were viewed as responding to social prejudice by evolving their own unique community with its distinctive patterns of personal and social life. These studies were typically organized around the premise, to quote the early study by Donald Webster Cory, that "we who are homosexual are a minority. . . . Our minority status is similar . . . to that of national, religious, and other ethnic groups, in the denial of civil liberties; in the legal, extra-legal and quasi-legal discrimination; in the assignment of an inferior social position; in the exclusion from the mainstream of life and culture."[37]

The conception of homosexuals as a socially oppressed minority gained quick acceptance in the developing subculture. In a review of the first decade of the Mattachine Society, the editors of the *Mattachine Review* characterized homosexuals as "one of the world's largest minorities."[38] Throughout the publication of the *Mattachine Review* and its lesbian counterpart, the *Ladder*, the notion of the homosexual as a minority is prominent. In an early editorial in the *Advocate*, Dick Michaels interpreted the very development of a homosexual subculture as an indicator of homosexuals' minority status. "Like any persecuted minority, homosexuals have created a subculture of their own."[39] In a classic statement of gay liberation, Dennis Altman interprets his own homosexual experience in terms of the minority concept. "Like most gay people, I know myself to be part of a minority feared, disliked and persecuted."[40] More than ten years later Altman could reflect on the changes in the meaning of homosexuality from a more dispassionate standpoint. "The seventies saw the beginnings of a large-scale transition to the status of homosexuality from a deviance or perversion, to an alternate life style or minority, as remarkable a change in the characterization of 'the homosexual' as was the original invention of that category in the nineteenth century."[41] By viewing themselves as a minority, homosexuals were able to interpret their discontents as social in origin. Moreover, if homosexuality is a natural sexual variation or an alternative lifestyle, discrimination against homosexuals is illegitimate. In a remarkable reversal, homosexuals proposed that it is society's response to homosexuality that is unhealthy and in need of reform. Such a reformation was to be achieved through the assertion of the interests and rights of the homosexual minority.

A variation of this political concept of homosexuality can be observed in the reconfiguring of the meaning of lesbianism in the 1960s and 1970s. For lesbians who "came out" in the midst of the women's movement, their sexual preference for women was frequently interpreted through the prism of feminism. To choose to bond primarily with women was viewed by many lesbians as a political act promoting sisterhood in the cause of all women's autonomy. Lesbianism was understood as a challenge to male hegemony which was maintained chiefly, so lesbian-feminists argued, through the institutions of heterosexuality, marriage and the family. "Every institution that feminists have shown to be oppressive to women . . . is also based on heterosexism, on the assumption that every woman either is or wishes to be bonded to a man both economically and emotionally. In order to effectively challenge our [women's] oppression . . . we must challenge the ideology of heterosexism."[42] Lesbianism was seen as a political act of resistance to male dominance. A woman had to choose to become a lesbian. This entailed acknowledging the integrity of her feelings of kinship for women and deciding to act upon them. This inevitably placed women in a struggle against men who, it was assumed, demanded the primacy of heterosexual bonding and the roles of wife and mother for women. "In our society . . . the Lesbian is in revolt. In revolt because she defines herself in terms of women and rejects the male definitions of how she should feel, act, look, and live. To be a Lesbian is to love oneself, a woman, in a culture that denigrates and despises women. The Lesbian rejects male sexual/political domination; she defies his world, his social organization, his ideology, and his definition of her as inferior. Lesbianism puts women first while the society declares the male supreme. Lesbianism threatens male supremacy at its core."[43] Accordingly, the choice to bond chiefly with women is an act of political resistance to male dominance; it is a choice to live for oneself and for other women. The lesbian appears as a symbol of all women's struggles for autonomy.

This political reconfiguring of the meaning of lesbianism is powerfully stated in a classic document of lesbian-feminism: the Radicalesbians' manifesto "The Woman Identified Woman." Rejecting sexual or psychological descriptions of the lesbian as an ideological strategy by men to frustrate women's struggle for autonomy and community, the Radicalesbians reconceived lesbianism as a political commitment by women to bond with each other against male domination. "What is a lesbian? A lesbian is the rage of all women condensed to the point of explosion. She is the women who . . . acts in accordance with her inner compulsion to be a more complete and freer human being. . . . These needs and actions . . . bring her into painful conflict with . . . the accepted ways of thinking and behaving. . . . She may not be fully conscious of the political implications of what for her began as personal necessity, but on some level she has not been able to accept the . . . female role. . . . She is forced to evolve her own life pattern. . . . The perspective gained from that journey, the liberation of self, the inner peace, the real love of self and of all women, is something to be shared with all women because we are all women."[44] The essential meaning of lesbianism was said to be women committed to each other in their common struggle for freedom and community. In this political transformation of the meaning of lesbianism, sexual feelings or behavior are secondary, if not irrelevant. Comments Ti-Grace Atkinson: "There are women who have never had sexual relations with other women, but who have made and lived a total commitment to this movement, these women are lesbians in the political sense."[45] Through journals and newspapers like the *Furies, Off Our Backs, Motive* and the writings of important lesbian-feminists such as Ti-Grace Atkinson,

Charlotte Bunch, Rita Mae Brown, Jill Johnston, Susan Griffin, Adrienne Rich and Andrea Dworkin, this political representation of lesbianism achieved cultural credibility in the 1970s.[46] For example, in a book of interviews with lesbians, one woman described lesbianism wholly in the language of women-identification. "My definition of a lesbian is a woman who identifies herself as a woman, a woman-identified-women. . . . She relates mostly to women on all levels: physical, spiritual, emotional, psychic, and sexual. When I think of a lesbian, I think of an independent, creative, individual, strong."[47] This social and political concept of the lesbian signaled a dramatic change in its meaning. The lesbian stepped forward as an heroic figure, pioneering for all women an independent, women-centered life.

In one crucial respect, the political reconfiguration of lesbianism coincides with reconstructions of homosexuality as a natural human sexual expression, lifestyle alternative or as an oppressed minority. Underlying all these conceptions of homosexuality is an affirmative attitude. Challenging the stigma implied in the medical model, these new discourses constructed homosexuality as potentially enriching and joyful.[48] The substitution of the term *gay* for *homosexual* symbolized this reassessment. "Gay" signified a personal identity and community affiliation.[49] In a memoir of her coming of age as a lesbian, Penelope Stanley nicely connects lesbianism to an affirmative identity and community affiliation. Recounting her introduction to the gay community, she recalls: "I had a new word for myself, gay. I wasn't 'homosexual', or 'queer.' I was 'gay.' It's hard to explain now the tremendous freedom that word bestowed in those years. . . . I now knew for sure that I was not alone. . . . Armed with my new identity, my new belonging [i.e., to a gay community], I sat my mother down one night and said, . . . 'Mother, I'm gay.'"[50] The demand to be called gay implied a demand to be treated with respect both for the ways lesbians and gay men are similar to heterosexuals and different from them. It is to this question of difference, at least with respect to intimate practices and ideals, that I now turn.

PATTERNS OF INTIMATE BEHAVIOR
Comparing Gays, Lesbians and Heterosexuals

One public stereotype in the 1960s and 1970s portrayed homosexual intimate conventions as the antithesis of the ideal heterosexual pattern. This stereotype held that in contrast to the heterosexual model, which imbues sex with romantic meaning and embeds sex in a stable social arrangement, the homosexual pattern was imagined as little more than a promiscuous quest for pleasure. Even homosexuals, it was argued, who try to elude this lifestyle discovered that homosexual intimacy is typically unstable, short-term and unsatisfactory. This is due, it was often assumed, to the inherently promiscuous, carnal nature of homosexual desire, a sign of its pathological or deviant status.

Like most stereotypes, this one contains an insight: homosexuals, at least male homosexuals in this period, did have significantly more sex partners than heterosexuals. This description does not, however, typically apply to their lesbian counterparts. Moreover, evidence points to a substantial segment of the gay male population whose intimate behavioral patterns closely resembled the heterosexual ideal. Finally, many gay men who were "promiscuous" were also romantically bonded. This suggests that though the stereotype of the promiscuous homosexual is misleading, perhaps there are certain ways in which homosexual intimate life was unique in this period.

The theme of the similarities and differences between gay, lesbian and heterosexual normative and behavioral patterns of intimacy is the focus of this section. In particular, the question of a unique gay male intimate culture will be explored in this and the subsequent section. Throughout this discussion I must emphasize that I am describing primarily patterns that obtained in the predominantly white middle-class gay urban subcultures of the 1960s and 1970s. We are, in other words, depicting a historically unique, socially circumscribed culture of intimacy.

I have argued that by the mid-twentieth century a culture of eroticism materialized in the United States. Valuing sex for its sensually pleasurable, expressive or communicative qualities acquired some social acceptance. This encouraged a focus on the erotic aspects of the body and on the mechanics of sex. It promoted a spirit of sexual experimentation and play. Survey research charts changes in heterosexual behavior which documents the development of the erotic aspects of sexuality. These changes include, for example, longer and more elaborate foreplay activity, increased oral-genital sex, experimentation with nonconventional sex acts and positions, and the use of sex aids. The legitimation of eroticism was rationalized, we recall, initially by framing sex as a medium of love. By the 1960s, however, there appeared discourses and representations providing rationales for eroticism solely on the grounds of its pleasurable, individualizing or communicative qualities.

As we turn to homosexual intimate patterns we find a parallel culture of eroticism. Confining ourselves to survey data, we can identify behavioral patterns among lesbians and gay men that, in terms of relating sex to erotic pleasure, resemble their heterosexual counterparts. For example, in *Homosexualities,* a publication of the Kinsey Institute for Sex Research, a majority of both white male homosexuals and white female homosexuals reported that in the past year they had regularly engaged in mutual masturbation and performed and received oral-genital sex. Many of the men said they regularly practiced anal intercourse.[51] In a subsequent national survey that focused more on sexual expression, Karla Jay and Allen Young found that among gay men the overwhelming majority engaged in fellatio and over 90 percent of them positively evaluated this behavior.[52] About 50 percent of these men reported regularly participating in anal intercourse with over 90 percent approving of this behavior.[53] Finally, many of these men reported experiencing finger-fucking (30 percent), rimming (30 percent), sadomasochism (40 percent), bondage (30 percent), fist-fucking (20 percent), and using a variety of sex aids to augment sexual pleasures (e.g., porn, nipple-clamps, vibrators).[54] The point does not need to be belabored; lesbians and gay men shared with heterosexuals an approach to sex as a sphere of pleasure and play. Gays, lesbians and heterosexuals participated in a common culture of intimacy that valued eroticism and a spirit of sexual experimentation.

Although lesbians and gay men valued the erotic aspects of sex, researchers have shown the centrality of intimate bonding and sex as a medium of love for homosexuals. For example, *The Gay Report* found that 83 percent of the gay men and 97 percent of the lesbians surveyed said that emotional involvement with their sex partner was important.[55] In their open-ended comments, lesbians and gay men often related sex to love. "Sex is important to me. . . . Sex is one way I have of telling my partner how much I love her. It feels good and I like it, as part of our total friendship."[56] A gay man commented: "Sex for sex's sake is unimportant to me—making love is important as it's emotional as well as sexual. I feel that emotions are an important factor."[57] Typically, sex was framed as a symbol of love and a way to enact love. "For me, the highest most complete expression of love is sex. Having sex with a person one loves is the closest I can get to that person."[58] For lesbians, sexual expression seemed less definitive of love. "Sex is one of the possible expressions of love, though not a necessary one."[59] Another lesbian observed, "Sex can be a tool in the growth of love. I experienced this by relating sexually to a friend. . . . We had been close but not really intimate. During the months we spent together as lovers we became very close emotionally, when the sexual aspect of the relationship ended, the closeness and love did not subside."[60]

When we consider some of the behavioral dynamics of homosexual intimacy in this period, we can detect some basic similarities with heterosexual patterns. Long-term, intimate relationships were an integral part of homosexual life. *Homosexualities* reported that over 90 percent of the male and female homosexuals surveyed had at least one long-term homosexual relationship in their lifetime.[61] At the time of the survey (1970), about one-half of the male homosexuals and 75 percent of the female homosexuals said they were currently involved in a homosexual relationship.[62] Statistical comparisons of gays and lesbians show little difference in terms of the number of affairs they had. For example, roughly 43 percent of the male homosexuals reported three or fewer affairs, compared to 44 percent of the female homosexuals.[63] Similarly, there is little difference in the duration of affairs between male and female homosexuals.[64] Thirty-eight percent of the male homosexuals reported that their first affair lasted between one and three years, compared to 42 percent of the female homosexuals. A comparison of homosexuals with heterosexuals reveals a significant difference in this regard. In *American Couples*, Philip Blumstein and Pepper Schwartz found that marriage typically lasted longer than homosexual relationships. Whereas 4 percent of the married couples who were together less than two years and 6 percent who were together between two and ten years broke up during the course of the study, the figure for male homosexuals was, respectively, 16 percent and 15 percent.[65] Interestingly, the figures for lesbians (22 percent and 20 percent) and cohabitors (17 percent and 12 percent) approximated those of homosexual men, suggesting that unique social forces were at work in sustaining heterosexual marriages.[66]

Considering the dynamics of intimacy, research reveals basic similarities between lesbians, gay men and heterosexuals in terms of the motivations for entering a relationship, the emotional and moral meaning of intimacy, and levels of personal satisfaction. In a series of studies of lesbian, gay male and heterosexual relationships, the psychologist Letitia Anne Peplau and her associates found few differences in terms of individual efforts to balance intimacy and companionship—"Dyadic attachment"—with individual independence—"the personal autonomy" value. "The lesbians and gay men we studied were generally very satisfied with their relationships. Lesbians reported considerable closeness in the relationship, with a mean rating of 7.7 on a nine-point scale, and a high degree of satisfaction, with a mean of 7.1. Gay men rated their relationships as being just as close (a 7.7 mean score) and very satisfying (a mean of 7.7). These ratings (of closeness and satisfaction) are almost identical to those of our heterosexual respondents."[67] Peplau reports that "almost 75 percent of the lesbians said they were in love. . . . Among gay men 83 percent were in love. . . . We again found no differences between lesbians, gay men, and heterosexuals in the likelihood of being in love with a partner."[68] These findings are supported by survey data. For example, *Homosexualities* reported that of the majority of respondents who were currently involved in a homosexual affair, 84 percent of the male homosexuals and 86 percent of the female homosexuals indicated they were in love with their partner.[69] In response to the question "What [respondent] is getting out of the current affair," almost 80 percent of the male and female homosexuals said "love, warmth, friendship," compared to just 20 percent who said sexual satisfaction.[70]

Comparing lesbians, gay men and heterosexuals in terms of the intensity of their romantic attachment or level of intimacy by using "Rubin's love scale," Dr. Peplau found "no differences . . . in the depth of love or liking felt by lesbian's, gay men, or heterosexuals in our study."[71] Finally, comparing lesbians, gay men and heterosexuals in terms of levels of relational commitment, her research showed no significant differences. For example, taking willingness to sacrifice for the relationship as an indicator of commitment, Peplau found that "almost 28% of the lesbians said they would definitely move in order to continue the relationship. . . . About half the gay men said they would either definitely (25%) or probably (23%) move."[72] Summarizing her research, Peplau writes "The men in this sample reported that their current relationships were extremely close and personally rewarding. While this finding may not characterize the relationships of all gay men, it clearly indicates that gay men can and do establish intimate and satisfying relationships. In many respects, the descriptions gay men gave of their current love relationships were remarkably similar to those of lesbians and of heterosexual college students who have participated in similar studies. For example, gay men's reports of closeness, love and satisfaction, actual and desired sexual frequency, and the balance of power were highly similar to those of lesbians and of heterosexual dating couples who have answered similar questions about their relationships."[73]

Keeping in mind these similarities in the dynamics of intimacy between lesbians, gay men and heterosexuals, we can likewise observe some differences. I'll comment on two of these.

Whereas heterosexual couples of the period typically took marriage with its bipolar gender role system as a model, lesbians and gay men overwhelmingly abandoned it—in principle and practice. Drawing conclusions from a study of the intimate behavior of about 130 gay men and the same number of lesbians and heterosexuals, Peplau found that contemporary gays and lesbians reject "marriage as a model for love relationships. . . . We found few signs of masculine/feminine role playing. The lesbians and gays we studied espoused an ideal of egalitarianism for their relationship, wanting partners to share power and responsibilities. ... A high percentage of our respondents reported that they shared cooking, decorating, cleaning, and they live more or less equally."[74] To the extent that lesbians and gay men rejected crucial elements of the marriage model, they had to create new conventions. Peplau describes these new patterns as exemplifying a companionate and egalitarian ideal. "Among the gay men and lesbians we studied, relationships often resembled best friendships. A friendship model promotes equity in love relationships."[75] Peplau explains these patterns of homosexual intimacy by their unique gender dynamics. "Same-sex friends often have similar interests, skills, and rescources—in part because they are exposed to the same gender-role socialization in growing up. It is easier to share responsibilities in a relationship when both partners are equally skilled—or inept—at cooking, making money, disclosing feelings, or whatever."[76]

Although many lesbians and gay men repudiated the gender-role conventions of the marriage model, there is evidence that this was true of broad segments of the heterosexual population as well. Sociologists have noted a trend toward a more equalitarian, companionate ideal among the middle class in the 1970s.[77] Indeed, we have documented that this ideal extends back decades in the U.S. Peplau presents no evidence to suggest, moreover, that lesbians and gay men have discarded the dominant heterosexual ideal of emotional exclusiveness and couple separation that differentiates it from a collegial, work or friendship relationship. Indeed, she offers evidence that lesbians and gay men, like heterosexuals, associated love with sexual expression, intimacy, companionship, shared responsibilities and so on.

Although gay and lesbian romantic relationships did not completely abandon the marriage model, at least one gay male pattern of the period rejected one of its crucial features: the norm of sexual monogamy. Observers of gay men's intimacy patterns in the 1960s and 1970s have frequently commented on the way they combined the emotional exclusiveness typical of heterosexual romantic love patterns with sexual nonmonogamy. For example, in *American Couples*, Philip Blumstein and Pepper Schwartz found that 26 percent of the heterosexual husbands and 21 percent of the heterosexual wives reported instances of nonmonogamy, compared to 82 percent of the gay men.[78] The figure for lesbians was 28 percent.[79] Moreover, of those heterosexual men who were nonmonogamous, 71 percent reported five or fewer sex partners; only 7 percent said they had more than twenty partners.[80] Eighty-three percent of heterosexual women reported fewer than five sex partners.[81] Of gay men, 27 percent reported fewer than

5 partners, while 43 percent said they had more than twenty sex partners. The lesbian pattern approximated that of heterosexual women. Peplau and Cochran believe that this pattern of sexual non-monogamy was unique to gay male relationships. "Where gay men appeared to differ most from lesbian and heterosexual individuals . . . was in their behavior outside their primary relationship. For example, when asked if they had had sex with someone other than their primary partner during the past two months, 54 percent of the gay men said they had, compared to only 13 percent of the lesbians and 14 percent of the college-aged dating [heterosexual] men and women. . . . Thus, it is in the general area of autonomy, and more specifically in the area of sexual exclusivity, that the largest differences between gay men's relationships and those of others have been documented to date."[83]

To grasp this divergence in intimate patterns, some researchers have proposed a unique life-cycle pattern to gay male intimacy. Its early stages were thought to be comparable to heterosexual marriage, with its heightened romanticism and its sexually monogamous character. In the course of the relationship, romance passes into a friendship-like bond; the relationship is gradually desexualized and the norm of sexual fidelity is replaced by one of sexual openness.[84] Blumstein and Schwartz document this progressive "desexualization" of gay intimacy. They found that about 3 percent of the gay male couples who had reported to have been together for less than two years had sex once a month or less. For gay male couples who said they were together for more than two years but less than ten years, the figure jumped to 13 percent. About 33 percent of the gay male couples surveyed who were together for more than ten years reportedly had sex once a month or less, compared to 15 percent of married heterosexual couples.[85] The reverse side to this trend is the weakening of the norm of sexual monogamy. Confirming previous studies, the sociologist Joseph Harry found that the norm of sexual fidelity in the early phases of gay romance gradually passes into a pattern of sexual infidelity. "It is clear that actual fidelity declines substantially after two years of [gay] marriage."[86] Harry conjectured that given the "great opportunities for [sexual] infidelity [in the gay subculture] . . . we suggest that fidelity, rather than infidelity contributes to the disruption of a relationship."[87] Infidelity contributed to maintaining gay intimate relationships, he thought, provided that the sex outside the primary relationship was deromanticized and therefore presumably not a threat to the emotional and social ties of the primary bond.

In his early research, Harry doubted whether a norm of sexual infidelity, even in a setting of abundant sexual opportunities, was functional in the long run. His own research confirmed what others had reported: gay romance seemed to lack the stability and longevity of heterosexual marriage. Gay intimacies were typically short-lived. In a conclusion to his early research, Harry judged this to be an undesirable state explained primarily by the failure of the gay community to provide institutional support and cultural guidelines for intimate behavior.[88] In his subsequent research, Harry reversed himself somewhat. He found that the gay subculture did provide institutional and normative guidance. Yet, gay romances were still short-lived. "It was found that those gay men who were committed to the gay world were more likely to be interested in emotionally intimate relationships . . . [and] be more sexually exclusive during their liaisons . . . [and] share a common residence with their lovers . . .; [yet] our hypothesis . . . that those committed to a gay community would have more lasting relationships was not confirmed."[89] Harry concluded that "while it does seem that the gay community legitimates the sexual unions of gay men . . ., it does not employ the same institutional meanings to define the gay marriage. Hence, it is only with risk that one may transfer such concepts as intimacy and infidelity from the heterosexual to the homosexual liaison."[90] Harry opined that gay men had evolved an alternative intimate pattern to the marriage model. This model had institutional support and legitimation within the gay subculture.

The suggestion by researchers that a unique gay male pattern of intimacy could be detected was observed by insiders to this community. For example, the novelist and commentator on gay affairs Edmund White argued that at least some gay men had innovated an alternative pattern to the marriage model. "Sex [for gay men] is casual, romance short-lived, the real continuity in many [gay] people's lives comes from their friends. Better to enjoy romance in the form of successive 'affairlets,' each six months long and to find true security in friendships that sometimes endure for decades."[91] White proposed that gay men did not invest in a love relationship the same expectations as are implied in the conventional heterosexual model. Gay men did not necessarily expect from a romantic bond exclusive sexual and emotional intimacy or long-term security and companionship. They typically depended on friendship for long-term emotional support. Like marriage, these friendships were often long-term, stable and involved a dense web of obligations, rights and commitments. Although gay men pursued romance, the emotional intimacy of these involvements may not have included the degree of social exclusivity typical of marriage, as friendships remained the primary social and affective support unit. In short, whereas heterosexuals and most lesbians at least strived to integrate sex, romance and friendship in one inclusive intimate arrangement, some gay men separated these elements—each forming the basis for a particular type of relationship or combined in sometimes dazzling ways.[92]

Edmund White does not deny that there were many gay men of the period who were couple-oriented and who wished to integrate sex, romance and companionship in a marriage-like arrangement. He is underscoring the appearance of a uniquely indigenous pattern of intimate life in the gay subculture of the 1970s. His observations support, moreover, the findings of researchers who have emphasized key ways in which gay intimate patterns of this period were unique. Despite the varying interpretations that researchers and observers like White might offer, they seem to agree that central to the gay male pattern of the time was the apparently widespread social acceptance of sex outside intimate romantic bonds. In the final section of this chapter, I wish to explore the dynamics of "causal sex" in the gay subculture as a way to further consider the theme of the similarities and differences between lesbian, gay men and heterosexual intimate cultures.

SEX AS PLEASURE AND COMMUNITY
The Question of Casual Sex

An assimilationist wing of the gay community has often held that lesbians and gay men are like heterosexuals in every way except for their sexual behavior. In fact, the relevant research documents that lesbians, gay men and heterosexuals in the 1960s and 1970s shared a construction of sex as a medium of love and pleasure. All three populations approached love expecting emotional intimacy, companionship and sexual gratification. They shared, moreover, a strain toward separating sex from love. Yet, gay men reconfigured the relation between sex, romance and friendship in a singular manner.

To press further into the matter of differences in intimate culture, there is perhaps no observation more pertinent than that concerning the "promiscuity" of gay men. We will call sex that occurs outside an intimate, long-term relationship "casual sex." This term is not an especially accurate designation, since it wrongly implies that such sex is not serious or important. We will return shortly to the issue of conceptualizing casual sex. First we need to outline some broad quantitative patterns of casual sexual behavior.

In *Homosexualities*, Alan Bell and Martin Weinberg found that over 50 percent of white male homosexuals reported having more than fifty sex partners in the past year. The comparable figure for white female homosexuals was 5 percent.[93] About 76 percent of the men said they had more than one hundred sex partners during their lifetime.

Ninety-eight percent of the women reported fewer than one hundred lifetime sex partners.[94] Underscoring this difference between gay men and lesbians, 74 percent of the lesbians said they had fewer than fifteen sex partners in their lifetime, compared to about 6 percent of the gay men.[95] Figures for heterosexuals approximate those of lesbians. In his nationwide survey *Sexual Behavior in the 1970s*, Morton Hunt found that the mean number of sex partners reported in the past year by single heterosexual men under twenty five was two. The figure for the same population of men between twenty five and thirty four increased to four. Married men over thirty five reported a median of six premarital lifetime sex partners.[97] The figures for heterosexual women were comparable to those for heterosexual men. Hunt does report one group of heterosexuals who seemed to depart from this pattern. Divorced men had a median of eight coital partners a year. Yet this increase in sex partners does not appear to be part of an alternative intimate pattern. Instead, it is related to the search for the right woman; the pattern of sexual variety ceases once romance ensues. The comparatively high number of sex partners for gay men seems less narrowly tied to a quest for intimate bonding. Thus, about 80 percent of the gay men surveyed in *Homosexualities* indicated that most of their sex partners were strangers. Seventy percent of them reported that more than half of their sex partners were one-time episodes.[98] These figures underscore the point that sex between individuals who are neither friends, romantic partners nor lovers was a striking feature of the gay male subculture in the 1970s.

To avoid misconstruing this data, we need to introduce some qualifying considerations. There are sound reasons to approach this survey data with skepticism. For example, the *Homosexualities* survey was confined to a fairly select San Francisco population. If we turn to the nationwide survey the *Gay Report*, we find that gay men reported significantly less casual sex. About one-third of the gay men surveyed said they had more than one hundred lifetime sex partners, compared to the 75 percent figure in *Homosexualities*. Similarly, in the *Gay Report*, one-half of the gay men said they had fewer than fifty lifetime sex partners and about one-third said they had less than twenty five lifetime sex partners. In *Homosexualities* only 17 percent of the gay men reported fewer than fifty lifetime sex partners and only 9 percent said they had fewer than twenty-five lifetime sex partners.[99] These figures reveal significant discrepancies and raise doubts about the reliability of these surveys. Moreover, surveys of sex patterns have additional flaws. Although these surveys requested apparently similar information, we do not know if the meanings of the terms were the same for these diverse respondents. Was the meaning of "the number of sex partners" similar for heterosexual and homosexual respondents? What counts as a sex partner depends on the definition of a sex act. Unfortunately, these surveys never clarified what counted as a sex act. If gay men counted not only anal intercourse but all interpersonal sex (e.g., mutual masturbation, body rubbing, oral-genital sex, deep kissing) as a sex act, whereas heterosexuals only counted vaginal intercourse, then the figures regarding the number of sex partners will be skewed upward for gay men. Unfortunately, available surveys never define what counts as a sex act in soliciting information on the number of sex partners. What would the numbers look like if all noncoital sexual behavior had been figured into calculating sex partners for heterosexuals?

To avoid exaggerating the uniqueness of this gay male pattern, we must keep in mind our previous discussion. There is abundant evidence provided by survey data and popular cultural documents that the heterosexual and lesbian intimate cultures also included strains toward accepting casual sex. Thus, about one-third of the lesbians surveyed in *Homosexualities* reported that half of their sex partners were strangers.[100] In chapter 5 we identified a range of research findings which underscored the social acceptance of sexual behavior among heterosexuals, from petting to coitus, where no affection or ongoing relationship exists. Some survey data also discloses definite patterns of heterosexual casual sex. For example, the *Cosmo Report* found that 25 percent of the women surveyed had between eleven and twenty-five sex partners, and about 15 percent reported more than twenty-five lifetime sex partners.[101] The legitimation of heterosexual casual sex is in evidence as well in the proliferation of mass circulation sex magazines, sex videos and movies, in the nearly ubiquitous presence of prostitutes, massage parlors, escort services and sex clubs in metropolitan areas.

Underscoring some general similarities in sexual patterns does not, of course, allow us to ignore meaningful differences. Whereas surveys of heterosexuals and lesbians in this period might, at best, reveal small segments of a sexually "promiscuous" population, surveys of gay men suggest that casual sex was widespread. Thus, even *The Gay Report* documents that over 50 percent of the gay men surveyed reportedly had between twenty-six and fifty lifetime sex partners. Just 15 percent of the men surveyed had less than ten lifetime sex partners. Almost 35 percent of these gay men reported over one hundred sex partners.[102] In short, any attempt to understand gay intimate patterns in the late 1970s must clarify the phenomenon of casual sex.

The term *casual sex* is not terribly precise.[103] It is often used to cover a wide range of sexual behaviors, from a one-time, five-minute encounter where no words or affection are exchanged to a regular sexual liaison which is accompanied by mutual concern and caring but the arrangement is sexually focused. Whereas the former appears as the very antithesis of intimacy, the latter approximates it in certain key ways. Casual sex, then, can refer to a variety of behaviors, and the line between it and intimate bonds is sometimes difficult to draw. It is still useful to identify some general features of casual sex that seem relevant to understanding the intimate culture of gay men in this period.

Casual sex lacks the inclusive bonds of intimate affairs and the exclusive and long-term commitment implied in them. This does not mean that casual sex is merely anonymous sex that lacks moral and emotional decisions and commitments. As in romantic involvements, partners in casual sex are frequently chosen for their sexual, personal and social attributes. Casual sex is rarely, if ever, random; frequently it is highly selective and it is always imbued with layers of emotionally charged meaning. In addition, casual sex occurs in a moral framework which regulates the interpersonal dynamics of the encounter. To the extent that the rules of casual sex specify a general normative order, it is typically guided by norms of consent, mutual respect and reciprocity of pleasure. Of course, factors such as physical attractiveness or age may offset these egalitarian norms. This is no less true in intimate affairs. The distinctiveness of casual sex is that any expectations of intimacy, commitment and responsibility are restricted to the encounter. Claims made by partners beyond the event are not felt as morally compelling.

Casual sex is, in other words, a specialized or bounded social exchange centered on the sex act. Its specialized character implies more than circumscribed responsibilities and intimacy. It is typically an interchange focused on sexual pleasure, although its clear that non-erotic motivations are involved. Sexual pleasure is, at least, the principal intersubjective theme of the event.

It is the pleasure-centered, specialized character of casual sex that gives to it an impersonal tone. In his study of "tearoom sex," Laud Humphreys observed that communication during these encounters rarely extended beyond signaling sexual interest and negotiating the act. The act itself was rarely accompanied by nonsexual conversation or affectionate gestures. "Tearoom sex is distinctly less personal than any other form of sexual activity, with the single exception of solitary masturbation. . . . Often in tearoom stalls, the only portions of the player's bodies that touch are the mouth of the insertee and the penis of the insertor; and the mouths of these parties seldom open for speech."[104] Humphreys's observations on the impersonal social character of tearoom sex may be less typical of casual sex than is often imagined. The population he studied was quite unique, as it included a high percentage of older and married men who were not accepting of their homosexuality. Similarity, the site he studied entailed norms promoting depersonalization and anonymity. In a study of homosexual casual sex in a secluded wooded area, Richard Troiden noted that conversations and affectionate exchanges were frequent, even expected. "The shelter provided by the wood allows the players to create their own, private social worlds, within which, through shows of warmth and affection, they can invest their sexual encounters with great meaning and importance—however brief these episodes might be."[105] Troiden's suggestion that public sex need not be impersonal and dehumanizing, but that its interpersonal dynamics depends on its social context is supported by observations of sex in gay bathhouses. One study found that the apparent "market mentality" of the baths was often offset by expectations that sex be affectionate and playful.[106] The baths were often experienced by gay men as a self-accepting milieu where the maintenance of good manners, mutual affection and playfulness overshadowed its impersonal strains.[107] In surveys like *Homosexualities* and the *Gay Report*, many respondents spoke of casual sex as involving personal conversations which, at times, pass into highly intimate exchanges.[108] This suggests that though casual sex is a socially focused event, it can admit of significant elements of affection and intimacy. Casual sex need not be an impersonal encounter between anonymous partners, each objectified and dehumanized. To be sure, a certain amount of impersonality is built into casual sex by virtue of its being a goal-directed, socially circumscribed event. Whether this level of impersonality is degrading or not depends on the general social and moral context of this behavior.

Finally, casual sex is consensual. Consent can be assumed by the absence of external coercion and by the interplay of gestures and acts that are involved in negotiating a sexual encounter. Consent extends beyond a general willingness to participate in a sexual episode. Sex partners negotiate specific acts. These agreements form the immediate moral context of the encounter. They set out the reciprocal expectations that structure the event. Part of the tacit understandings that make casual sex possible is agreement about its bounded character. Each partner understands that having casual sex entails highly restricted expectations and obligations. At the end of the event, each partner may leave unencumbered by any emotional, moral or social debt. There is, of course, nothing to exclude the development of a more intimate bond. To the extent, however, that this possibility is built into the expectations of casual sex, it is imbued with a romantic anticipation. This would, of course, render casual sex more psychologically and socially ambiguous.

Casual sex entails a degree of impersonality but is not necessarily an emotionally empty, anonymous exchange. It is nevertheless, quite distinct from the current ideal of romantic love. Its prevalence among gay men as compared to lesbians and heterosexuals in this period is pertinent to the theme of the differences and similarities in intimate cultures. How do we explain the relatively high incidence of casual sex among gay men of this period?

One explanation of casual sex among gay men has been framed within a medical discourse. Some critics of this behavior argue that casual sex is a flight from feelings and commitment. Robert Boyers, editor of *Salmagundi*, remarked that participants in casual sex are "disturbed and crippled people enacting fantasies of release . . . that can at best relieve momentarily the fear or impotence they experience when they confront real people capable of making complex emotional demands."[109] Some homosexual critics concede the pathological character of casual sex, but explain it sociologically. They claim that the social hostility toward homosexuals forces them into a secretive, deviant lifestyle. One manifestation of their socially oppressed state is the substitution of casual sex for genuine intimacy. Moreover, social disapproval is said to be internalized as self-contempt, leaving homosexuals psychologically incapable of forming intimate ties. Homosexual desire evokes guilt and self-loathing which is said to be acted out in the degrading rituals of casual sex. The result of homosexual oppression is that sexual desire is split off from emotional needs for love and companionship. Casual sex represents, then, a flight from feelings; a repetition-compulsion of desire, guilt, and punishment. In an important study of homosexuals in the 1960s, Martin Hoffman proposed this thesis.

> Society rejects him and he, following this lead, rejects himself, his own sexual orientation, and in so doing, rejects himself as a person and precludes the possibility of any kind of meaningful relationship with another man. This tragic situation is due, in large measure, to the view of homosexuality which is prevalent in the larger society. Pressures exist, both external (such as a need for anonymity on the part of many men who would be socially vulnerable if their sexual orientation were known) and internal (the self-denigration and concomitant denigration of the partner), that promote sex which is isolated from the rest of these men's lives. This is alienation of the most terrible kind, for it tends to fragment the existence of the homosexual, and deprive him of the possibility—which heterosexuals take for granted—of integrating sex with love, and of working toward a devel-

opment of the self and a structuring of one's life which would lead to a whole, rich involvement with another person.[110]

Although this account introduces a social explanation and shifts the moral burden from the homosexual to society, it betrays the bias of assimilationists who uncritically endorse a "marital" intimate ideal. Accordingly, homosexual intimate patterns that depart from this model, especially if they separate sex from intimacy, are charged with a psychologically and morally inferior status.

Setting aside the moral standpoint of the social oppression explanation, it seems to apply primarily to socially isolated homosexuals who are not self-accepting and who lack a positive gay community affiliation. These homosexuals are likely to confine their homosexuality to furtive quests for sexual pleasure or relief in anonymous encounters to avoid the risks of exposure and self-identification as homosexuals. It is telling that this explanation gained prominence before gay liberation. This account would seem, at best, to describe a pre-gay liberation pattern of homosexual life.

The "social oppression" explanation is not applicable to many gay men in the 1970s who were self-accepting and yet continued to value casual sex. Casual sex cannot be simply described as a flight from intimacy since many gay men were simultaneously involved in long-term affairs. As I previously observed, casual sex and intimate relationships were not necessarily mutually exclusive among gay men of this period. Moreover, it is hardly credible to interpret casual sex among these individuals as an enactment of socially induced guilt or shame. Integrated into a community that furnished positive self-images, these gay men were typically self-accepting. Descriptions drawn from memoirs or autobiographies, fiction, surveys and ethnographic studies, show that gay men often described causal sex as a way to celebrate their body, sexuality and gay identity. Typical is the following comment made by a respondent in the *Gay Report*. "I enjoyed a period of exceeding promiscuity when I was coming out. . . . I discovered for the first time the freedom to be me, the freedom to meet lots of new men, the freedom to explore my sexuality, and it was a joyful thing."[111] This shift in the meaning of casual sex from a drama of self-loathing and flight from feelings to one of self-affirmation is symbolized by changes in the site of casual sex. A younger generation of homosexuals who came of age in the late 1960s, frequented public restrooms less and bathhouses more. In the baths, sexual encounters were often expressive, playful and self-affirming.[112] Moreover, symbolizing the more positive, celebratory self-image of homosexuals, the baths had been significantly upgraded in the seventies. Bathhouses frequented by a gay-identified clientele were often quite luxurious. Dennis Altman described one of these new gay baths. "It is not just a bathhouse, for you can eat snacks here, buy leather gear and inscribed T-shirts, even watch live cabaret performances on certain nights. . . . Most striking is a large disco floor on the top story, surrounded by enormous soft pillows, where men dance clad only in towels. . . . In the basement there is a small swimming pool, showers, and steam-rooms; the main floor is largely occupied by a maze of small rooms."[113] Bill McNeeley, who owned The Club Baths, commented on the symbolic and social role of the new baths. "We made the baths beautiful and clean and treated our customers as special human beings and made them feel good about themselves."[114]

If social oppression is the major source of casual sex, how to explain the case of lesbians? Lesbians, no less than gay men, were subject to discriminatory laws and stereotypes. Yet, survey data as well as autobiographical statements reveal sexual patterns that bear little resemblance to gay men. For example, the *Gay Report* found that whereas 15 percent of the gay men surveyed reported ten or fewer sex partners in their lifetime, the figure for lesbians was 62 percent. Only 14 percent of the lesbians said they had more than twenty-five lifetime sex partners, compared to 68 percent of the gay men.[115] There was, moreover, no counterpart in the lesbian community of the 1970s to gay bathhouses, backroom bars, sex shops and porn theatres. This suggests that a key explanation of gay men's sex patterns relates to gender considerations.

With the rise of lesbian-feminism in the 1970s, the differences in intimate patterns between lesbians and gay men were said to reflect general gender differences between men's and women's sexuality.[116] It was argued that men typically separate sexual desire from nonsexual feelings; they can and do, at times, relate to themselves and others in a narrowly sexual way. Men's disposition to sexualize their feelings, and to separate sex from nonsexual motivations, encourages them to approach sex as a sphere of pleasure and play. By contrast, women experience themselves in a more integrated and relational way. Sexual desires are interwoven with nonsexual feelings and motivations. Women are said to connect sex to relational considerations of building and maintaining intimacy. These gender differences are, it is argued, anchored in early childhood psychosexual dynamics and primary gender-role socialization processes, and are reinforced by institutional and cultural arrangements.

The thesis of the gendered nature of sexuality was discussed in the previous chapter. One does not, of course, need to hold to an extreme version of this thesis for it to be serviceable. The evidence underscoring the continuities in sexual patterns among men and among women in this period is considerable. This does not commit us, however, to the notion that lesbian and gay men's sexual patterns are simply an expression of this general gender pattern. The latter argument, which is at the core of the gender explanation of casual sex, is cogent but incomplete.

The "gender" explanation does not apply to many lesbians and gay men. Many gay men in the 1960s and 1970s were critical of casual sex. Typical is a comment by a gay man interviewed in the *Gay Report,* "I receive virtually no pleasure from one-night stands. I need a deeper involvement with a person in order to enjoy sex."[117] Furthermore, there is a fairly sizable portion of lesbians who exhibit patterns of casual sex somewhat resembling gay men. The *Gay Report* found that 24 percent of the lesbians surveyed indicated that they had between eleven and twenty-five lifetime sex partners, and 13 percent of them said they had over twenty-six lifetime sex partners.[118] In interviews, many lesbians indicated they had evolved arrangements that permitted nonmonogamy. Typical is the following comment: "I have sex outside the relationship, and we talk about it openly. So far it has had a positive effect. We both agree to be nonmonogamous and may or may not share our other sexual experiences."[119] Less directly bearing on behavior but still pertinent is the appearance in the late 1970s of a libertarian sexual discourse among lesbians affirming a sexually pluralistic lifestyle that includes casual sex.[120]

The gender explanation suffers from another shortcoming. It assumes that a social fact—sexual patterns of lesbians and gay men—can be explained by the abstract characteristics of its individual members, i.e., masculine and feminine gender traits. A subculture, however, is not simply the sum of the discrete characteristics of its individual members but is an emergent phenomenon. It has its own institutional and cultural dynamics which need to be understood to explain the attitudes and behavior of its individual members. Although these subcultural dynamics may relate to gender considerations in key ways, they cannot be explained by merely invoking the abstract concept of a male and female sexuality. We need to consider a "subcultural" explanation of casual sex.

The gay subculture of the 1970s has been described as achieving a level of "institutional completeness" found historically in various ethnic and religious communities. However, whereas ethnicity or a shared religious tradition functioned as a community-building force in these subcultures, in the gay community it was a common sexual orientation, an elaborate system of sexual exchanges and a heightened culture of eroticism that were the cohering factors. "It is," comments the sociologist John Lee, "sexual pluralism and the emergence of public territories for the facilitation of numerous casual sex encounters which ultimately energizes the development of the gay community."[121] This was made possible by an elaborate "gay sexual supply system" which included "gay bars, discos, baths, moviehouses, washrooms, cruising streets and parks, gymnasiums and health clubs, beaches, parking lots, bookstores, shopping malls, and classified newspaper advertisements."[122] Within this dense network of sexually based social ties, sex acquired a value as a medium of both individualism and community. Discourses and representations appeared that imbued casual sex with social importance related to promoting individual happiness, social liberation and social solidarity. To be sure, we have observed parallels in the heterosexual intimate culture. Yet, the unique social role of sex in the gay subculture as a community-building agent gave casual sex a significance lacking in the heterosexual and lesbian intimate cultures. Briefly, I wish to allude to some of these discourses that imbued casual sex with personal and social significance.

As in the broader culture, sex in the gay subculture was constructed as a domain of pleasure and communication which carried its own value. Casual sex was thought of as standing alongside other "recreational" activities which are justified because they are pleasurable or productive of social bonds. The emotionally and socially circumscribed character of its interpersonal dynamics were said to be akin to other recreational activities. Dennis Altman proposed a recreational rationale for sex. "Once sex is desacralized and separated from its procreative function, it becomes evident that there is no reason to regard it as a form of behavior set apart from all others. It is regarded as legitimate to have a 'meaningful' discussion with someone one meets on a voyage and will never see again, why can't it be as equally meaningful to have a fuck with someone in similar circumstances?"[123] Altman assumes that sex carries multiple meanings and values, one of which is as a medium of pleasure and play. "Sex can be a very significant and intimate expression of love, but it can also be fun, pleasure, release, adventure and a good way to establish contact with someone.... Sex is not a unitary phenomenon with one meaning, one appropriate form, or one correct context."[124] As long as an exchange of mutual consent, respect and reciprocity was maintained, casual sex was considered as legitimate a way to receive and give pleasure or communicate as, say, sports or intellectual exchange.

The defense of casual sex as a medium of pleasure and self-expression was, at times, elevated into the claim that it was productive of a liberated sexuality. "Gay men now lead the way in the development of sexual life. Since we found ourselves outside the rigid institutions developed by the straight world . . . we have been able to produce new institutions to fit modern sexuality. . . . Not only do we have the baths, but the baths themselves have become more sophisticated and specialized, raising the potential of erotic life to new levels of fantasy and experience."[125] Because gay men were less constrained by social conventions, they were, in fact, positioned to fully exploit the general trend toward exploring the erotic aspects of sex. With their private clubs and bathhouses, what Foucault once called "laboratories of sexual experimentation," gay men, at times, viewed themselves as a sexual vanguard leading the way to the development of humanity's sensual, expressive side.[126] Subcultural discourses describe gay men as pioneering the movement towards a nonphallic, body-centered, experimental sexuality driven by fantasy and an ethic of sexual play-fulness. By separating sex from its intimate romantic bonds, gay men thought they could prefigure a liberated sexuality. Casual sex, in other words, was imbued with higher purposes relating to sexual and personal fulfillment and liberation.

Defending sex for promoting hedonistic and expressive values does not mean that gay men endorsed an anarchic vision of a free-floating, promiscuous sexual desire. The carnal and expressive pleasures of casual sex were not justified as a substitute for more stable, long-term intimate arrangements but as their complement. Moreover, gay men often claimed that the option of casual sex made possible more flexible, diverse and healthy forms of intimate life. Freed from social pressures to adopt a marriage model, gay men thought they had more latitude to innovate intimate arrangements that were responsive to their singular needs for security and companionship but also independence and sexual variety.

These subcultural discourses underscored the communitarian role of sex. Casual sex was viewed as a primary community-building force in gay life. Through casual sex, gay men were said to experience heightened feelings of brotherhood and male solidarity. "I feel an element of brotherhood with the men I've shared sex with, something that transcends the boundaries of class or race or creed."[127] Barriers of age, class, education and sometimes race were said to be weakened as individuals circulated in this system of sexual exchange; competition and rivalry between men might give way to bonds of affection and kinship. Casual sex was imagined to be a way gay men could build and sustain a common life. Through casual sex, networks of acquaintances, sex partners, friends and lovers, a unique collective life was said to materialize. Commenting on the communitarian role of sex in gay life, the *Village Voice* columnist Richard Goldstein writes:

"For many gay men, fucking satisfies a constellation of my needs that are dealt with in straight society outside the arena of sex. For gay men, sex, that most powerful instrument of attachment and arousal, is also an agent of communion."[128] Indeed, the very continuity and coherence of the gay subculture was thought to revolve around its system of sexual exchanges. "Sexual promiscuity ... has for a long time now been the essential glue holding the urban gay ghetto together."[129]

The dense network of sexual exchanges that formed in the urban gay subculture of the 1970s was accompanied by discourses and representations that imbued this sexual system with social importance. Casual sex was imagined as a site that was pregnant with possibilities for personal happiness, sexual liberation as well as productive of diverse social bonds. Such sexual representations gave to casual sex a higher personal and social significance than a mere physical release.

To be sure, not all gay men shared this sexual construction. As is evidenced in the novels of Larry Kramer and Andrew Holleran, two of the most popular writers of the 1970s, this sexual system was troubling to many gay men.[130] Even prior to AIDS, there were many gay critics of the post-liberation gay male sexual culture. Some critics interpreted these sexual patterns as a flight from intimacy or a symptom of narcissism.[131] Marxists assailed its anonymity and one-sided hedonism as marking the colonization of gay life by capitalism.[132] Casual sex and the heightened culture of eroticism were viewed by them as illustrating the logic of commodity fetishism, as thinking, feeling and willing persons disappeared behind the hegemony of organs, orifices and technique. Others criticized the emotional callousness and dehumanizing aspects of casual sex. In surveys and interviews, these criticisms are echoed by gay men who assail the lack of intimacy, the instrumentalism, the emotional shallowness or the one-sided emphasis on pleasure in casual sex.[133] In short, gay critics of casual sex seemed to more or less share a romantic sexual ethic. This ideology holds that sex is legitimate only in a committed relationship of love; sexual intimacy is but one aspect of a broader emotional, moral and social bond. Sex simultaneously symbolizes this intimacy and reinforces it. It is, in essence, an act of caring and its qualities should exhibit this. Sex should be tender and nurturing; sex partners should always be approached as whole persons.

The dispute over casual sex in the gay male subculture reveals a conflict between two sexual ethics. Defenders of casual sex argue that in this behavior individuals appear as bearers of general rights and sexual needs whose satisfaction is a condition of happiness. The sexual exchange is aimed at inducing and receiving pleasure in a context guided by norms of mutual consent, respect and reciprocity. If these moral conditions are met, casual sex is considered a legitimate mode of self-expression or social bonding. Critics argue that even if casual sex is not intended to be an alternative to romantic love, it is morally objectionable. Sex always touches upon an individual's basic feelings and wishes. Sex should be a special way to express intimacy or love. From this standpoint, casual love amounts to the rendering of acts of interpersonal affection and love into instrumental exchanges between anonymous persons. It is inherently dehumanizing and degrading.

The clash over the meaning and morality of casual sex is important because it indicates a basic conflict of sexual ideologies in the gay subculture of the 1970s. While this cultural conflict is revealed in the debate over casual sex in the gay community, it was evident among heterosexuals in debates about teen sexuality, contraception and birth control, divorce and recreational sex. In other words, *we can detect in American middle-class culture in the contemporary period (1960–1980) a basic conflict between a "romantic" and "libertarian" sexual ideology.* Whereas previously individuals may have experienced a conflict between a normative order that tied sex to romance and love and their longing for sexual variety and pleasure, it was only in the contemporary period that discourses and representations appeared that legitimated sex for nonromantic reasons. It was only with these discourses that conflicting individual impulses could become a source of ideological and political conflict.

By the end of the 1970s, sex carried two public meanings. Sex was framed as a medium of intimacy and love; it carried deeply felt romantic expectations and longings. Sex was, simultaneously, valued for its pleasurable, expressive and communicative qualities alone; it was conceived of as a medium of self-fulfillment. These two ideologies engendered personal and social confusions and conflicts. The two constructions of sex entailed two distinct meanings and behavioral norms. If sex is both a way to express intimacy and a deromanticized medium of pleasure and play, then sex can become a domain of heightened ambiguity, tension and anomie. Does a satisfying sexual exchange signal a deeper intimacy, or does it represent little more than a fortunate meshing of bodily pleasures? Does unsatisfying sex indicate some underlying relational incompatibility, or does it reveal perhaps a temporary or unfortunate sexual maladjustment?

Sexual conflicts surfaced at a social structural and political level between sexual romanticists and libertarians. Sexual political struggles around teen sex, contraception, sex education, abortion, pornography and prostitution seem, in part, to be anchored in basic disputes regarding the meaning and morality of sex. For example, the ideological and policy debates over teen access to contraceptives and birth control divides between romanticists and libertarians. The former oppose such access, as it is presumed to legitimate and encourage casual sex. Romanticists tend to favor a norm of abstinence until teens are mature enough to value sex as part of an intimate loving bond. Libertarians may prefer that sex be embedded in a social configuration of intimacy, but they value sex for its pleasurable and communicative qualities alone. They would, in general, support the right of teens to choose to have sex so long as it is safe, consensual and mutual. Access to cheap and safe contraceptives would be considered essential for teens to exercise their sexual rights in an autonomous and responsible way.

Many of the sexual and social conflicts of the 1970s relate to the emergence of discourses offering postromantic constructions of sex. This is true in the gay subculture as well as in the larger society. However, with the rise of the AIDS epidemic and an observable conservative social drift in the 1980s, American intimate culture may be at a critical juncture. The merits of a sexual politics centered on an expansive notion of choice and pleasure is now being debated. Indeed, the culture of eroticism developed in the twentieth century is being held responsible for a wide range of current social ills.

CONCLUSION

Between the mid-nineteenth century and the post–World War II period, the meaning of same-sex intimate behavior and its social role changed dramatically. In nineteenth-century, white, middle-class culture, same-sex intimacy was socially acceptable. It was, however, more acceptable for women and only legitimate as an expression of love. Finally, it was accepted only as a supplement, as it were, to heterosexual marriage, not as an alternative. Indeed, it was precisely the perception in the early twentieth century that fewer men and women were marrying or staying married and more of them, especially women, were living with other women that prompted the labelling of same-sex longings as perverse and pathological.

The early decades of the twentieth century saw the growing public authority of a medical-scientific discourse that conceived of same-sex desire as an abnormal psychosexual condition. The bearers of this desire stepped forward as a new, pathological human type: the homosexual. This period witnessed the emergence of the concepts of heterosexuality and homosexuality as the master categories of a sexual regime that defined the individual's sexual and personal identity and normatively regulated intimate desire and behavior. In this chapter we have sketched a third equally momentous change: the de-medicalization of homosexuality and its transformation into an affirmative identity and community.

I have avoided comparisons between heterosexual and homosexual cultures of intimacy in the "Victorian" and "modern" periods. In part, this reflects considerations of evidence and documentation. It also relates to the lack of an elaborated homosexual subculture in these periods. It was not until the contemporary period that homosexuals created affirmative models of intimacy. In addition, a plethora of survey and research data and easily accessible documents (memoirs, novels, ethnography) permits us to examine not only general normative patterns but attitudes and behavior. Because most of this documentation relates to homosexuals who are affiliated with the subculture, it is not clear that my analysis can be generalized beyond this segment of the homosexual population.

Drawing on these empirical sources, I have criticized views which exaggerate either the similarities or the differences between heterosexual and homosexual patterns of intimacy in the 1960s and 1970s. Against a perspective that accentuates the uniqueness of homosexuals, I have emphasized common normative patterns between heterosexuals, gay men and lesbians. For example, all three populations value long-term love relationships, invoke sexual satisfaction and companionship as standards of love, aspire to egalitarian ideals and experience similar tensions around balancing intimacy and personal independence. Although we have noted some differences between heterosexual and homosexual patterns relating to role playing or the duration of love relationships, we have focused on a somewhat distinctive pattern among gay men.

Whether gay men were in romantic relationships or not, they participated in casual sex and did so at a rate that was not comparable to heterosexuals or lesbians. Gay men of this period did not typically combine emotional exclusiveness in a relationship with sexual monogamy. More importantly, the role of sex in gay men's lives and therefore their intimate conventions depart in key ways from the experience of many heterosexuals and lesbians. The intimate ideal that companionship, romance and sex be combined in one long-term relationship is less descriptive of at least some gay men in the 1970s. In this period, many gay men evolved interpersonal arrangements in which companionship and ongoing emotional support was provided by friendship networks, while sex was casual. Intermittently, the companionship and intimacy of friendship and the eroticism of casual sex were united in romantic affairs. Yet, even in these romances, casual sex continued. Presumably, casual sex did not threaten romance since it was approached as a nonromantic domain of pleasure and play.

The fact that casual sex was not, in principle, disruptive to intimate bonds does not explain its prevalence among gay men. Various explanations, from invoking social oppression or gender dynamics to subcultural considerations have been reviewed. I have underscored the importance of discourses issuing forth from the center of the gay subculture. These representations imbued casual sex with positive meaning ranging from anticipations of exalted pleasures to a quest for authenticity, self-fulfillment, liberation and brotherhood.

Even prior to AIDS, however, many in the subculture voiced serious reservations about aspects of its intimate culture. Like heterosexual and lesbian sexual romanticists, some gay men assailed the separation of sex from intimacy and romantic bonds; they protested the so-called objectification, instrumentalism, one-dimensional hedonism and emotional callousness of casual sex. With the AIDS epidemic, the romanticists were no longer on the defense. The post-liberationist culture of eroticism was linked to AIDS.

By the mid-1980s, we can observe a movement supported by many gay men, lesbians and heterosexuals to delegitimate the construction of sex as a realm of pleasure and self-expression valued solely for its individuating or communitarian qualities. Contemporary sex reformers are highlighting the spiritual aspects of romance; they are projecting sex exclusively as a medium of love and intimacy. The likelihood of a change in American intimate conventions is the theme of the epilogue.

Epilogue

From today's vantage point we can observe a series of purity movements beginning in the late 1970s. Campaigns against alcohol, drugs and unhealthy foods and a heightened emphasis on physical and mental fitness are typical of purity crusades in the United States.[1] They are one response to anxieties elicited by social changes. They are efforts to ward off chaos and perceived social decline by intensifying discipline and self-control. It is as if disturbing social events can be controlled by individuals imposing upon themselves regimes of discipline and healthful living.

The domain of sexuality is especially susceptible to purity campaigns.[2] The control of carnal desire has figured prominently in the history of these movements. This is evident, for example, in the current campaign against pornography, the crusade for teen chastity and the efforts to medicalize casual sex as a "compulsion" or "addition." These purity campaigns have spearheaded an assault upon the culture of intimacy that has evolved in late twentieth-century America. The expansion of sexual individualism and pluralism, and the growing public authority of a libertarian hedonistic ethic, are being held responsible for a range of current ills in our intimate culture, from teen pregnancy and divorce to herpes and AIDS. Comments the psychiatrist and popular author Willard Gaylin, "The only empirical results of . . . the sexual revolution seem to be the spread of . . . genital herpes and AIDS; an extraordinary rise in the incidence of cancer of the cervix; and a disastrous epidemic of teenage pregnancies."[3] Although contemporary criticism of the American culture of intimacy ranges from right-wing assaults on eroticism to feminist criticisms of sexual objectification or left-wing attacks on the merging of sex and commercialization, demands to reform American intimate culture have converged around the notion that in light of the dangers of sex that have recently become evident greater restrictions need to be placed on sexual choice and diversity.

My own assessment of the American culture of intimacy is far more positive. I am not convinced by critics who presume a tight causal tie between expanded sexual choice, a culture of eroticism and a range of social ills. Divorce, for example, seems more related to the changing economic and social position of women and to the mounting pressures on couples to provide emotional and social support than to the sexualization of love or the emphasis placed on the erotic aspects of marital sex. Indeed, the dramatic rise in divorce rates began at the turn of the century, prior to the establishment of a culture of eroticism. Moreover, the social and moral meaning of divorce is ambiguous. Research shows that most divorcees remarry, suggesting that divorce does not promote anomie or social disorder but permits individuals to reestablish social units that are more fulfilling than their current intimate ties.[4] Similarly, it is a mistake to interpret AIDS as a product of a permissive sexual culture. Heterosexuals, even those whose sexual patterns involved multiple sex partners, have not been the primary victims of HIV. Male homosexuals have been the chief population that has been at risk through the sexual transmission of HIV. It is not, moreover, their "promiscuity" per se that accounts for the high numbers of gay men who have suffered from AIDS. Rather, it was the introduction of HIV into an urban gay male subculture that cohered around a system of sexual exchanges that explains the high numbers of gay men with AIDS.

Critics of the contemporary American culture of intimacy frequently overlook its beneficial aspects. It has encouraged the development of the sensual expressive side of the individual. Accordingly, it has been productive of new forms of self-expression and pleasure. The cultivation of sexual desires and behaviors has given rise to new affirmative identities and ways of life, e.g., among gays and lesbians or in contributing to the formation of a leather, S/M culture. Finally, our intimate culture has been productive of new social bonds and types of collective life. The reconfiguring of sex in the twentieth century as a medium of love and romantic bonding rendered sex a powerful socially unifying force. Sex created binding affective and moral ties within a romantic unit. Further, while the separation of sex from romance created opportunities for individualism, it also functioned as a medium through which strangers might communicate and form connecting ties. Casual sex has been productive of a multiplicity of social formations. Through casual sex, regular sexual liaisons, romances or friendships may develop as well as give rise to more elaborate social networks or organizations. For example, in the gay male subculture, an organized collective life emerged from casual sexual liaisons and exchanges. The role of sex as an agent of community building seems to be the case with other marginal and unconventional sexualities, for example, sadomasochists or swingers.[5] Critics of the American intimate culture have not sufficiently appreciated that while expanded sexual freedom and a culture of eroticism may have some costs, the benefits—including expanded freedom and diversity, new sites of pleasure and self-expression and the creation of new identities and communities—are considerable.

Setting aside the debate over the moral meaning of the American intimate culture, the movements to reform it, especially in the context of AIDS, are likely to have some lasting impact. In the remainder of the Epilogue, I wish to briefly address the question, What changes in the American intimate culture are presently occurring and what can we expect in the near future?

I detect two major current trends that run somewhat counter to the evolution of American middle-class intimate culture as I have charted it. First, there is a movement to stigmatize casual sex as symptomatic of an individual or social pathology. Sex outside of a romantic, intimate relationship is being described as narcissism, an immature flight from feelings and commitment or a sign of the decline of the moral authority of key institutions (e.g., the family, church, schools).[6] Casual sex is now often constructed as a domain of danger, as is evidenced in popular movies like *Fatal Attraction* and *Dangerous Liaisons*.[7] AIDS is regularly invoked as proof of the danger of causal sex. "AIDS remains a prominent skeleton at the feast of sexual liberation," intone the editors of the *National Review*.[8] The link between permissiveness and AIDS is not made only by conservatives. B. D. Colon of the *Rolling Stone* commented: "A lifestyle that involves hundreds of sexual contacts . . . appears to be as much a phenomenon of the modern 'sexual revolution' as is AIDS."[9] Nor is this recourse to AIDS to relate a tale of the dangers of casual sex confined to heterosexual critics. The AIDS activist Michael Callen finds in AIDS a message of sexual ethics. "Promiscuity has become a narcotic for many promiscuous gay men. And AIDS is merely the logical conclusion of a decade of unprecedented promiscuity."[10] To be sure, AIDS does require Americans, especially gay men, to change specific behaviors. It requires safe sex practices; it does not demand, on health grounds, the abandonment of casual sex, since AIDS does not mean that casual sex is necessarily dangerous. This is a construction placed upon AIDS in order to legitimate reforming our intimate culture.[11]

The other side to interpreting casual sex as dangerous is the legitimation of sex exclusively as a medium of romance and love. Reminiscent of the early decades of the twentieth century, we can observe a campaign to restrict legitimate sexual expression to long-term, intimate relationships. Sexual and self-fulfillment are being identified with a concept of sex that defines it as necessarily intertwined with the emotional and social life of the individual. For example, George Leonard, former apostle of the sexual liberation, now maintains that a sexual ethic that encourages the separation of sex from intimacy is dangerous.

> We are beginning to realize, in fact, that sexual liberation divorced from love and creation is not a revolution at all but . . . leads to a depersonalization and devaluation of relationships and thus of life itself, which leads in turn to . . . despair and anomie . . . It is even possible to see the recent . . . tolerance of loveless sex as one of those desperate attempts at adaptation that have often marked the death throes of any line of cultural, biological, or artistic development.[12]

In place of an ideology of expanded sexual choice and diversity, Leonard advocates an ideal of "erotic love." The latter re-establishes the tight link between sex and intimacy; it emphasizes the social and spiritual aspects of sex.

Related to efforts to reconfigure sex exclusively as a domain of love is a new emphasis placed upon courtship, romance and monogamy. "Recreational sex . . . has led to a frantic aimless search for sensation and . . . to a dissociation of courtship and romance, desecration of courtship and romance," remarks Leonard.[13] He recommends a renewal of romance and a new ideal of "high monogamy" which embeds sex in a long-term intimate, monogamous, loving relationship. Dr. Gaylin's *Rediscovering Love* prescribes romance for an intimate culture that, he believes, has been devastated by the quest for pleasure and its confusion of sensuality and love. "The romantic element must be restored to modern life. It must be added to our relationships to reinstate human love to its central position in human experience. . . . Romance must be rediscovered . . . in order to overcome the mounting sense of isolation, purposelessness, and ennui."[14] In the gay male culture, the campaign to rediscover the virtues of a more social and spiritual concept of romance and intimacy has assumed a redemptive significance. This is especially evident in writings by gay men on AIDS. Long-term activist and writer Arthur Bell interprets AIDS as entailing a beneficial effect in that it promotes romance and commitment instead of promiscuity. "Indiscriminate sex with phantom partners in backrooms is beginning to diminish. . . . Barbarity is on the way out. Romance [is] . . . on the way in."[15] David Goodstein, the recently deceased owner and editor of the *Advocate*, joins a critical view of the pre-AIDS period to the prospects for spiritual renewal instigated by AIDS. "During the last half of the 1970s, it wasn't chic in gay male circles to place a high value on life-companions or close friendships. Now we have another chance for progress: to acknowledge the value of intimate relationships."[16] Both heterosexual and gay critics of casual sex advocate a renewal of a more spiritual notion of romance and love; they defend a couple-centered, monogamous intimate norm in which the emphasis shifts from the erotic aspects of sex to its social and spiritual aspects. Reformers imbue this intimate ideal with expectations of health, moral order and social progress.

Reformers' efforts to legitimate sex exclusively in a context of love and revitalize rituals of romance have promoted the respiritualization of sex and love. By this I mean less the desexualization of love than an emphasis on the social and spiritual aspects of sex. While some reform discourses continue to highlight the importance of erotic pleasure as a mainstay of love, there is a trend to underscore its spiritual qualities.

These cultural shifts are clearly in evidence in the advice literature of the 1980s. Dagmar O'Connor announces that her book *How to Make Love to the Same Person for the Rest of Your Life* "is for those of us in the eighties who believe in sexual commitment again. . . . It is for all of us . . . who have finally rejected one-night stands and serial affairs, secret infidelities and open marriages and who now yearn for one complete and lasting sexual relationship."[17] O'Connor promises the reader erotic pleasure and adventure, but only "in an on-going sexual relationship."[18] Heterosexual marriage represents her intimate ideal. "Marriage truly is the best possible arrangement for enjoying the most exciting sex there is."[19] Whereas O'Connor still invokes erotic pleasure as a rationale for marriage, the chief trend in current advice texts is to offer more spiritual constructions of love and intimacy. Paul Pearsall begins his enormously popular *Super Marital Sex: Loving for Life* by juxtaposing the joys of spiritual intimacy to the emptiness of promiscuity. "Super marital sex is the most erotic, intense, fulfilling experience any human being can have. Anonymous sex with multiple partners pales by comparison, an empty imitation of the fulfillment of a sexuality of intimacy and commitment to one person for life."[20] Pearsall is not justifying intimacy by its erotic payoff but claiming that sex is fulfilling in this context precisely because of its spiritual and social role. Super marital sex is not sex that heightens sensual pleasure but sex that intensifies an intimate loving marital bond. Super marital sex "transcends eroticized, genitalized sex for a marital experience of intimacy that far exceeds what is possible in any less committed relationship."[21] Super marital sex represents a "new model of intimacy" in which sex functions as a medium of trust, solidarity and commitment.

In *Lifemates: The Love Fitness Program for a Lasting Relationship,* Drs. Harold Bloomfield and Sirah Vettese urge the spiritualization of sex and love in response to the moral bankruptcy of the sexual ideals of the '60s and '70s. "We now see that 'liberated sex' has bred sexual exploitation, performance fears . . ., unwanted pregnancies, boredom . . ., spiritual maliase [and] AIDS."[22] In place of the false ideal of sexual liberation as erotic pleasure and variety, they propose an ideal of a lifetime heterosexual love bond which they call "lifemates." For lifemates, a spiritual notion of love is the basis of intimacy. Sex functions as a medium of spiritual union. "Intimate sex is a spiritual joining to discover how open, sensitive, caring and loving you and your lifemate can be."[23] The lifemate ideal carries a norm of sexual monogamy." Monogamy . . . becomes a spiritual quest. . . . You must go deep within yourself and your love partner. . . . When you and your lover can share your passion without fear, and with patience, commitment, and trust, you may discover a state of sexual grace. . . . Once you discover this level of intimacy with your lifemate, monogamy loses all sense of bondage and becomes a source of liberation."[24] Given this spiritual reconfiguration of the meaning of sex and love, the lifemate ideal involves a renewal of the importance of courtship and romance. The authors invoke AIDS to recommend "the return of monogamy but also the return of good old-fashioned courtship. The era of multiple partners . . . may have run its course. . . . The data suggests the old-fashioned idea that sex should not be enjoyed without a substantial emotional commitment. . . . When it comes to safe sex, the best medical advice may be to fall in love before you fall into bed."[25]

The titles of the bestsellers in this genre indicate at least a partial normative shift in our intimate culture. Whereas the bestsellers of the 1960s and 1970s had such titles as *The Joy of Sex, The Sensuous Man, The Sensuous Woman* and *The Pleasure Bond;* the titles that have captured the public in the '80s are *I Love You, Let's Work It Out, Lifemates, Intimate Play, The Lifelong Lover, How to Put the Love Back into Making Love* or *How to Make Love to the Same Person for the Rest of Your Life.* These advice texts are indicative of a reaction in American intimate culture against the legitimation of sex for its pleasurable or expressive qualities alone. Casual sex is being framed as dangerous and pathological. The erotic aspects of sex are being downplayed, while its social and spiritual aspects are being emphasized.

Many critics evaluate the sexual trends of the postwar years unfavorably. I am more ambivalent. I concur with the aim of halting a trend toward the sexualization of pleasure and the overinvestment in the importance of sexual pleasure. Sex can and, in my view, should function as a sphere of pleasure, but inflating its role risks creating unrealistic expectations. We should not look to sex to satisfy a range of needs and pleasures that can best be met elsewhere. Moreover, while sex can and should be an agent of romantic bonding, exaggerating its role in creating and sustaining intimate ties threatens to conflate sex and love and to neglect other powerful sources of emotional and social bonding. Discourses that highlight the affective and socially bonding aspects of love may promote communication about the moral and interpersonal aspects of intimacy. Finally, critics have forced us to address the downside of pursuing sex for its sensually pleasurable qualities. Concerns about heightening performance anxieties, objectifying individuals as mere bodies and organs and promoting sexually transmitted disease in a culture that values erotic pleasure and variety cannot be ignored. There are, then, drawbacks and costs to expanding sexual choice and to valuing sex as a medium of erotic pleasure.

I am worried, however, about the social implications of these normative shifts in our intimate culture. They entail restrictions on sexual freedom and diversity which, I believe, are undesirable. Lifestyle options are greatly circumscribed by legitimating sex exclusively as an intimate expression confined to long-term, loving relationships. Sex will no longer serve as a way individuals can initiate and build relationships or as one medium to establish different types of social bonds. Lifestyles that depart from this intimate ideal will undoubtedly be labeled deviant. Individuals who participate in nonconventional lifestyles will be stigmatized as abnormal, immature, perverse, socially dangerous or morally inferior. This is already evident in the construction of casual sex as a sphere of danger and pathology. Sexual minorities such as lesbians and gay men, swingers and sadomasochists, as well as other socially marginal populations whose intimate cultures may be unconventional, will suffer the most from this shift to a restrictive intimate ideal. In fact, in current advice texts the ideal of a lifetime marriage pattern is urged in a much more unidimensional and insistent way than in the literature of the recent past. Its likely that this restrictive intimate ideal will be used to attack sexual minorities as well as other marginal groups who may seem threatening to a society that is obsessed with discipline, fitness, self-control and lifestyle uniformity as a means to promote personal health, social stability and progress.

Paralleling this restrictive cultural movement, we can identify discourses and representations defending an expansive notion of sexual choice and diversity. These cultural expressions are particularly visible among minority communities. My comments will be confined to these cultural expressions in the feminist, lesbian and gay male communities.

As we saw in chapter 5, there emerged in the 1970s at least one current of feminism that highlighted the dangers of sex. Sex was viewed by some radical feminists as a sphere of gender conflict in which men sought to exercise power over women. Female desire was described as scripted by men in order to reproduce male dominance. The norm of heterosexuality and marriage, of vaginal intercourse and orgasm, was interpreted as imposed by men for their benefit. Within this radical feminist framework, pornography and all efforts to separate sex from intimate relationships were defined as promoting men's sexual values and interests. A feminist sexual ethic crystallized that framed sex as a medium for expressing bonds of intimacy. Sex was to be nurturing and tender so as to exhibit and reinforce the intimate, loving qualities of a relationship.

For those women whose struggle for autonomy included a struggle for different sexual and intimate practices, this radical feminist sexual ideology was judged to be unnecessarily constraining. Feminists who retained strong ties to a prefeminist lesbian culture, feminists who identified with the gay movement, and liberal, socialist and even some radical feminists who were troubled by any lifestyle orthodoxy, objected to this feminist sexual ethic. By the early 1980s, local ideological skirmishes escalated into a virtual sex war. As Ann Ferguson has noted, the major division was between "romanticists" who framed sex as an expression of an intimate, committed relationship and "libertarians" for whom sex could legitimately have multiple meanings and social occasions.[26] Critics of sexual romanticism took the offensive. They produced a vast discursive outpouring that defended an expansive concept of sexual freedom, diversity and pleasure. The two volumes *The Powers of Desire* and *Pleasure and Danger*, along with the special "sex issue" of *Heresies* and the anti-antiporn anthology *Against Censorship*, defended an intimate culture that permits a wide latitude of sexual and intimate lifestyles.[27] Whether it was Joan Nestle's celebration of a dyke culture in which lesbians are sexually aggressive and powerful, Gayle Rubin's theoretical defense of radical sexual pluralism, Amber Hollibaugh's urging women to own up to their own carnal desires or Paula Webster's discerning in porn a liberating erotic possibility, these critics of sexual romanticism affirmed feminism as a movement of sexual liberation which endorsed women's right to choose the meaning and context of sex.[28]

These critics of a feminist romantic sexual ethic proposed an alternative libertarian sexual ideology. Sex was framed less as a realm of gender power struggle than as a complex, heterogeneous field of meaning and social practice. Sex could legitimately have multiple meanings and a plurality of appropriate social settings. In the forefront of this movement of sexual radicalism were a group of lesbian sadomasochists. The San Francisco group Samois, with its brilliant theoreticians Pat Califia and Gayle Rubin, pressed a feminist libertarian sexual ideology to its furthest conclusion.[29] They proposed, in effect, that there should be no binding norms of sexual behavior beyond those agreed upon by the sex partners themselves. They sought to degender the meaning of sex or at least to depoliticize specific sexual desires and acts. Sex was defended as a realm of pleasure and self-expression, not simply as an enactment of gender scripts and conflicts. Thus, whereas feminist critics saw in lesbian S/M a reiteration and reinforcement of a bipolar gender order that privileges and empowers men,[30] libertarians emphasized the playfulness of role playing and argued that the eroticization of power and role playing is not necessarily associated with masculine or feminine gender roles. Roles are playful, fluid and often reversible and do not, typically, extend beyond the S/M scene. "S/M is a consensual form of activity intended for the pleasure of all participants. . . . S/M does involve power and power roles in a temporary situation. Many anti-S/M feminists have the mistaken notion that we live the roles 24 hours a day. S/M is not in itself a lifestyle. It is a sexual preference. . . . In a S/M scene . . . both the top and bottom exercise power. The roles have been agreed on. . . . The roles do not correspond to male dominant-female submissive social patterns. I've seen many feminine lesbian tops and many butch lesbian bottoms. . . . Each of us in our S/M scene is concerned with her own pleasure and with her partner's pleasure. . . . Sometimes we are casual sex partners. Sometimes we are friends. Sometimes we are lovers."[31]

By the mid-1980s these feminist libertarian themes had moved into mainstream culture. For example, *Re-making Love*, published by Doubleday as a mass circulation trade book written by three prominent feminists, amounts to a defense of an intimate culture of expanded freedom and diversity. Contrary to the radical or cultural feminist orthodoxy, these authors insist that women have been pioneers of a sexual revolution that affirms pleasure, variety and choice. Their book aims to recover the initial impulse of the women's movement as a sexual liberation movement. In the women's sexual revolution, "women have won a new range of sexual rights—to pleasure, to fantasy and variety."[32] The right of female sexual autonomy, they insist, should cover the option of casual sex. "Casual sex should be a choice. .... Women have come too far to surrender the range of possibilities opened up by their sexual revolution."[33]

The defense of an expansive concept of sexual choice noted among feminists and lesbians is equally visible in the gay male subculture. AIDS and the resurgence of political and cultural conservatism in the '80s encouraged many gay men to adopt a monogamous, marital intimate ideal. In fact, reformers in the gay community have mounted a sustained campaign to promote this ideal on health and moral grounds. Yet, the affirmation of sexual freedom, variety and erotic pleasure remains integral to this subculture.

AIDS has contributed to changes in sexual behavior among gay men. Researchers have documented that at least through the mid-1980s on the average gay men have fewer sex partners and engage in less high-risk sexual behavior.[34] As much as AIDS has occasioned a discourse of restraint and the spiritualization of intimacy in the gay community, it has also given rise to a renewed commitment to sexual freedom and to exploring new forms of eroticism.

At the center of the gay male response to AIDS has been the concept of "safe sex." This refers to sex acts that are thought to involve no significant risks of receiving or transmitting the HIV. By framing the implications of AIDS within a discourse that divides sex acts into safe and high-risk, it was possible to avoid imbuing all sex with danger. If some sex acts are "safe," appeals to AIDS-related health risks cannot warrant a specific sexual and intimate lifestyle. A sexual ethic that restricts lifestyle choices, not simply sex act choices, cannot be defended on the grounds of the health concerns raised by the HIV. It remains the responsibility of individuals to choose the meaning and role of sex in their lives.

The defense of a libertarian sex ethic in the gay community is less evident in elaborated discourses than in pamphlets, brochures and advertisements on safe sex. Typical is the following advertisement in *The Advocate*, a national gay magazine.

The Safer
The Sex,
The Better!
The *Advocate* believes in and supports informed personal choice in sexual matters. During the AIDS crises, we encourage you to practice the safest sex possible.[35]

In its "Safer Sex Guidelines," *Outweek*, a New-York lesbian and gay weekly, offers the following advice: "Remember, sex is good, and gay sex is great. Don't avoid sex, just avoid the virus. Learn to eroticize safe sex and you can protect others, remain safe and have fun."[36] The message in these ads is that AIDS obligates us to rely on medical knowledge of HIV transmission to guide our choice of sex acts, not its meaning, or our intimate arrangement.

The emphasis on safe sex in the gay male subculture has encouraged a heightened concentration on safe sex acts; it has led to the innovation of new forms of eroticism. In diverse gay-oriented representations and discourses, we can observe an intensification of the erotic potential of language, fantasy, autoeroticism, nongenital sex and role playing. This is evident in the proliferation of phone sex businesses targeting the gay male consumer. Phone sex exploits the erotic qualities of language and fantasy; it is pleasure-centered, autoerotic, casual and safe. In the age of AIDS, many gay men continue to affirm an expansive notion of sexual freedom, variety and pleasure. They maintain that the spread of HIV requires only a change in specific sex acts or the deployment of special precautions, not a change in the meaning of sex or its role in fashioning an intimate lifestyle.

Sexual minority communities such as feminists or lesbians and gay men are important carriers of an expansive and open intimate culture.[37] Yet, between the battle at the extremes of choice and restraint, intimacy and pleasure, it is the great cultural mainstream which shows little sympathy for overturning an intimate culture that, though messy and costly at times, gives most Americans the kind of personal choice and gratification we seem to want.

As we move into the 1990s, the intimate culture that has evolved in the United States over the last century is unlikely to undergo another great transformation akin to the changes I have charted. The legitimation of sexual choice and variety, and the value placed on sex as both a medium of intimacy and a pleasure have enormous social support today. Of course, Americans will continue to disagree over the extent of permissible choice and the range of permissible diversity. Social conflicts will not abate over the morality of eroticism and the dangers of allowing some slippage between sex and intimacy. Today, reformers campaigning to restrict choice and variety and to spiritualize intimacy are on the offensive. Those most threatened by movements of restriction and discipline have responded with their own defense of choice, variety and erotic pleasure. How these minorities fare will tell us a lot about the fate of choice and diversity in American intimate culture in the near future.

Notes

INTRODUCTION

1. For general statements on cultural analysis, see Clifford Geertz, *The Interpretation of Cultures* (New York: Basic Books, 1973) and *Local Knowledge* (New York: Basic Books, 1983); Janet Dolgin et al. (eds.), *Symbolic Anthropology* (New York: Columbia University Press, 1977) and Jeffrey Alexander and Steven Seidman (eds.), *Culture and Society: Contemporary Debates* (Cambridge: Cambridge University Press, 1990).

2. Cf. Sherry Ortner and Harriet Whitehead (eds.), *Sexual Meanings: The Cultural Construction of Gender and Sexuality* (Cambridge: Cambridge University Press, 1981); Carroll Smith-Rosenberg, *Disorderly Conduct* (New York: Oxford University Press, 1985); Rosiland Coward, *Female Desires* (New York: Grove Press, 1985).

3. See Carl Degler, "What Ought to Be and What Was: Women's Sexuality in the Nineteenth Century." *American Historical Review* 79 (Dec. 1974).

4. See Estelle Freedman, "Sexuality in Nineteenth-Century America: Behavior, Ideology and Politics," *Reviews in American History* 10 (Dec. 1982); John D'Emilio and Estelle Freedman, *Intimate Matters* (New York: Harper & Row, 1988).

5. Obviously, I am not saying that AIDS is an acceptable cost for expanded sexual choice. My claim is that the widespread circulation of HIV requires "safe-sex" practices, not necessarily the restriction of intimate lifestyle options. See Steven Seidman, "Transfiguring Sexual Identity: AIDS and the Construction of Homosexuality," *Social Text* 19–20 (Fall 1988).

CHAPTER 1

1. See, for example, Vernon Louis Parrington, *The Colonial Mind*, vol. 1 of *Main Currents in American Thought* (New York: Harcourt, Brace, 1972) and "The Puritan Diaries, 1620–1720," in *The Cambridge History of American Literature*, ed. William Trent et al. (New York: G. P. Putnam's Sons, 1971); James Truslow Adams, *The Founding of New England* (Boston: Atlantic Monthly Press, 1921); and H. L. Mencken, "Puritans as a Literary Force," in *A Book of Prefaces* (New York: Knopf, 1917).

2. Edmund Leites, *The Puritan Conscience and Modern Sexuality* (New Haven: Yale University Press, 1986), p. 12.

3. Ibid., p. 76.

4. Ibid., p. 15.

5. Ibid., p. 16.

6. Edmund Morgan, *The Puritan Family* (New York: Harper & Row, 1966), p. 48.

7. William and Mallville Haller, "The Puritan Art of Love," *Huntington Library Quarterly* 5 (Oct. 1941), p. 257.

8. Roger Thompson, *Sex in Middlesex: Popular Mores in a Massachusetts County, 1649–1699* (Amherst: University of Massachusetts Press, 1986), p. 73. On sodomy laws in the colonial era, see Jonathan Katz, *Gay/Lesbian Almanac* (New York: Harper & Row, 1983).

9. Thompson, *Sex in Middlesex*, p. 128. Also, see John D'Emilio and Estelle Freedman, *Intimate Matters* (New York: Harper & Row, 1988), p. 28.

10. D'Emilio and Freedman, *Intimate Matters*, p. 19. Cf. John Demos, *A Little Commonwealth* (New York: Oxford University Press, 1970), pp. 95–97.

11. Quoted in Morgan, *The Puritan Family*, pp. 47–49.

12. Morgan, *The Puritan Family;* Carl Degler, *At Odds*, (New York: Oxford University Press, 1980), pp. 70–72.

13. Philip Greven argues that only the evangelical Puritans were truly ascetic and held "sex-negative attitudes." See his *The Protestant Temperament* (New York: Alfred A. Knopf, 1977).

14. Kathleen Verduim, " 'Our Cursed Natures': Sexuality and the Puritan Conscience," *New England Quarterly* 56 (June 1983), p. 226.

15. Ibid., p. 223.

16. The classic statement remains Steven Marcus, *The Other Victorians* (New York: Basic Books, 1964).

17. Carl Degler, *At Odds* and "What Ought to Be and What Was: Women's Sexuality in the Nineteenth Century," *American Historical Review* 79 (Dec. 1974). Peter Gay, *The Bourgeois Experience*, vol. 1, *The Education of the Senses* (New York: Oxford University Press, 1984); Ellen Rothman, *Hands and Hearts* (Cambridge, Mass.: Harvard University Press, 1987). For one dissenting view, see Carol Zisowitz Stearns and Peter Stearns, "Victorian Sexuality: Can Historians Do It Better?" *Journal of Social History* 18 (Summer 1985).

18. Degler, *At Odds*, p. 70.

19. See Verduin, " 'Our Cursed Natures'," p. 237.

20. Frederick Hollick, *The Marriage Guide, or Natural History of Generation* (New York: Arno Press, 1974 [1885]), p. 356. Cf. Joseph Howe, *Excessive Venery, Masturbation and Continence* (New York: Arno Press, 1974 [1887]), p. 24. Charles Knowlton, *Fruits of Philosophy* (New York: Arno Press, 1972 [1832]), p. 52.

21. Elizabeth Blackwell, *Counsel to Parents* 8th ed. (London, 1913) p. 1.

22. James Ashton, *The Book of Nature* (New York, 1870), p. 35.

23. William Acton, *The Functions and Disorders of the Reproductive Organs*, 3rd ed. (Philadelphia, 1865), p. 204.

24. Henry Guernsey, *Plain Talk on Avoided Subjects* (Philadelphia, 1907 [1882]), p. 60.

25. Edward B. Foote, *Plain Home Talk* (New York; 1891 [1870]), p. 172.

26. Robert Dale Owen, *Moral Philosophy* (New York: Arno Press, 1972 [1830]), p. 11.

27. R. T. Trall, *Sexual Physiology and Hygiene* (New York: Arno Press, 1974 [1886]), p. 236. Cf. Charles Meigs, *Lecture on Some of the Distinctive Characteristics of the Female* (Philadelphia, 1847), p. 6–7.

28. James Foster Scott, *The Sexual Instinct* (New York, 1898), p. 138.

29. Ibid., p. 117.

30. O. S. Fowler, *Love and Parentage,* (New York, 1850), p. 131.

31. Dio Lewis, *Chastity or, Our Secret Sins* (New York: Arno Press, 1974 [1874]), pp. 27–28.

32. Blackwell, *Counsel to Parents,* p. 39.

33. Samuel Bayard Woodward, *Hints for the Young in Relation to the Health of Body and Mind* (Boston, 1856 [1838]), p. 7. Cf. Wesley Grindle, *New Medical Revelations* (Philadelphia, 1857), p. 70.

34. Ashton, *The Book of Nature,* pp. 42–43.

35. Sylvester Graham, *A Lecture to Young Men* (New York: Arno Press, 1974 [1834]), pp. 42–43.

36. Ibid., pp. 48–49.

37. Ibid., p. 35. Cf. O.S. Fowler, *Amativeness, or Evils and Remedies of Excessive and Perverted Sexuality,* 13th ed. (New York: 1850 [1844]), pp. 20–40.

38. Graham, *Lecture to Young Men,* p. 45; Cf. Foote, *Plain Home Talk,* p. 607.

39. Augustus Gardner, *Conjugal Sins* (New York, 1870), p. 84.

40. R. T. Trall, *Sexual Physiology and Hygiene* (New York: Arno Press, 1974 [1866]), p. 234.

41. J. H. Kellogg, *Plain Facts for Old and Young* (New York: Arno Press, 1974 [1877]), p. 346.

42. The causal tie between sexual excess and the destiny of humanity reflects as well the social hereditarian assumptions that virtually all advice writers accepted. It was thought that the physical, mental and spiritual characteristics of the parents, especially at the moment of conception, are transmitted to the child. A parent who practiced sexual excess or unnatural sex would transmit to his or her offspring a constitutional disposition toward vice and perversion. See Charles Rosenberg, *No Other Gods* (Baltimore: Johns Hopkins University Press, 1976). Typical is the statement by Dr. Kellogg: "It is an established physiological fact that the character of offspring is influenced by the mental as well as the physical conditions of the parents at the moment of the performance of the generative act. . . . By debasing the reproductive function to an act of selfish animal indulgence, they imprinted upon their children an almost irresistible tendency to vice." He continues, "It cannot be doubted that the throngs of deaf, blind, crippled, idiotic unfortunates who were 'born so,' together with a still larger class of dwarfed, diseased, and constitutionally weak individuals, are the lamentable results of some sexual law on the part of their progenitor." Through the hereditary transmission of a disposition to perversion, sexual excess and the misfortune and misery it brings bind generations to a social dynamic of personal degeneration and social decline. Henry Kellogg, *Plain Facts,* pp. 448–449. Also, Trall, *Sexual Physiology,* p. xii; Ashton, *Book of Nature,* pp. 21–22.

43. Graham, *Lecture to Young Men*, p. 50.

44. Lewis, *Chastity*, p. 26.

45. Kellogg, *Plain Facts*, p. 169.

46. See G. J. Barker-Benfield, *The Horrors of the Half-Known Life* (New York: Harper & Row, 1976).

47. Acton, *Reproductive Organs*, p. 169. Also, Duffey, *Relations of the Sexes*, (New York, 1876), p. 179; Foote, *Plain Home Talk*, p. 543; Hollick, *The Marriage Guide*, pp. 364–365.

48. Ashton, *The Book of Nature*, p. 20.

49. Hollick, *The Marriage Guide*, p. 183.

50. Foote, *Plain Home Talk*, p. 617.

51. George Henry Napheys, *The Physical Life of Women: Advice to the Maiden, Wife, and Mother* (Philadelphia, 1870), p. 80.

52. Graham, *Lecture to Young Men*, p. 80. Also, Kellogg, *Plain Facts*, pp. 375, 453 and Duffey, *The Relations of the Sexes*, p. 221.

53. Acton, *Reproductive Organs*, p. 133. Cf. Fowler, *Love and Parentage* p. 88; James Ashton, *The Book of Nature*; Thomas Hersey, *The Midwife's Practical Directory* (New York: Arno Press, 1974 [1834]), p. 63.

54. Dio Lewis, *Chastity*, p. 117.

55. Elizabeth Blackwell, *The Human Element in Sex, Being a Medical Inquiry into the Relation of Sexual Physiology to Christian Morality*, 2d ed. (London, 1894), p. 49. Also *Counsel to Parents*, p. 79.

56. Eliza Duffey, *The Relations of the Sexes*, p. 208.

57. Ibid., p. 219. Cf. Alice Stockham, *Tokology* (Chicago, 1892 [1883]), pp. 249, 323. Cf. Elizabeth Evans, *The Abuse of Maternity* (New York: Arno Press, 1974 [1875]), p. 43.

58. Acton, *Reproductive Organs*, p. 151.

59. Ashton, *The Book of Nature*, p. 47.

60. Kellogg, *Plain Facts*, p. 115.

61. Acton, *Reproductive Organs*, p. 102.

62. Ibid., p. 108.

63. Ibid., p. 110.

64. Ibid.

65. Ibid.

66. Ibid., p. 122.

67. Graham, *A Lecture to Young Men*, p. 59.

68. Ibid., p. 61. Cf. William Alcott, *The Young Man's Guide*, 2d ed. (Boston, 1834 [1833]), pp. 296–297.

69. Fowler, *Love and Parentage*, p. 20.

70. Ibid., p. 122.

71. Ibid., p. 137.

72. Ibid., p. 67.

73. Ibid., p. 68.

74. Ibid.

75. Ibid., p. 75.

76. Ibid., p. 68.

77. Ibid., p. 83.

78. Ibid., p. 100.

79. Ibid., p. 132.

80. Ibid., p. 69.

81. Ibid., p. 132.

82. Guernsey, *Plain Talk on Avoided Subjects*, p. 59.

83. Ibid., p. 93.

84. Ibid., p. 94.

85. Ibid., p. 92.

86. Ibid., p. 89.

87. Ibid., p. 91. Cf. John Humphrey Noyes, *Male Continence* (New York, 1872).

88. Duffey, *The Relations of the Sexes*, p. 210.

89. Ibid., p. 211.

90. Ibid., p. 96.

91. Ibid., p. 212.

92. Henry Chevasse, *Physical Life of Man and Woman* (Cincinnati, 1871), p. 38.

93. Ibid., p. 74.

94. Ibid., p. 38.

95. Ibid., p. 39.

96. Ibid., p. 46.

97. See, for example, Degler, *Ad Odds;* Nancy Cott, "Passionlessness: An Interpretation of Victorian Sexual Ideology, 1790–1850," *Signs* 4 (1979). Daniel Scott Smith, "Family Limitations, Sexual Control, and Domestic Feminism in Victorian America," in *Clio's Consciousness Raised* ed. Mary Hartman and Lois Banner (New York: Harper & Row, 1974).

98. Duffey, *The Relations of the Sexes*, p. 230.

99. Ibid., p. 231.

100. Ibid., p. 248.

101. John Cowan, *The Science of a New Life* (New York, 1871), p. 27.

102. Ibid., p. 29.

103. Ibid., p. 46.

104. Ibid., p. 41.

105. Estelle Freedman, "Sexuality in Nineteenth-Century America: Behavior, Ideology, and Politics," *Reviews in American History* 10 (Dec. 1982). Also see John and Robin Haller, *The Physician and Sexuality in Victorian America* (Urbana: University of Illinois Press, 1974).

106. James Reed, *From Private Vice to Public Virtue.* (New York: Basic Books, 1970), p.

19. John Spurlock, *Free Love: Marriage and Middle-Class Radicalism in America, 1820–1860* (New York: New York University Press, 1988).

107. Degler, *At Odds*, p. 250.

108. See, for example, Barbara Ehrenreich and Deidre English, *For Her Own Good* (New York: Doubleday, 1979). For a more general overview of the failure of the regulars to establish dominance, which, in turn, allowed for the proliferation of medical ideologies and practices, see Richard Harrison Shryock, *Medicine and Society in America, 1660–1860* (New York: New York University Press, 1960). Also see Paul Starr, *Social Transformation of American Medicine* (New York: Basic Books, 1982).

109. See Stephen Nissenbaum, "Careful Love: Sylvester Graham and the Emergence of Victorian Sexual Theory in America, 1830–1840," (Ph.D. Diss. University of Wisconsin, 1968), pp. 223–239.

110. Smith-Rosenberg, *Disorderly Conduct*, p. 302; also see John and Robin Haller, *The Physician and Sexuality in Victorian America*, chap. 3.

111. See, for example, David Pivar, *Purity Crusade: Sexual Morality and Social Control, 1868–1900* (Westport, Conn.: Greenwood Press, 1973).

112. Mary Ryan, "The Power of Women's Networks: A Case Study of Female Moral Reform in Antebellum America," *Feminist Studies* 5 (Spring 1979), p. 77.

113. Paul Boyer, *Urban Masses and Moral Order in America, 1820–1920* (Cambridge, Mass.: Harvard University Press, 1978).

114. Linda Gordon, *Woman's Body, Woman's Right* (New York: Penguin, 1977), p. 119. Also see William Shade. "A Mental Passion: Female Sexuality in Victorian America," *International Journal of Women's Studies*, vol. 1 (Jan–Feb. 1978).

115. Chevasse, *Physical Life*, p. 424.

116. Scott, *Sexual Instinct*, p. 419.

CHAPTER 2

1. Cf. John D'Emilio and Estelle Freedman. *Intimate Matters* (New York: Harper & Row, 1988), p. 72.

2. Sarah Grimké, "Marriage" in Gerda Lerner (ed.), *The Female Experience: An American Documentary* (Indianapolis: Bobbs-Merrill, 1977), p. 95.

3. Ibid., pp. 93–94.

4. Quoted in Lerner, *The Female Experience*, p. 84.

5. Ibid.,

6. As this book was in press, an important reinterpretation of Victorian intimacy appeared whose main thesis departs from my own. In *Searching the Heart: Women, Men, and Romantic Love in Nineteenth-Century America*, (New York: Oxford University Press, 1989), Karen Lystra argues that sex and eroticism were an accepted part of Victorian love. Historians have failed to appreciate this because they have relied primarily upon public documents, especially popular medical and advice literature. Drawing on love letters written between 1830 and 1900, Lystra purports to discover an intimate culture that, at least with respect to the meaning of sex, closely resembles contemporary middle-class American society. If the Victorians did not announce this sexualized intimacy to the world, as we do today, it was,

she thinks, because they viewed sexual expression as a very personal expression of the self.

This book is by far the strongest argument advanced by the revisionists—e.g., Gay, Degler, Rothman—highlighting the parallels between the Victorians and contemporary Americans. It shares, however, the shortcomings of much of this history. First, Lystra all too often leaves sexual meanings unanalyzed, especially in relation to love. Typically, she quotes letters that refer to physical gestures of intimacy as if their meaning is self-evident. In fact, she appears to read contemporary meanings into these gestures. When Lystra does relate these sexual meanings to their historical setting, she regularly emphasizes that sex functioned as a symbol of love or a medium of spiritual union, not as a sphere of erotic joy. Indeed, its hard to see how sex could have been viewed in any other way, given Lystra's insistence that love was viewed basically as a spiritual and religious experience.

Second, if sex and eroticism were an integral aspect of Victorian love, we would expect to find expressions of this in the public culture of the time. Indeed, Lystra cannot seriously maintain her thesis without discovering public discourses and representations that articulate these meanings. Lystra turns to popular medical and advice literature to try to make her case. Given the dominant interpretation of this literature as representing an ideology of restraint and the spiritualization of intimacy, her strategy is to distinguish various ideological strains in these discourses. She argues that only one current—the "restrictionist"—advocated a repressive, spiritual intimate ideal. For reasons she does not explain, historians have taken the restrictionist ideology as reflecting mainstream opinion and accordingly have produced a stereotype of the "repressed Victorian." This, she believes, has been an error. It was the "moderates," a group valuing sex as an expression of love, who represented mainstream opinion. Thus, Lystra claims to have uncovered a cultural consistency between the private world of love letters and public discourses.

This argument, however, is very weak. Given the importance of demonstrating this consistency, it is surprising how cursory her analysis is of these public texts. More to the point, my own research suggests that her effort to differentiate ideological currents is not credible. For example, she describes Fowler as an "enthusiast," Duffey and Trall as "moderates," and Blackwell and Alcott as "restrictionists." Yet, my own research shows that, on the issue of sex and love, there are no significant differences among them. Though they all acknowledged the beneficial role of sex in marriage, love was construed as essentially spiritual. Sex, at best, symbolized a spiritual union or functioned as a spiritual act. In none of these discourses, and indeed, in none of the popular medical advice literature I consulted, was eroticism ever framed as essential to the meaning of intimacy or as a basis of love. This is a critical issue. If we cannot locate meanings in public discourses that are presumably widely shared in private life, then that presumption must be seriously challenged. In the end, Lystra's research is, in my view, important and challenging to an argument like my own, but her conclusions are grossly overstated given her narrowed evidentiary base and the problems I've referred to.

7. Byron Caldwell Smith, *The Love-Life of Byron Caldwell Smith* (New York: Antigone Press, 1930), p. 4.

8. Ibid., p. 5

9. Ibid., p. 4.

10. Ibid.

11. Ibid., p. 5.

12. Ibid., p. 8.

13. Ibid.

14. Ibid., p. 9.

15. Ibid., p. 49.

16. Ibid., pp. 141–142.

17. Ibid., p. 13.

18. Ibid., p. 73.

19. Ibid.

20. Ibid., p. 74.

21. Ibid., p. 74.

22. *Letters of Theodore D. Weld, Angelina Grimké Weld and Sara Grimké, 1822–1844*, ed. Gilbert Barnes and Dwight Dumond (New York: Appleton-Century, 1934), 625.

23. Ibid., p. 588.

24. Ibid., p. 583.

25. Ibid.

26. Ibid., p. 588.

27. Ibid., p. 583.

28. Ibid., p. 554.

29. Ibid.

30. Ibid., p. 582.

31. Ibid.

32. Ibid., p. 583.

33. Ibid., p. 588. Cf. Julia Newberry, *Diary* (New York: W. W. Norton, 1933 [1871]), p. 157.

34. Ibid., pp. 598–599.

35. Ibid., p. 586. On the importance of this ordeal of mutual self-disclosure in the dynamics of intimacy, see Lystra, *Searching the Heart*, chaps. 2 and 6.

36. Ibid., p. 588.

37. Ibid., p. 586.

38. Ibid., p. 600.

39. Ibid., p. 636.

40. Maud, *Diary*, ed. Richard L. Strout (New York: Macmillan, 1939).

41. Ibid., p. 108.

42. Ibid.

43. Ibid., p. 113.

44. Ibid., p. 202.

45. Ibid., p. 114.

46. Ibid.

47. Ibid., p. 203.

48. Ibid., p. 202.

49. Carroll Smith-Rosenberg, "The Female World of Love and Ritual." My focus is on intimate relations between women. Some research suggests that there are strong parallels in relations between men. Anthony Rotundo's research points to the existence of "romantic friendships" between men. Yet, in contrast to relations between women, intimacies between men were apparently confined to one distinct phase in the life cycle—youth. See Rotundo's "Romantic Friendship: Male Intimacy and Middle-Class Youth in the Northern United States, 1800–1930," *Journal of Social History* 23 (Fall 1989); also, see Martin Bauml Duberman, *About Time: Exploring the Gay Past* (New York: A Sea Horse Book, 1986), and Jonathan Katz, *Gay/Lesbian Almanac* (New York: Harper & Row, 1983).

50. Smith-Rosenberg, "The Female World," p. 55.

51. Ibid., p. 56.

52. Ibid.

53. Lillian Faderman, *Surpassing the Love of Men* (New York: Morrow, 1981), p. 161.

54. *The Making of A Feminist: Early Journals and Letters of M. Carey Thomas*, ed. Marjorie H. Dobkin (Ohio: Kent State University Press, 1979).

55. Smith-Rosenberg, "The Female World," p. 61.

56. Ibid., p. 60.

57. The view that Victorian men and women occupied separate spheres and roles which led to formal gender relations has been challenged by, among others, Carl Degler, *At Odds* (New York: Oxford University Press, 1980; Peter Gay, *The Bourgeois Experience*, vol. 2, *The Tender Passion* (New York: Oxford University Press, 1986); and Ellen Rothman, *Hands and Hearts* (Cambridge, Mass.: Harvard University Press, 1987). For an overview of this discussion, see Linda Kerber, "Separate Spheres, Female Worlds, Woman's Place: The Rhetoric of Woman's History," *Journal of American History* 75 (June 1988).

58. Faderman, *Surpassing the Love of Men*, p. 159.

59. Nancy Sahli, "Smashing: Women's Relationships Before the Fall," *Chrysalis* 8 (1979), p. 26.

60. Quoted in Smith-Rosenberg, "The Female World," p. 74.

61. Quoted in Faderman, *Surpassing the Love of Men*, p. 160.

62. *Early Journals and Letters of M. Carey Thomas*, p. 229.

63. Quoted in Lerner, *The Female Experience*, p. 94.

64. *Elizabeth Cody Stanton as Revealed in Her Letters, Diary, and Reminiscences*, ed. T. Stanton and H. Stanton Blatch (New York: Harper & Row, 1922), vol. 2, p. 156.

65. Peter Gay, *The Tender Passion*, p. 219.

66. Discussions of a spiritual and moral notion of womanhood can be found in Barbara Welter "The Cult of True Womanhood: 1820–1860" in *The American Family in Social-Historical Perspective*, ed. Michael Gordon, 3d ed. (New York: St. Martin's Press, 1983); Jan Lewis, "Mother's Love: The Construction of an Emotion in Nineteenth-Century America," in *Social History and Issues in Human Consciousness*, ed. Andrew Baines and Peter Stearns (New York: New York University Press, 1989). Among these historians who argue that women voluntarily adopted the spiritual and moral definition of womanhood as a way to enhance their power are Carl Degler, *At Odds* and Nancy Cott, *The Bonds of Womanhood* (New Haven: Yale

University Press, 1977). Those historians who highlight the coercive or male imposed character on this female gender identity are, for example, Mary Ryan, *Womanhood in America* (New York: New Viewpoints, 1975) and Barbara Ehrenreich and Deidre English, *For Her Own Good* (New York: Doubleday, 1979).

67. See Rothman, *Hands and Hearts*, part 2, and Lystra, *Searching the Heart*, chap. 6.

68. Maud, *Diary*, p. 202. Women's ambivalence toward marriage was reinforced by Victorian didactic and advice literature which frequently depicted the dark side of marriage. This ambivalence was heightened by women's literature which often spoke of the possibilities of self development, doing good deeds and independence as a single woman. See Lee Virginia Chambers-Schiller, *Liberty, A Better Husband* (New Haven: Yale University Press, 1984).

69. (New York: 308.

70. Elizabeth Cody Stanton, "Address, First Annual Meeting of the Woman's State Temperance Society, Rochester, N.Y., June 1, 1857," in *The Concise History of Woman Suffrage*, ed. Mari Jo and Paul Buhle (Urbana: University of Illinois Press, 1978), p. 175.

71. Sarah Grimké, "Marriage," pp. 95–96.

72. Nancy Cott, "Passionlessness: An Interpretation of Victorian Sexual Ideology, 1790–1850," *Signs* 4 (1979).

73. Charles Rosenberg, "Sexuality, Class and Role in 19th-Century America," *American Quarterly* 25 (May 1973), p. 137.

74. Gay, *The Tender Passion*, p. 50.

75. Leslie Wheeler (ed.), *Loving Warriors: Selected Letters of Lucy Stone and Henry B. Blackwell, 1853–1893* (New York: Dial Press, 1981), pp. 155–156.

76. Richard Sewall (ed.), *The Lyman Letters* (Amherst, Mass.: University of Massachusetts Press, 1965), p. 39.

77. J. Marion Sims, *The Story of My Life* (New York: De Capo Press, 1968) p. 397.

78. This is a point emphasized by Steven Marcus, *The Other Victorian* (New York: Basic Books, 1964). See also G. J. Barker-Benfield, "The Spermatic Economy," *Feminist Studies* 1 (Summer 1972).

79. Cf. Stephen Nissenbaum, *Sex, Diet and Debility in Jacksonian America* (Westport, Conn.: Greenwood Press, 1980); Jayme Sokolow, *Eros and Modernization: Sylvester Graham, Health Reform, and the Origins of Victorian Sexuality in America* (Rutherford, N.J.: Farleigh Dickenson University Press, 1983); Michel Foucault, *The History of Sexuality*, vol. 1, *An Introduction* (New York: Vintage, 1980).

80. See, for example, Marcus, *The Other Victorians;* David Pivar, *Purity Crusade, Sexual Morality and Social Control, 1868–1900* (Westport, Conn.: Greenwood Press, 1973); William Sanger, *The History of Prostitution* (New York: American Medical Press, 1895 [1858]).

81. Pivar, *Purity Crusade*, p. 57.

82. See, for example, D'Emilio and Freedman, *Intimate Matters;* Walter Kendrick, *The Secret Museum* (New York: Viking/Penguin, 1987); Pivar, *Purity Crusade;* Mark Connelly, *The Response to Prostitution in the Progressive Era* (Chapel Hill: University of North Carolina Press, 1980); Paul Boyer, *Purity in Print: The Vice-Society Movement and Book Censorship in America* (New York: Scribner's 1968); Linda

Gordon, *Woman's Body, Woman's Rights: A Social History of Birth Control in America* (New York: Grossman, 1976).

CHAPTER 3

1. See, for example, Elaine Tyler May, *Great Expectations: Marriage and Divorce in Post-Victorian America* (Chicago: University of Chicago Press, 1980); James McGovern, "The American Women's Pre–World War I Freedom in Manners and Morals," in *Our American Sisters*, ed. Jean Friedman and William Shade (Boston: Allyn and Bacon, 1973); John Burnham, "The Progressive Era Revolution in American Attitudes Toward Sex," *Journal of American History* 59 (March 1973). For attempts to relate the discussion of sexuality to a crisis in intimate life, see James Reed, *From Private Vice to Public Virtue* (New York: Basic Books, 1978), 54, and Barbara Epstein, "Family, Sexual Morality, and Popular Movements in Turn-of-the-Century America," in *Powers of Desire: The Politics of Sexuality*, ed. Ann Snitow et al. (New York: Monthly Review Press, 1983).

2. Agnes Repplier, "The Repeal of Reticence," *Atlantic Monthly Review* 113 (1916).

3. See Jeffrey Weeks, *Sexuality and Its Discontents* (London: Routledge and Kegan Paul, 1985). Sheila Ronbotham and Jeffrey Weeks, *Socialism and the New Life* (London: Pluto Press, 1977).

4. Robert Wiebe, *The Search for Order, 1877–1920* (New York: Hill and Wang, 1967). Cf. Gilman Ostrander, *American Civilization in the First Machine Age: 1890–1940* (New York: Harper & Row, 1970) and Louis Galambos and Joseph Pratt, *The Rise of the Corporate Commonwealth* (New York: Basic Books, 1988).

5. Stuart Ewen, *Captains of Consciousness: Advertising and the Social Roots of Consumer Culture* (New York: McGraw-Hill, 1976). T. J. Jackson Lears, "From a Salvation to Self-Realization: Advertising and the Therapeutic Roots of the Consumer Culture, 1880–1930," in *The Culture of Consumption*, ed. R. W. Fox and T. J. Jackson Lears (New York: Pantheon, 1985). T. J. Jackson Lears, *No Place of Grace* (New York: Pantheon, 1981); Roland Marchand, *Advertising the American Dream* (Berkeley: University of California Press, 1986); Warren Susman, *Culture as History: The Transformation of American Society in the Twentieth Century* (New York: Pantheon, 1984).

6. See, for example, Peter Carroll and David Noble, *The Free and the Unfree* (New York: Penguin, 1977), pp. 271–272.

7. Alfred Kinsey et al., *Sexual Behavior in the Human Female* (Philadelphia: W. B. Saunders, 1953), p. 300.

8. *Ibid.*, 331.

9. G. V. Hamilton, *A Research in Marriage* (New York: Lear, 1948), p. 120.

10. Robert Latou Dickinson and Lura Beam, *A Thousand Marriages: A Medical Study of Sex Adjustment* (Baltimore: The Williams and Wilkins Co., 1932), p. 443–444.

11. See, for example, Carl Degler, *At Odds* (New York: Oxford University Press, 1980), pp. 376–377.

12. Elaine Tyler May, *Great Expectations*, p. 51.

13. Degler, *At Odds*, p. 384.

14. William Henry Chafe, *The American Woman* (New York: Oxford University Press, 1972), pp. 89–90.

15. Ibid.

16. See, for example, Mabel Newcomer, *A Century of Higher Education for American women* (New York: Harper, 1959), p. 46.

17. Chafe, *The American Woman*, p. 60.

18. See Carroll Smith-Rosenberg, *Disorderly Conduct* (New York: Oxford University Press, 1985). Also see Jill Conway, "Women Reformers and American Culture, 1870–1930" *Journal of Social History* 5 (Winter 1971).

19. Smith-Rosenberg, *Disorderly Conduct*, p. 253.

20. Mary Ryan, *Womanhood in America* (New York: New Viewpoints, 1975), p. 236.

21. Joseph Kirk Folsom, *The Family* (New York: John Wiley & Sons, 1934), p. 417.

22. Hamilton, *A Research in Marriage*, p. 496.

23. Katherine Bement Davis, *Factors in the Sex Life of Twenty-two Hundred Women* (New York: Harper & Brothers, 1929), p. 247.

24. Ibid., pp. 247–248.

25. Ibid., p. 254.

26. On the link between the growing empowerment of women and the homosexual threat to marriage and the family, see Lisa Duggan, "The Social Enforcement of Heterosexuality and Lesbian Resistance in the 1920s," in *Class, Race and Sex: The Dynamics of Control*, ed. Amy Swerdlow and Hanna Lessinger (Boston: G. K. Hall, 1983); Rayna Rapp and Ellen Ross, "The Twenties Backlash: Compulsory Heterosexuality, The Consumer Family, and the Waning of Feminism," in *Powers of Desire*. Christina Simmons, "Companionate Marriage and the Lesbian Threat," *Frontiers* 4 (Fall 1979); Carroll Smith-Rosenberg, "The New Woman as Androgyne: Social Disorder and Gender Crisis; 1870–1936," in *Disorderly Conduct;* Nancy Sahli, "Smashing: Women's Relationships Before the Fall," *Chrysalis* 8 (1979). Women's changing social position has been also linked to a crisis in masculinity. See Michael Kimmel, "The Contemporary 'Crisis' of Masculinity in Historical Perspective," in *The Making of Masculinities*, ed. Harry Brod (Boston: Allen & Unwin, 1987) and Joe Dubbert, "Progressivism and the Masculinity Crisis," in *The American Man*, ed. E. Pleck and J. Pleck (Englewood Cliffs, N.J.: Prentice-Hall, 1980). Although many men reacted defensively to women's challenge to a Victorian gender system, some men rallied behind women and became ardent feminists. See the Kimmel essay, as well as William Leach, *True Love and Perfect Union* (New York: Basic Books, 1980) and S. Strauss, *Traitors to the Masculine Cause* (Westport, Conn.: Greenwood Press, 1983).

27. McGovern, "The American Woman's Pre–World War I Freedom," p. 242.

28. Lewis Erenberg, *Steppin' Out: New York Nightlife and the Transformation of American Culture, 1890–1930* (Westport, Conn.: Greenwood Press, 1981), p. 114. Also see Larry May, *Screening out the Past: The Birth of Mass Culture and the Motion Picture Industry* (New York: Oxford University Press, 1980); Alice Marquis, *Hopes and Ashes: The Birth of Modern Times, 1929–1939* (New York: Free Press, 1986); for a parallel analysis of working-class youth, see Kathy Peiss, " 'Charity Girls' and City Pleasures: Historical Notes on Working Class Sexuality, 1880–1920," in *Powers of Desire*.

29. See Erenberg, *Steppin' Out; * Ostrander, *American Civilization in the First Machine Age*.

30. See Paula Fass, *The Damned and the Beautiful* (New York: Oxford University Press, 1977); Ellen Rothman, *Hands and Hearts;* and Elaine May, *Great Expectations.*

31. Alfred Kinsey, *Sexual Behavior in the Human Female*, pp. 298–299, 392–400. Also see Edwin O. Smigel and Rita Seiden, "The Decline and Fall of the Double Standard," in *Our American Sisters*, ed. Jean Friedman and William Shade (New York: Allyn and Bacon, 1973).

32. Some contemporary feminist historians have emphasized that this turn to a new style of sexuality was not a form of gender rebellion but a diversion from the evolving radical politics of the women's movement in the pre–World War I period. These women's preoccupation with sexuality left intact the structural sources of gender injustice; moreover, the sexualization of femininity became a new basis of male social control. Women are defined primarily by their sexual attractiveness and their competence in giving and receiving sexual pleasure. See, for example, Mary Ryan, *Womanhood in America*, pp. 258–265. Also see the interesting essay by Christina Simmons, "Modern Sexuality and the Myth of Victorian Repression," in *Passion and Power: Sexuality in History*, ed. Kathy Peiss and Christina Simmons (Philadelphia: Temple University Press, 1989). While not wishing to dispute the politically ambiguous meaning of this phenomenon, I would press the point that the de-eroticization of female sexuality and the absence of sexual choice is one aspect of the denial of women's autonomy. When women challenge traditional masculine privileges, regardless of whether it is in the economic, political or sexual sphere, it is a serious form of gender rebellion.

33. William O'Neill, *Divorce in the Progressive Era* (New Haven: Yale University Press, 1967), p. 20.

34. Ernest Groves and William Ogburn, *American Marriage and Family Relationships* (New York: Henry Holt, 1928), p. 127. Also see Robert and Helen Lynd, *Middletown* (New York: Harcourt, Brace, 1929), p. 121.

35. For general overviews of this discussion, see O'Neill, *Divorce in the Progressive Era;* Fall, *The Damned and the Beautiful*, and Christina Simmons, "Marriage in the Modern Manner: Sexual Radicalism and Reform in America, 1914–1941" (Ph.D. diss.: Brown University, 1982).

36. On the sex education movement, see John Burnham, "The Progressive Era" and Bryan Strong, "Ideas of the Early Sex Education Movement in America, 1890–1920," *History of Education Quarterly*, Summer 1972.

37. Cf. Fass, *The Damned and the Beautiful*, pp. 75–79; Rothman, *Hands and Hearts*, pp. 242, 267–268.

38. Joseph Kirk Folsom, *The Family* (New York: John Wiley & Sons, 1934), p. 408.

39. See, for example, Robert Bell, *Premarital Sex in a Changing Society* (Englewood Cliffs, N.J.: Prentice-Hall, 1966); Winston Ehrmann, *Premarital Dating Behavior* (New York: Henry Holt, 1959); Ira Reiss, *Premarital Sexual Standards in America* (Glencoe, Ill.: Free Press, 1960).

40. Ernest Groves, *Marriage* (New York: Henry Holt, 1933), pp. 3–4.

41. Marie Carmichael Stopes, *Married Love* (London: Putnam, 1931 [1918]), p. xiii.

42. Alice Stockham, *Karezza* (Chicago: Leonidas, 1896), p. 75.

43. Isabel E. Hutton, *The Sex Technique in Marriage*, 3d ed. (New York: Emerson Books, 1932), p. 26.

44. Rachelle T. Yarros, *Modern Women and Sex: A Feminist Physician Speaks* (New York: The Vanguard Press, 1933), p. 12.

45. Robert Street, *Modern Sex Techniques*, (New York: Lancer Books, 1959), p. 187.

46. Theodore Van de Velde, *Ideal Marriage: Its Physiogomy and Technique* (Westport, Conn.: Greenwood Press, 1950 [1930]), p. 6.

47. Margaret Sanger, *Happiness in Marriage* (New York: Blue Ribbon Books, 1926), p. 17.

48. Wilfrid Lay, *A Plea for Monogamy* (New York: Boni and Liveright, 1923), p. 3.

49. H. W. Long, *Sane Sex Life and Sane Sex Living* (New York: Eugenics Publishing Co., 1919), p. 16.

50. Van de Velde, *Ideal Marriage*, pp. 3–4.

51. M. J. Exner, *The Sexual Side of Marriage* (New York: W. W. Norton, 1932), pp. 19–20.

52. Hannah Stone and Abraham Stone, *A Marriage Manual* (New York: Simon and Schuster, 1939), pp. 114, 188. Cf. Oliver Butterfield, *Sexual Harmony in Marriage* (New York: Emerson Books, 1953), p. 22.

53. Hutton, *The Sex Technique in Marriage*, p. 26.

54. L. T. Woodward, *Sophisticated Sex Techniques in Marriage* (New York: Lancer Books, 1967), p.

55. Van de Velde, *Ideal Marriage*, p. 3.

56. Thurman Rice, *The Age of Romance* (Chicago: American Medical Association, 1933), p. 43.

57. Esther Tietz and Charles Weichert, *The Art and Science of Marriage* (New York: Wittlesey House, 1938), p. 5.

58. Maxine Davis, *Sexual Responsibilities in Marriage* (New York: Dial Press, 1963), p. 24.

59. Alice Stockham, *Karezza*, p. 78.

60. Exner, *The Sexual Side of Marriage*, p. 173.

61. See for example, Ernest Groves, *Marriage*, p. 10.

62. Davis, *Sexual Responsibilities in Marriage*, p. 20.

63. Van de Velde, *Ideal Marriage*, pp. 5–6, 16–17.

64. Yarros, *Modern Women and Sex*, p. 74.

65. Davis, *Sexual Responsibilities in Marriage*, p. 27.

66. Ibid., p. 33.

67. Mary S. Calderone, *Release from Sexual Tensions* (New York: Random House, 1960), p. 166.

68. Tietz and Weichart, *The Art and Science of Marriage*, p. 7.

69. Exner, *The Sexual Side of Marriage*, pp. 19–20.

70. Sanger, *Happiness in Marriage*, p.

71. Marie Carmichael Stopes, *Enduring Passion* (London: G. P. Putnam's Sons, 1929 [1928]), p. 22.

72. Hutton, *The Sex Technique in Marriage*, p. 26. Cf. Sanger, *Happiness in Marriage*, p. 107.

73. Long, *Sane Sex Life*, p. 56.

74. Stopes, *Enduring Passion*, p. 19.

75. Hannah and Abraham Stone, *A Marriage Manual*, p. 303.

76. Ibid., p. 203.

77. Ibid., p. 204. My emphasis.

78. Van de Velde, *Ideal Marriage*, p. 6.

79. Ibid.

80. Ibid., p. 17.

81. Eustare Chesser, *Love without Fear: How to Achieve Sex Happiness in Marriage* (New York: Roy Publishers, 1947 [1940]), p. 82.

82. Long, *Sane Sex Life*, p. 44. Cf. Helen Wright, *The Sex Factor in Marriage* (New York: The Vanguard Press, 1938), pp. 80–81.

83. Long, *Sane Sex Life*, p. 144.

84. W. F. Robie, *The Art of Love* (Boston: The Gorham Press, 1921), p. 124.

85. William Lee Howard, *Sex Problems Solved* (New York: Edward J. Clode, 1915), p. 5.

86. Exner, *The Sexual Side of Marriage*, p. 161. Cf. Sanger, *Happiness in Marriage*, p. 19; Wright, *The Sex Factor in Marriage*, pp. 80–81.

87. William Robinson, *Woman: Her Sex and Love Life*, 17th ed. (New York: Eugenics Publishing Co., 1929 [1917]), p. 368. My emphasis.

88. Groves, *Marriage*, p. 264.

89. Davis, *Sexual Responsibilities in Marriage*, p. 27.

90. Ibid., p. 33.

91. Ibid., pp. 97–98.

92. Ibid., pp. 20, 26.

93. Ibid., p. 20.

94. Robinson, *Woman*, p. 363.

95. Ibid., p. 365.

96. Butterfield, *Sexual Harmony in Marriage*, p. 22.

97. Chesser, *Love without Fear*, p. 104.

98. Robert Chartham, *Sex for Advanced Lovers* (New York: New American Library, 1970), p. 9.

99. Robinson, *Woman*, p. 363.

100. Woodward, *Sophisticated Sex Techniques in Marriage*, p. 11.

101. Davis, *Sexual Responsibilities in Marriage*, p. 184.

102. Van de Velde, *Ideal Marriage*, p. 124.

103. Stopes, *Enduring Passion*, pp. 16–17.

104. Chesser, *Love without Fear*, p. 84.

105. Van de Velde, *Ideal Marriage*, p. 15.

106. Ibid., p. 17.

107. Hutton, *The Sex Technique in Marriage*, p. 47.

108. Hannah and Abraham Stone, *A Marriage Manual*, p. 218. Cf. Elizabeth and Forrester MacDonald, *Homemaking* (Boston: Marshall Jones Co., 1927), p. 49.

109. Ibid., p. 217.

110. Davis, *Sexual Responsibilities in Marriage*, p. 110.

111. Ibid., p. 118.

112. Van de Velde, *Ideal Marriage*, p. 126.

113. Hannah and Abraham Stone, *A Marriage Manual*, p. 77.

114. Hutton, *The Sex Technique in Marriage*, p. 76.

115. To be sure, gender Victorian gender roles persisted, e.g., men were expected to initiate sex, their satisfaction was defined as more essential for their happiness than it was for women's, men were still viewed as more lustful. On the persistence of Victorian gender codes in the twentieth century, see Peter Gabriel Filene, *Him/Her/Self: Sex Roles in Modern America* (New York: New American Library, 1974).

116. Hannah and Abraham Stone, *A Marriage Manual*, p. 215. Cf. Lena Levine, *The Doctor Talks with the Bride* (New York: Planned Parenthood, 1938), p. 6.

117. Exner, *The Sexual Side of Marriage*, p. 97; Long, *Sane Sex Life*, p. 136.

118. Tietz and Weichart, *The Art and Science of Marriage*, p. 37.

119. Robie, *The Art of Love*, p. 104. Sanger. *Happiness in Marriage*, pp. 139–140.

120. Sanger, *Happiness in Marriage*, p. 21.

121. Van de Velde, *Ideal Marriage*, p. 6.

122. Ibid., p. 17.

123. Ibid., p. 101.

124. Ibid., pp. 109–116.

125. Ibid., p. 101.

126. Ibid., p. 178.

127. Ibid., p. 101.

128. Long, *Sane Sex Life*, p. 132. Cf. Wright, *The Sex Factor in Marriage*, p. 86.

129. Hannah and Abraham Stone, *A Marriage Manual*, p. 222.

130. Ibid., p. 271.

131. Calderone, *Release from Sexual Tension*, p. 66. The movement of a medical conception of homosexuality into popular culture is documented by Jonathan Katz, *Gay/Lesbian Almanac* (New York: Harper & Row, 1983). See also Lillian Faderman, "Lesbian Magazine Fiction in the Early Twentieth Century," *Journal of Popular Culture* 11 (Spring 1978).

132. See, for example, Sahlie, "Smashing" and Smith-Rosenberg, "The New Women as Androgyne" in *Disorderly Conduct*.

133. Hannah and Abraham Stone, *A Marriage Manual*, p. 301.

134. Van de Velde, *Ideal Marriage*.

135. Ibid., p. 235.

136. Wright, *The Sex Factor in Marriage*, p. 98.

137. Sanger, *Happiness in Marriage*, p. 14.

138. Ben Lindsey and Wainwright Evans, *The Companionate Marriage* (New York: Boni & Liveright, 1927), p. 65.

CHAPTER 4

1. See, for example, Peter Filene, *Him/Her/Self* (New York: New American Library, 1974).

2. See Elaine Tyler May, *Great Expectations* (Chicago: University of Chicago Press, 1980).

3. Hutchins Hapgood, *A Victorian in the Modern World* (New York: Harcourt, Brace Company, 1939). Cf. Catherine Drinker Bowen, *Family Portrait* (Boston: Little, Brown, 1970).

4. Helen Bevington, *Charley Smith's Girl: A Memoir* (New York: Simon and Schuster, 1965), p. 184. Cf. Olive Clapper, *One Lucky Woman* (New York: Doubleday, 1961).

5. See, for example, Floyd Dell, *Homecoming* (New York: Farrar & Rinehart, 1933), p. 18, and Raymond Fosdick, *Chronicle of a Generation: An Autobiography* (New York: Harper & Row, 1958).

6. See Rheta Dorr, *A Woman of Fifty* (New York: Funk & Wagnalls, 1924); Maud Nathan, *Once Upon a Time and Today* (New York: G. P. Putnam's Sons, 1933); Vida Dutton Scudder, *On Journey* (New York: Dutton, 1937); Lawrence Langner, *The Magic Curtain* (New York: E. P. Dutton & Co., 1951); Edward Weeks, *My Green Age* (Boston: Little, Brown, 1973).

7. Hapgood, *A Victorian in the Modern World*, p. 587.

8. Ibid., p. 588.

9. Henry Seidel Canby, *American Memoir* (Boston: Houghton Mifflin, 1947), p. 81.

10. Ibid.

11. Ibid., pp. 85–86.

12. Clelia Duel Mosher, *The Mosher Survey: Sexual Attitudes of Forty-five Victorian Women*, ed. James Mahood and Kristine Wenburg (New York: Arno Press, 1980).

13. See Carl Degler, *At Odds* (New York: Oxford University Press, 1980), pp. 262–266, and Peter Gay, *The Bourgeois Experience*, vol. 1, *Education of the Senses* (New York: Oxford University Press, 1984), pp. 135–144. A less sanguine view is offered by Rosiland Rosenberg, *Beyond Separate Spheres* (New Haven: Yale University Press, 1982), pp. 181, 197.

14. See Steven Seidman, "Sexual Attitudes of Victorian and Post-Victorian Women: Another Look at the *Mosher Survey*," *Journal of American Studies*, 23 (April 1989).

15. G. V. Hamilton, *A Research in Marriage*, (New York: Lear Publications, 1948).

16. Ibid., p. 60.

17. Ibid.

18. Ibid., p. 66.

19. Ibid., pp. 71–72.

20. Robert Latou Dickinson and Lura Bean, *A Thousand Marriages: A Medical Study of Sex Adjustment* (Baltimore: Williams & Wilkins Co., 1932), p. 442.

21. Ibid., p. 56.

22. Katherine Benent Davis, *Factors in the Sex Life of Twenty-Two Hundred Women* (New York: Harper & Brothers, 1929), p. 38.

23. Alfred Kinsey et al., *Sexual Behavior in the Human Female* (Philadelphia: W. B. Saunders, 1953), p. 392.

24. Ibid., pp. 268, 392–393, 400.

25. Max Eastman, *Enjoyment of Living* (New York: Harper & Row, 1948).

26. Ibid., p. 321.

27. Ibid.

28. Ibid., p. 323.

29. Ibid., p. 324.

30. Ibid.

31. Ibid., p. 353.

32. Ibid., p. 336.

33. Ibid., p. 357.

34. Ibid., p. 358.

35. Ibid., p. 343.

36. Ibid., p. 321.

37. Ibid., p. 343.

38. Ibid., p. 510.

39. Dori Schaffer, *Dear Deedee: From the Diaries of Dori Schaffer* (New Jersey: Lyle Stuart, 1978).

40. Ibid., p. 30.

41. Ibid.

42. Ibid., p. 31.

43. Ibid., p. 43.

44. Ibid., p. 90.

45. Ibid., p. 92.

46. Ibid., p. 93.

47. Ibid., p. 97.

48. Ibid., p. 108.

49. Ibid., p. 133.

50. Ibid.

51. Ibid., p. 142.

52. Ibid., p. 194.

53. Eastman, *Enjoyment of Living*, p. 343.

54. On the feminist argument regarding the historicity of gender, see the fine collection *Woman, Culture and Society*, edited by Michelle Zimbalist Rosaldo and Louise Lamphere (Stanford, Calif.: Stanford University Press, 1974). Especially important are Linda Nicholson's *Gender and History* (New York: Columbia University Press, 1986) and Joan Scott's *Gender and the Politics of History* (New York: Columbia University Press, 1988).

55. On the different gender styles and meanings of love, see Francesca Cancian, *Love in America* (Cambridge: Cambridge University Press, 1987); also see *Changing Boundaries* ed. E. Allgeier and N. McCormick (Palo Alto, Ca.: Mayfield, 1983) and *Sex and Love*, ed. Sue Cartledge and Joann Ryan (London: Women's Press, 1983).

56. Eastman, *Enjoyment of Living*, p. 486.

57. Eastman, *Love and Revolution*, p. 4.

58. Eastman, *Enjoyment of Living*, p. 489.

59. Eastman, *Enjoyment of Living*, p. 487.

60. There is a substantial psychoanalytical literature on this topic. An excellent recent overview of this dynamic from an object-relations perspective is to be found in Nancy Chodorow, *The Reproduction of Mothering* (Berkeley: University of California Press, 1978) and "Oedipal Asymmetries and Heterosexual Knots," *Social Problems* 4 (1976).

61. Ben Hecht, *A Child of the Century* (New York: Simon & Schuster, 1954).

62. Ibid., p. 25.

63. Ibid.

64. Ibid.

65. Ibid., p. 24.

66. Ibid., p. 25.

67. Ibid., p. 24.

68. Hutchins Hapgood, *The Story of a Lover* (New York: Boni and Liveright, 1919). Also see Neith Boyce and Hutchins Hapgood, "Enemies," in *The Provincetown Plays*, ed. George Cram Cook and Frank Shay (Cincinnati: Stewart Kidd Company, 1921).

69. Edgar Lee Masters, *Across Spoon River* (New York: Farrar & Rinehart, 1936), p. 248.

70. Ibid.

71. Max Eastman, *Love and Revolution* (New York: Random House, 1964), p. 112.

72. Hecht, *A Child of the Century*, p. 21. See also Dell Floyd's *Homecoming*, where the quest for sexual adventure seems closely related to the wish for individual separateness and autonomy.

73. Masters, *Across Spoon River*, p. 230.

74. Ibid., pp. 235–240.

75. See, for example, Gussie Kimball, *Gitele* (New York: Vantage Press, 1960).

76. Rose Talbot, *No Greater Challenge* (New York: Vantage Press, 1955), p. 58.

77. Ibid., p. 59.

78. Ibid., p. 69.

79. E.g. Ursula Greenshaw Mandel, *I Live My Life* (New York: Exposition Press, 1965).

80. Hortense Odlum, *A Woman's Place* (New York: Charles Scribner's Sons, 1939), p. 45.

81. Ibid., p. 45.

82. Agnes Meyer, *Out of These Roots* (New York: Arno Press, 1980 [1965]), p. 98.

83. Richard Drinnon and Anna Drinnon (eds.), *Nowhere at Home: Letters from Exile of*

Emma Goldman and Alexander Berkman (New York: Schocken Books, 1975), p. 133.

84. Dori Schaffer, *Dear Deedee*, p. 98.

85. Ibid., p. 90.

86. Ibid.

87. Ibid., p. 100.

88. Ibid., p. 108.

89. Ibid., p. 134.

90. Ibid., p. 181.

91. Fannie Hurst, *Anatomy of Me* (New York: Doubleday, 1958), p. 105.

92. Ibid., p. 224.

93. Ibid., pp. 272–273. Cf. Helen Hull, *Labyrinth* (New York: Macmillan, 1923).

94. See Lillian Fadermann, *Surpassing the Love of Men* (New York: Morrow, 1981) and Carroll Smith-Rosenberg "The New Woman as Androgyne: Social Disorder and Gender Crisis: 1870–1936," in *Disorderly Conduct* (New York: Oxford University Press, 1985). George Chauncey, Jr., "From Sexual Inversion to Homosexuality: Medicine and the Changing Conceptualization of Female Deviance," *Salmagundi* 58–59 (Fall–Winter 1983).

95. On the scientific-medical discourse on homosexuality, see Michel Foucault, *The History of Sexuality, vol. 1, An Introduction* (New York: Random House, 1980); David Greenberg, *The Construction of Homosexuality* (Chicago: University of Chicago Press, 1988), and Jeffrey Weeks, *Sexuality and Its Discontents* (London: Routledge & Kegan Paul, 1985); Michael Lynch, " 'Here Is Adhesiveness': From Friendship to Homosexuality," *Victorian Studies* 29 (Autumn 1985). For an interesting analysis of the social prominence of a science of sex in this period, see Lawrence Birken, *Consuming Desire* (Ithaca: Cornell University Press, 1988).

96. Documentation of the penetration of the scientific-medical image of homosexuality into popular culture is provided by Jonathan Katz, *Gay/Lesbian Almanac* (New York: Harper & Row, 1983). Also see note 94.

97. Of course, not all same-gender eroticism and intimacy in all groups were similarly affected. Evidence shows that working-class men and women, in particular, but also some middle-class people, drew on more local, folk traditions and images to define their desires and behavior in ways that differed significantly from the medical model. See, for example, George Chauncey, Jr., "Christian Brotherhood or Sexual Perversion? Homosexual Identities and the Construction of Sexual Boundaries in the World War One Era," *Journal of Social History* 9 (1985). Also, see the unpublished study cited by Vern Bullough and Bonnie Bullough in "Lesbianism in the 1920s and 1930s: A New Found Study," *Signs* 2 (Summer 1977).

98. See Foucault, *The History of Sexuality*, p. 43; Jeffrey Weeks, *Sex, Politics and Society* (New York: Longman, 1981), pp. 96–121. Although Greenberg agrees with this analysis, he challenges the claim made by Foucault and Weeks that homosexuality became self-defining only with its medicalization. See Greenberg, *The Construction of Homosexuality*, pp. 301–346.

99. Mary Maclane, *The Story of Mary Maclane* (Chicago: Herbert S. Stone, 1902), p. 38.

100. Ibid., p. 39.

101. Ibid., p. 41.

102. Mary Maclane, *I, Mary Maclane* (New York: Frederick A. Stokes Co., 1917).

103. Ibid., p. 276.

104. Ibid., The problematicization of female intimacy can be seen in two novels: Harvey O'Higgins, *Julie Cane* (New York: Harper & Brothers, 1924) and Rose Franken, *Intimate Story* (New York: Doubleday, 1955).

105. Wanda Fraiken, *Neff, We Sing Diana* (New York: Houghton Mifflin, 1928), p. 105.

106. Ibid., p. 57.

107. Ibid., p. 199.

108. Ibid.

109. Charlotte Armstrong, *The Unsuspected* (New York: Coward-McCann, 1945).

110. Ibid., p. 38.

111. Ibid., p. 52.

112. Ibid., p. 93.

113. Ibid.

114. Ibid.

115. Ibid., pp. 94–95.

116. Ibid., p. 95.

117. Ibid., p. 153.

118. Ibid., p. 190.

119. Ibid., p. 161.

120. Diana Frederics, *Diana: A Strange Autobiography* (New York: Arno Press, 1975 [1939]). Compare the diary of the political analyst and writer Dorothy Thompson, excerpts of which can be found in Jonathan Katz, *Gay American History* (New York: Harper & Row, 1976), pp. 556–562.

121. Ibid., p. 18.

122. Ibid., p. 19.

123. Ibid., p. 21.

124. Ibid., p. xi.

125. Ibid., p. 63.

126. Ibid., p. 69.

127. Ibid., p. 79.

128. Ibid., p. 80.

129. Ibid., p. 81.

130. Ibid., p. 82.

131. Ibid., p. 110.

132. Ibid.

133. Ibid., p. 113.

134. Ibid., p. 114.

135. Ibid., p. 196.

136. Ibid., p. 197. The negative side of lesbian love is chronicled in the novels of Gale

Wilhelm, especially *Torchlight to Valhalla* (New York: Random House, 1975 [1938]) and *We Too Are Drifting* (New York: Random House, 1975 [1935]). The classic text in this regard is Radclyffe Hall, *The Well of Loneliness* (New York: Pocket Books, 1975 [1975]). See Lillian Faderman, "Radclyffe Hall and the Lesbian Image," *Conditions* 1, (April 1977).

137. Ibid., p. 158.

138. Ibid.

139. Ibid., p. 219.

140. Cf. Diane Hames, " 'I Am a Woman': Ann Bannon and the Writing of Lesbian Identity in the 1950s," in *Lesbian and Gay Writing*, ed. Mark Lilly (Philadelphia: Temple University Press, 1990). Jeff Weinstein, "In Praise of Pulp: Bannon's Lusty Lesbians," *Voice Literary Supplement* no. 20 (Oct. 1983).

141. Ann Bannon, *Odd Girl Out* (New York: Arno Press, 1975 [1957]).

142. Ibid., p. 14.

143. Ibid., pp. 54–55.

144. Ann Bannon, *I Am a Woman* (New York: Arno Press, 1975 [1959]).

145. Ibid., p. 92.

146. Ibid.

147. Ibid., p. 105.

148. Ibid., p. 137.

149. Ibid.

150. Ann Bannon, *Women in the Shadows* (New York: Arno Press, 1975 [1959]).

151. Ibid., p. 8.

152. Ibid., p. 22.

153. Ibid., p. 3.

154. See, for example, Diana Frederics, *Diana: A Strange Autobiography;* Mary Casal, *The Stone Wall* (New York: Arno Press, 1975 [1930]); also, see the essays collected in *Carol in a Thousand Cities*, ed. Ann Aldrich (Greenwich, Conn.: Fawcett, 1960).

155. See note 94. Also, Rayan Rapp and Ellen Ross, "The Twenties Backlash: Compulsory Heterosexuality, the Consumer Family, and the Waning of Feminism," in *Class, Race and Sex*, ed. Amy Swerdlow and Hanna Lessinger (Boston: G. K. Hall, 1983) and Lisa Duggan, "The Social Enforcement of Heterosexuality and Lesbian Resistance in the 1920s," in *Class, Race and Sex.*

156. See Katz, *Gay/Lesbian Almanac*, pp. 213–214, 219, 235, 258, 294, 299, 327. Cf. Chauncey, "Christian Brotherhood of Sexual Perversion."

157. Foucault, *The History of Sexuality*. Cf. John D'Emilio, *Sexual Politics, Sexual Communities* (Chicago, University of Chicago Press, 1983).

158. See, for example, Paul Fass, *The Damned and the Beautiful* (New York: Oxford University Press, 1977); Ellen Rothman, *Hands and Hearts* (Cambridge: Harvard University Press, 1987); Robert and Helen Lynd, *Middletown* (New York: Harcourt, Brace, 1929); Robert Bell, *Premarital Sex in a Changing Society* (Englewood Cliffs, N.J.: Prentice-Hall, 1966); Ira Reiss, *Premarital Sex Standards in America* (New York: Free Press, 1960).

CHAPTER 5

1. See the recently released 1970 Kinsey Institute sponsored survey *Sex and Morality in the U.S.* by Albert Klassen, Colin Williams and Eugene Levitt (Middletown, Conn.: Wesleyan University Press, 1989), chap. 1. The authors dissent from the view proposed here. "Our data have shown that the patterns of sexual morality in the United States in 1970 tended to be quite conservative. The findings do not support the contention that a 'Sexual-Revolution' had occurred in 1970. . . . They do suggest a continuity in sexual norms that appears remarkable in its consistency and persistence" (p. 267). This conclusion, however, can be challenged in at least two ways. First, the survey is biased towards this conclusion. For example, 90 percent of the respondents were married or had been married at the time of the survey. Similarly, the authors do not isolate the sexual attitudes of the generation born after 1945. The general category they use, "under 35," does not adequately capture the changes among the youth who came of age in 1970. Second, the data does not really support the conclusion of continuity in sexual morality. For example, 45.7 percent of the respondents said they felt they were more approving of premarital and extramarital sex than their parents; 25 percent of them said they were more approving of same-sex intimate behavior than their parents (p. 20). When one compares the responses of those "under 35" with those respondents "65 and older," the younger generation is substantially more liberal. Whereas 50.3 percent of the younger generation say prostitution is always wrong, 71.5 percent of the older generation say this. Again, whereas 24.9 percent of the younger generation say premarital sex by teenage boys in love is always wrong, the figure for the older population is 51.5 percent. In short, along virtually every key dimension of sexual behavior, the younger respondents are much more liberal than the older ones (pp. 25–27). Had the authors isolated the attitudes of the young (under 30) and the single population, their findings would have been even more obviously inconsistent with their conclusion.

2. Paul Gebhard, "Sexuality in the Post-Kinsey Era," in *Changing Patterns of Sexual Behavior*, ed. Wilt C. Arnytage, R. Chester and John Reel (New York: Academic Press, 1980), pp. 47–48.

3. See the essays in *Changing Boundaries*, ed. E. Allgeies and N. McCormick (Palo Alto, Ca.: Mayfield, 1983); Cf. Barbara Ehrenreich, Elizabeth Hess, Gloria Jacobs, *Re-Making Love* (New York: Doubleday, 1987); also see chap. 3.

4. See John D'Emilio, *Sexual Politics, Sexual Communities* (Chicago: University of Chicago Press, 1983). On the concept of a homosexual identity as a historical creation, see Jeffrey Weeks, *Sexuality and Its Discontents* (London: Routledge & Kegan Paul, 1985) and *Sex, Politics and Society* (London: Longman, 1981); Jonathan Katz, "The Invention of the Homosexual, 1880–1950," in *Gay/Lesbian Almanac* (New York: Harper & Row, 1983).

5. D'Emilio, *Sexual Politics*. Also see Dennis Altman, *The Homosexualization of America* (Boston: Beacon Press, 1983), Barry Adam, *The Rise of a Gay and Lesbian Movement* (Boston: Twayne, 1987).

6. On the intersection of commerce and sex in the postwar years, see Dennis Altman, *The Homosexualization of America*, chap. 3; Barbara Ehrenreich and Deirdre English, *For Her Own Good* (New York: Doubleday, 1978), chap. 8.

7. Jeffrey Weeks, *Sexuality and Its Discontents*, p. 25.

8. See, for example, Richard Wightman and T. Jackson Lears (eds.), *The Culture of*

Consumption (New York: Pantheon, 1985); Estelle Freedman and John D'Emilio, *Intimate Matters* (New York: Harper & Row, 1988).

9. Cf. Christopher Lasch, *The Culture of Narcissism* (New York: Norton, 1977). Daniel Scott Smith, "The Dating of the Sexual Revolution: Evidence and Interpretations," in *The American Family in Socio-Historical Perspective*, ed. Michael Gordon (New York: St. Martin's Press, 1973).

10. For example, Herbert Marcuse, *One-Dimensional Man* (Boston: Beacon Press, 1964); Michael Schneider, *Neurosis and Capitalism* (New York: Seabury Press, 1975); Wolfgang Haug, *Commodity Aesthetics, Ideology and Culture* (New York: International, 1985).

11. See Paul Fass, *The Damned and the Beautiful* (New York: Oxford University Press, 1977) and Ellen Rothman, *Hands and Hearts* (Cambridge, Mass.: Harvard University Press, 1987); John Modell, "Dating Becomes the Way of American Youth," in *Essays on the Family and Historical Change*, ed. Leslie Page Moch and Gary Stark (College Station: Texas A&M University Press, 1983); John Modell, "Normative Aspects of American Marriage Timing Since World War II," *Journal of Family History* 5 (1980).

12. See Robert S. and Helen Lynd, *Middletown* (New York: Free Press, 1929); see note 11.

13. See Gerald Marriner, "The Estrangement of the Intellectuals in America: The Search for New Life Styles in the Early Twentieth Century" (Ph.D. diss., University of Colorado, 1972); Christina Simmons, "Marriage in the Modern Manner: Sexual Radicalism and Reform in America, 1914–1941," (Ph.D. diss., Brown University, 1982); Ellen Kay Trimberger, "Feminism, Men, and Modern Love: Greenwich Village, 1900–1925," in *Powers of Desire*, ed. Ann Snitow, Christine Stansell, and Sharon Thompson (New York: Monthly Review Press, 1983).

14. See Kenneth Kenniston, *The Young Radicals* (New York: Harcourt, Brace and World, 1968); Theodore Roszak, *The Counter Culture* (New York: Doubleday, 1969).

15. Alex Comfort (ed.), *The Joy of Sex* (New York: Simon & Schuster, 1970), p. 15.

16. Ibid.

17. David Reuben, *Everything You Always Wanted to Know about Sex (But Were Afraid to Ask)* (New York: Bantam, 1969), p. 4.

18. Ibid., pp. 53–55.

19. Ibid., p. 55.

20. Ibid., p. 58.

21. Alex Comfort (ed.), *More Joy of Sex* (New York: Simon & Schuster, 1977), p. 96.

22. Ibid., p. 97.

23. *The Joy of Sex*, p. 10.

24. Ibid., p. 11.

25. David Reuben, *Everything*, p. 60.

26. "M," *The Sensuous Man* (New York: Dell, 1971), p. 14.

27. Reuben, *Everything*, p. 214.

28. "J," *The Sensuous Women* (New York: Dell, 1969), p. 149.

29. *The Joy of Sex*, p. 13.

30. Ibid., pp. 54–55.

31. Ibid., p. 168.

32. Ibid., p. 169.

33. *More Joy of Sex*, p. 90.

34. *The Joy of Sex*, p. 227.

35. William Masters and Virginia Johnson, *The Pleasure Bond* (Boston: Little, Brown, 1970), p. 23.

36. Ibid., p. 48.

37. *The Joy of Sex*, p. 153.

38. *The Sensuous Man*, p. 180.

39. Ibid., p. 14.

40. Masters and Johnson, *The Pleasure Bond*, p. 15.

41. *The Joy of Sex*, p. 56.

42. Ibid., p. 9.

43. Masters and Johnson, *The Pleasure Bond*, p. 238.

44. Reuben, *Everything*, chap. 8.

45. *The Joy of Sex*, pp. 60, 225, 235.

46. *More Joy of Sex*, p. 68.

47. Irving Bieber et al., *Homosexuality* (New York: Basic Books, 1962). Edmund Berger, *Homosexuality: Disease or Way of Life?* (New York: Hill & Wang, 1956).

48. For a more critical analysis of current sex manuals, see Meryl Altman, "Everything They Always Wanted You to Know: The Ideology of Popular Sex Literature," in *Pleasure and Danger*, ed. Carole Vance (Boston: Routledge & Kegan Paul, 1984); and Rosalind Brunt, "An Immense Verbosity: Permissive Sexual Advice in the 1970s," in *Feminism, Culture and Politics*, ed. R. Brunt and C. Rowan (London: Lawrence and Wishart, 1982).

49. Barbara Ehrenreich, *The Hearts of Men* (New York: Doubleday, 1983).

50. My comments are based on an examination of *Playboy* from its initial appearance in 1953 through the early 1970s.

51. Hugh Hefner, "The Playboy Philosophy," *Playboy* 9 (Dec. 1962), p. 169.

52. Hefner, "The Playboy Philosophy," *Playboy* 10 (Feb. 1963), p. 48.

53. Ibid.

54. Ibid.

55. Ibid.

56. Freedman and D'Emilio, *Intimate Matters*, p. 287.

57. U.S. Commission on Obscenity and Pornography, *The Report of the Commission on Obscenity and Pornography* (New York: Random House, 1970).

58. Ibid., p. 24.

59. Ibid., p. 25.

60. Ibid., p. 58.

61. Ibid., p. 54.

62. Ibid., p. 85.

63. Alan Soble, *Pornography* (New Haven: Yale University Press, 1986), p. 75.

64. Ibid., p. 21.

65. Ibid., p. 95.

66. Ann Barr Snitow, "Mass Market Romance: Pornography for Women Is Different," in *Powers of Desire*, ed Ann Snitow et al (New York: Monthly Review Press, 1983), p. 261.

67. Betty Friedan, *The Feminine Mystique* (New York: Dell, 1963), chap. 11.

68. Ibid., p. 250.

69. Ibid., p. 258.

70. Ibid., p. 253, 265.

71. Kate Millet, *Sexual Politics* (New York: Ballentine, 1978 [1969]), p. 86. For a comprehensive analysis of the diverse strains of early radical feminism, see Alice Echols, *Daring to be Bad* (Minneapolis: University of Minnesota Press, 1989).

72. Shulamith Firestone, *The Dialectic of Sex* (New York: Morrow, 1970).

73. The Boston Women's Health Book Collective, *Our Bodies, Ourselves* (New York: Simon and Schuster, 1971).

74. Kate Millet, *Sexual Politics*, part 3.

75. See Anne Koedt, "The Myth of the Vaginal Orgasm," in *Radical Feminism*, ed Anne Koedt, Ellen Levine and Anita Rapone (New York: Quadrangle, 1973).

76. Andrea Dworkin, "Phallic Imperialism: Why Economic Recovery Will Not Work for Us," *Ms.* 5 (Dec. 1976), p. 101.

77. Ti-Grace Atkinson, *Amazon Odyssey* (New York: Links Books, 1974), p. 86.

78. Dana Densmore, "Independence from the Sexual Revolution," in *Radical Feminism*, pp. 113–114.

79. Ibid., p. 114.

80. Robin Morgan, *Going Too Far* (New York: Random House, 1977), p. 181.

81. Shulamith Firestone, "The Women's Rights Movement in the U.S.; New View," in *Voices from Women's Liberation*, ed Leslie B. Tanner (New York: New American Library, 1971), p. 442.

82. Robin Morgan, "Rights of Passage," *Ms.* 4 (Sept. 1975), p. 75.

83. Sandra Coyner, "Women's Liberation and Sexual Liberation," in *Marriage and Alternatives*, ed. Roger Libby and Robert Whitehurst (Glenview, Ill,: Scott, Foresman, 1977), p. 217.

84. Ibid., p. 221.

85. For an overview of the radical feminist critique of pornography, see Ann Ferguson, "Pleasure, Power, and the Porn Wars," *The Women's Review of Books* 3, no. 8, (May 1986); Deirdre English, "The Politics of Porn," *Mother Jones* April 1980; Paula Webster, "Pornography and Pleasure," *Heresies* 3, no. 12 (May 1981); Donna Turley, "The Feminist Debate on Pornography: An Unorthodox Interpretation," *Socialist Review* 87 (May–August 1986); Ellen Willis, "Feminism, Moralism and Pornography," in *Beginning to See the Light* (New York: Alfred A. Knopf, 1981).

86. Irene Diamond, "Pornography and Regression: A Reconsideration of 'Who' and What," in *Take Back the Night*, ed. Laura Lederer (New York: Morrow, 1980), p. 188.

87. Diana E. H. Russell, "Pornography and the Women's Liberation Movement," in *Take Back the Night*, p. 304.

88. Ibid., p. 314; Laura Lederer, "Introduction," pp. 19–20.

89. Susan Brownmiller, excerpt on pornography from *Against Our Will: Men, Women and Rape*, in *Take Back the Night*, pp. 19–20.

90. Helen Longino, "Pornography, Oppression, and Freedom: A Closer Look," in *Take Back the Night*, p. 42.

91. Beverly LaBell, "The Propaganda of Misogyny," in *Take Back the Night*, p. 176.

92. Beatrice Faust, *Women, Sex and Pornography* (New York: Macmillan, 1980), p. 80.

93. Diana E. H. Russell with Laura Lederer, "Questions We Got Asked Most Often," in *Take Back the Night*, p. 27.

94. Susan Lurie, "Pornography and the Dread of Women: The Male Sexual Dilemma," in *Take Back the Night*, p. 160.

95. Andrea Dworkin, "Why So-called Radical Men Love and Need Pornography," in *Take Back the Night*, p. 152.

96. Kathleen Barry, *Female Sexual Slavery* (New York: New York University Press, 1984), p. 266.

97. Ibid., p. 267.

98. Ibid.

99. Ibid.

100. Ibid., p. 268.

101. Helen Gurley Brown, *Sex and the Single Girl* (New York: Pocket Books, 1962), p. 246.

102. Ibid., p. 4.

103. Ibid., p. 209.

104. Ibid., p. 207.

105. Ingrid Bengis, "Love," *Ms.* (Nov. 1972), p. 66.

106. M. Petchesky, Review of *The Joy of Sex*, *Ms.* Sept. 1973.

107. Barbara Grizzuti Harrison, "Talking Dirty," *Ms.* Oct. 1973, p. 41.

108. Ibid.

109. Robin Morgan, "Rights of Passage, *Ms.* Sept. 1975, p. 75.

110. Andrea Dworkin, "Phallic Imperialism: Why Economic Recovery Will Not Work for Us." *Ms.* Dec. 1976, p. 101.

111. Robin Morgan, "How to Run Pornography Out of Town," *Ms.* Nov. 1978, p. 55.

112. Edna O'Brien, "Live for the Moment . . . or at least for the Night: A Defense of the Brief Encounter," *Cosmopolitan*, Dec. 1967, p. 68.

113. Alma Birk, "The Sexual Drive in Women (Greater, Equal, or Inferior to Men's?)," *Cosmopolitan*, Feb. 1968, p. 72.

114. Ibid.

115. Gael Green, "How Sexually Generous Should a Girl Be?," *Cosmopolitan*, May 1968, p. 138.

116. Ibid.

117. Ibid., p. 139.

118. "J," *The Sensuous Woman*, p. 69.

119. Ibid., p. 159.

120. Eva Margolies, *Sensual Pleasure: A Woman's Guide* (New York: Avon Books, 1981), p. xiv.

121. Ibid., p. 10.

122. Ibid., p. 12.

123. Ibid.

124. Ibid., p. 87.

125. Ibid., p. 88.

126. Ibid., p. 89.

127. Ehrenreich et al., *Re-making Love*, p. 108.

128. Georgia Dullen, "X-rated 'Couple Films' Finding a New Market," *New York Times*, Oct. 6, 1986.

129. Ibid.

130. Nancy Friday, *My Secret Garden: Women's Sexual Fantasies* (New York: Pocket Books, 1974).

131. Ehrenreich et al., *Re-making Love*, p. 96.

132. Lonnie Barbach, *Yourself: The Fulfillment of Female Sexuality* (New York: Doubleday, 1975), p. xvi.

133. Ibid., p. 197.

134. Lonnie Barbach, *Pleasures: Women Write Erotica* (New York: Harper & Row, 1984).

135. Ann Barr Snitow, "The Front Line: Notes on Sex in Novels by Women, 1969–1979," in *Women: Sex and Sexuality*, ed. Catherine R. Stimpson and Ethel Specter Person (Chicago: University of Chicago Press, 1980).

136. Erica Jong, *Fear of Flying* (New York: Nott, Rinehart and Winston, 1973), p. 44.

137. Ibid., p. 74.

138. Erica Jong, *How to Save Your Own Life* (New York: Signet, 1977) pp. 262–264.

139. Ira Robinson, Karl King, Jack Balswick, "The Premarital Sexual Revolution among College Females," in *Intimate Lifestyles*, ed. Jack Delora and Jonna Delora (Pacific Palisades, Calif.: Goodyear, 1975), p. 456.

140. Ibid., p. 457.

141. Carol Tauris and Susan Sadd, *Redbook Report on Female Sexuality* (New York: Delacorte, 1977), p. 159. Cf. Wolfe, *The Cosmo Report*, p. 404.

142. Ibid.

143. Ibid., p. 161.

144. Ibid. Cf. *The Cosmo Report*, p. 342, and Shere Hite, *The Hite Report* (New York: Dell, 1976), p. 630.

145. Ibid. Cf. *The Cosmo Report*, p. 358.

146. Ibid., p. 165.

147. Ibid., p. 167.

148. Morton Hunt, "Sexual Behavior in the 1970s; Part II; Premarital Sex," *Playboy*, Nov. 1973, p. 75.

149. Morton Hunt, *Sexual Behavior in the 1970s* (New York: Playboy Press, 1974), p. 135.

150. Wolfe, *The Cosmo Report*, p. 390.

151. Philip Blumstein and Pepper Schwartz, *American Couples* (New York: Morrow, 1983), p. 255.

152. Hunt, *Sexual Behavior in the 1970s*, p. 204.

153. Carol Tauris, "The New Redbook Report," *Redbook*, Feb. 1978, p. 111.

154. Hite, *The Hite Report*, p. 421.

155. Hunt, *Sexual Behavior in the 1970s*, p. 117.

156. Ibid., p. 134.

157. Hunt, "Premarital Sex," p. 74.

158. Linda Wolf, *The Cosmo Report*, p. 374. Cf. Lenore Walker, *The Battered Woman* (New York: Harper & Row, 1979); S. Steinmetz and M. Strauss (eds.), *Violence in the American Family* (New York: Harper & Row, 1974); M. Strauss, R. Gelles and S. Steinmetz, *Behind Closed Doors: Violence in the American Family* (Garden City, N.Y.: Anchor Press, 1980); Susan Brownmiller, *Against Our Will* (New York: Simon and Schuster, 1975).

159. Paula Webster, "Pornography and Pleasure," p. 50. Also see Judith Long Laws and Pepper Schwartz, *Sexual Scripts* (Hinsdale, Ill.: Dryden Press, 1977).

160. There are good reasons to believe that the psychological sources of women's sexual ambivalence goes beyond learned behavior. Psychoanalytic perspectives suggest that in a normatively heterosexual and male-privileged society, intrafamilial dynamics produce differences in the psychosexual orientation of middle-class boys and girls. I only wish to comment on one theme that bears on the issue at hand. Both boys and girls typically have their primary love relationship with their mother or a female surrogate. However, the psychosexual implications are different. The heterosexual and male-privileged structure of our society encourages the mother and father to induce in the boy an experience of his sexuality as integral or primary in his sense of self and connection to others. The mother incites his sexuality by responding to the boy as a developing man and as a substitute for her husband. The father encourages and approves of a boy's sexual expression and assertiveness as a sign of masculinity. In other words, the boy experiences his sexual feelings and their expression in a genital and aggressive way as a positive sign of his entitlement to the privileges of adult heterosexuality and manhood. By contrast, the girl is pressured to sublimate her sexual desires into an emotional-moral longing. Enforcing the heterosexual norm, the mother defuses her daughter's developing sexual feelings to her. The mother further desexualizes the girl's experience of herself by inducing in her the ideal feminine traits which defocalize her sexuality and focalize her spiritual, moral or aesthetic feelings. Finally, the one relationship in which girls are encouraged to be sexual, in which they experience themselves as a potent sexual being, is with their fathers. And this relationship is often imbued with an aura of danger. The very condition of intimacy between a father and a daughter may evoke suspicions of sexual seduction and exploitation. This induces an anxiety or sense of danger surrounding the girl's sexual feelings toward her father. In short, her sexuality is not experienced as self-affirming or empowering but as bearing psychic risk and danger.

See, for example, Nancy Chodorow, *The Reproduction of Mothering* (Berkeley: University of California Press, 1978); Dorothy Dinnerstein, *The Mermaid and the Minotaur* (New York: Harper & Row, 1976); Juliet Mitchell, *Psychoanalysis and Feminism* (New York: Random House, 1975); Ethel Spector Person, "Sexuality as a Mainstay of Identity: Psychoanalytic Perspectives," in *Women: Sex and Society,* ed. Catherine Stimpson and Ethel Specter Person.

CHAPTER 6

1. Working-class intimate cultures have only begun to be analyzed. Some interesting historical work has been done. See Christine Stansell, *City of Women: Sex and Class in New York, 1789–1860* (New York: Alfred A. Knopf, 1986) and Kathy Peiss, *Cheap Amusements: Working Women and Leisure in Turn-of-the-Century New York* (Philadelphia: Temple University Press, 1986). Some useful observations can also be found in John D'Emilio and Estelle Freedman, *Intimate Matters* (New York: Harper & Row, 1988). Some sociological work has been done but remains quite cursory. See, for example, Mira Komarovsky, *Blue-Collar Marriage* (New York: Random House, 1964); Lee Rainwater, *And the Poor Get Children* (Chicago: Quadrangle, 1960); and Lillian Rubin, *Worlds of Rain* (New York: Basic Books, 1976).

2. Mary Casal, *The Stone Wall* (New York: Arno Press, 1975 [1930]), p. 50.

3. Ibid.

4. Ibid., p. 92.

5. Ibid., p. 180.

6. Ibid., p. 147.

7. Diana Frederics, *Diana: A Strange Autobiography* (New York: Arno Press, 1975 [1939]), p. 21.

8. Ibid., p. 81.

9. Ibid., p. 82.

10. Ibid., p. 79.

11. Louis Hyde (ed.), *Rat and Devil: Journal Letters of F. O. Mattheissen and Russell Cheney* (Boston: Alyson, 1978), p. 47.

12. Ibid., p. 29.

13. Ibid., pp. 87–88.

14. Casal, *The Stone Wall*, p. 185.

15. Frederics, *Diana*, p. 83.

16. Glimpses into the experience of homosexuality as an individual problem can be found in Robert Reinhart, *A History of Shadows* (Boston: Alyson, 1986); Keith Vacha, *Quiet Fire: Memoirs of Older Gay Men* (New York: Crossing Press, 1985); Jonathan Katz, *Gay/Lesbian Almanac* (New York: Harper & Row, 1983); Martin Duberman, *About Time* (New York: Seahorse, 1986). Also, see novels of the period referred to in chapter 4. The critical role of a subculture in developing and maintaining positive images of homosexuality in the face of social disapproval is underscored by Lillian Faderman, *Surpassing the Love of Men* (New York: Morrow, 1981), p. 368. Also see Dennis Altman, Introduction to *The Gay Liberation Book*, ed. Len Richmond and Gary Noguera (San Francisco: Ramparts, 1973), p. 15.

17. See John D'Emilio, *Sexual Politics/Sexual Communities: The Making of a Homosex-*

ual Minority in the United States, 1940–1970 (Chicago: University of Chicago Press, 1983) and D'Emilio and Freedman, *Intimate Matters.*

18. Cf. Michael Foucault, *The History of Sexuality*, vol. 1, *An Introduction* (New York: Pantheon, 1978); Jeffrey Weeks, *Sex, Politics and Society* (London: Longman, 1981), and *Sexuality and Its Discontents* (London: Routledge and Kegan Paul, 1985).

19. D'Emilio, *Sexual Politics, Sexual Communities*, chap. 2, and Allan Bérubé, "Marching to a Different Drummer: Lesbian and Gay GIs in World War II," in *Powers of Desire*, ed. Ann Snitow et al. (New York: Monthly Review Press, 1983).

20. D'Emilio, *Sexual Politics, Sexual Communities*, chap. 3.

21. See Barry Adam, *The Rise of a Gay and Lesbian Movement* (Boston: Twayne, 1987); Lillian Faderman, *Surpassing the Love of Men;* Jeffrey Weeks, *Coming Out: Homosexual Politics in Britain From the Nineteenth Century to the Present* (London: Quartet Books, 1977).

22. John Lee, "The Gay Connection," *Urban Issues* 8 (July 1979), pp. 179–180. Cf. Laud Humpreys, "Exodus and Identity: The Emerging Gay Culture," in *Gay Men*, ed. Martin Levine (New York: Harper & Row, 1979).

23. James Baldwin, *Giovanni's Room* (New York: Dial Press, 1956); Gore Vidal, *The City and the Pillar* (New York: Dutton, 1984); Tennessee Williams, *Hard Candy* (New York: New Directions, 1954) and *Streetcar Named Desire* (New York: New Directions, 1947).

24. Edmund White, *A Boy's Own Story* (New York: Dutton, 1982); Andrew Holleran, *Dancer from the Dance* (New York: Morrow, 1978); Jane Rule, *Desert of the Heart* (New York: W. W. Norton, 1976); Rita Mae Brown, *Rubyfruit Jungle* (Plainfield, Vt.: Daughters, Inc., 1973); Adrienne Rich, *On Lies, Secrets and Silence* (New York: W. W. Norton, 1979); Larry Kramer, *Faggots* (New York: Random House, 1978).

25. Donald Webster Cory (pseud. Edward Sagarin), *The Homosexual in America* (New York: Greenberg, 1951); Evelyn Hooker, "Male Homosexuals and Their Worlds," in *Sexual Inversion*, ed. Marmor Judd (New York: Basic Books, 1965); Martin Hoffman, *The Gay World* (New York: Basic Books, 1968).

26. Dennis Altman, *Homosexual Oppression and Liberation* (New York: Avon, 1971); Jonathan Katz, *Gay American History* (New York: Thomas Crowell, 1976); Lillian Faderman, *Surpassing the Love of Men;* Adrienne Rich "Heterosexuality and Lesbian Existence," in *Powers of Desire*, ed. Ann Snitow et al.

27. See Dennis Altman, *The Homosexualization of America* (Boston: Beacon Press, 1983) and Michael Bronski, *Culture Clash* (Boston: South End Press, 1984).

28. Alfred Kinsey, et al., *Sexual Behavior in the Human Male* (Philadelphia: W. B. Saunders, 1948) and *Sexual Behavior in the Human Female* (Philadelphia: W. B. Saunders, 1953); Evelyn Hooker, "The Adjustment of The Male Overt Homosexual," *Journal of Projective Techniques* 21 (1957).

29. Peter Jackson, "The Tender Trap," *Mattachine Review* 3 (February 1957), p. 12.

30. William Baker, "A Step Towards Acceptance," *Mattachine Review* 3 (December 1957), pp. 15–16.

31. For an analysis of the Mattachine Society, see D'Emilio, *Sexual Politics, Sexual Communities* and Toby Marotta, *The Politics of Homosexuality* (Boston: Houghton Mifflin, 1981).

32. Luther Allen, "If the Cat Can Look at the King," *Mattachine Review* 3 (May 1957), p. 12.

33. Charles Thorp, "Leadership and Violence," in *Out of the Closets*, ed. Karla Jay and Allen Young (New York: Douglas/Links, 1972), p. 353. For another relevant document of the time that expresses the view of homosexuality as a positive identity and lifestyle, see Del Martin and Phyllis Lyon, *Lesbian/Woman* (San Francisco: Glide, 1972). See the anthologies *Out of the Closets, The Gay Liberation Book*, and *Lavender Culture* (New York: Praeger, 1971); Dennis Altman, *Homosexual Oppression and Liberation*.

34. Dick Michaels, "Editorial," *The Advocate*, Dec. 1968, p. 2.

35. Dick Michaels, "Editorial," *The Advocate*, Feb. 12. 1765.

36. David Goodstein, "Editorial," ibid.

37. Cory, *The Homosexual in America*, pp. 120–121.

38. Editors, "Editorial," *Mattachine Review* 6 (April 1960), p. 27.

39. Dick Michaels, *The Advocate*, Aug. 1969, p. 12.

40. Altman, *Homosexual Oppression and Liberation*, p. 13. Cf. Murphy, *Homosexual Liberation*, p. 21.

41. Altman, *The Homosexualization of America*, p. 2. Phyllis Lyon and Del Martin, "Realities of Lesbianism," in *Lesbians Speak Out*, ed The Women's Collective, 2d ed. (Oakland, Calif.: Women's Press Collective, 1974). D'Emilio interprets the making of a homosexual community and politic around the concept of the homosexual as a minority. See *Sexual Politics, Sexual Communities*, pp. 30–34.

42. Charlotte Bunch, "Learning from Lesbian Separatism," in *Lavender Culture*, pp. 438–439.

43. Charlotte Bunch, "Lesbians in Revolt," in *Lesbianism and the Women's Movement*, ed. Nancy Myron and Charlotte Bunch (Baltimore: Diana Press, 1975), p. 29.

44. Radical lesbians, "The Woman Identified Woman," in *Radical Feminism*, ed. Anne Koedt et al. (New York: Quadrangle, 1973), pp. 240–241.

45. Ti-Grace Atkinson, "Lesbianism and Feminism," in *Amazon Expedition*, ed. Phyllis Birkby et al. (Washington, N.J.: Times Change Press, 1973), p. 12. Cf. Rita Mae Brown, "Take a Lesbian to Lunch," in *Out of the Closets*.

46. Ti-Grace Atkinson, *Amazon Odyssey* (New York: Links Books, 1974); Charlotte Bunch, "Learning from Lesbian Separation," in *Lavender Culture;* Andrea Dworkin, *Our Blood* (New York: Harper & Row, 1976); Rita Mae Brown, "The Shape of Things to Come," in *Lesbianism and the Women's Movement;* Jill Johnston, *Lesbian Nation* (New York: Simon & Schuster, 1973); Suan Griffin, *Women and Nature* (New York: Harper & Row, 1978); Adrienne Rich, "Heterosexuality and Lesbian Existence," in *Powers of Desire;* and Robin Morgan, *Going Too Far* (New York: Random House, 1978).

47. See the fine collection of interviews of lesbians in *Lesbian Crossroads*, ed. Ruth Baetz (New York: Morrow, 1980), p. 61.

48. For expressions of affirmative, indeed celebratory notions of homosexuality in the period, see Jonathan Katz, *Coming Out!* (New York: Arno Press, 1975); Murphy, *Homosexual Liberation*, Arthur Bell, *Dancing the Gay Lib Blues* (New York: Simon & Schuster, 1971); Kay Robin and Randy Wicker, *The Gay Crusaders* (New York: Arno Press, 1975 [1972]); Martha Shelly, "Gay Is Good," in *Out of the Closets;* Carl Wittman, "A Gay Manifesto," in *Out of the Closets*.

49. On the meaning of gay, see Peter Fisher, *The Gay Mystique* (New York: Stein & Day, 1972), pp. 232–233; Jonathan Ned Katz, *Gay/Lesbian Almanac.*

50. Julia Penelope Stanley, "My Life as a Lesbian," in *The Coming out Stories*, ed. Susan Wolfe and Penelope Stanley (Watertown, Mass.: Persephone Press, 1980). Cf. Lenn Richmond, "Born Again," in *The New Gay Liberation*, ed. Len Richmond and Gary Noguera (Palo Alto, Calif.: Ramparts Press, 1979).

51. Alan Bell and Martin Weinberg, *Homosexualities* (New York: Simon & Schuster, 1978). pp. 328–329.

52. Karla Jay and Allen Young, *The Gay Report* (New York: Simon & Schuseter, 1977), p. 456.

53. Ibid., p. 480.

54. Ibid., p. 555.

55. Ibid., p. 171.

56. Ibid., p. 164.

57. Ibid., p. 168.

58. Ibid., p. 176.

59. Ibid., p. 177.

60. Ibid.

61. Bell and Weinberg, *Homosexualities*, p. 312.

62. Ibid.

63. Ibid.

64. Ibid., p. 314.

65. Phillip Blumstein and Pepper Schwartz, *American Couples* (New York: Morrow, 1983), p.

66. Ibid., p.

67. Letitia Anne Peplau, "What Homosexuals Want," *Psychology Today*, March 1981, p. 34.

68. Ibid.

69. Bell and Weinberg, *Homosexualities*, p. 319.

70. Ibid., p. 320.

71. Peplau, "What Homosexuals Want," p. 34.

72. Ibid.

73. Ibid., p. 37.

74. Ibid., p. 30.

75. Ibid., p. 32.

76. Ibid.

77. See, for example, Jean Lipman-Blumen and Ann Tickamyer, "Sex Roles in Transition: A Ten-Year Perspective," *Annual Review of Sociology* (1975); Arland Thornton and Deborah Freedman, "Changes in the Sex Role Attitudes of Women, 1962–1977; Evidence from a Panel Study," *American Sociological Review* 44 (Oct. 1979); Andrew Cherlin and Pamela Barnhouse Walters, "Trends in United States Men's and Women's Sex-role Attitudes: 1972 to 1978," *American Sociological Review* 46 (Aug. 1981).

78. Blumstein and Schwartz, *American Couples*, p. 273.

79. Ibid.

80. Ibid.

81. Ibid.

82. Ibid.

83. Letitia Anne Peplau and Susan D. Cochran, "Value Orientations in the Intimate Relationships of Gay Men,"; *Journal of Homosexuality* 6 (Spring 1981), p. 16.

84. See Carol Warren, *Identity and Community in the Gay World* (New York: John Wiley, 1974).

85. Blumstein and Schwartz, *American Couples*. Cf. Marcel Saghir and Eli Robbins, *Male and Female Homosexuality* (Baltimore: Williams and Wilkins, 1973); and Joseph Harry, "Marriage among Gay Males: The Separation of Intimacy and Sex," in *The Sociological Perspective*, ed. Scott McNall, 4th ed. (Boston: Little, Brown, 1977), p. 334.

86. Harry, "Marriage among Gay Males," p. 338.

87. Ibid., p. 336. Cf. Warren, *Identity and Community in the Gay World*.

88. Ibid., pp. 339–340.

89. Joseph Harry and Robert Lovely, "Gay Marriages and Communities of Sexual Orientation," *Alternative Lifestyles* 2 (May 1979), p. 198.

90. Ibid., p. 199.

91. Edmund White, *States of Desire*, p. 286.

92. Cf. C. A. Tripp, *The Homosexual Matrix* (New York: McGraw-Hill, 1975). Also, Edmund White, "Paradise Found," *Mother Jones* 8 (June 1983).

93. Bell and Weinberg, *Homosexualities*, p. 312.

94. Ibid., p. 308.

95. Ibid.

96. Morton Hunt, *Sexual Behavior in the 1970s* (Chicago, Ill.: Playboy Press, 1974), p. 152.

97. Ibid., p. 151–152.

98. Bell and Weinberg, *Homosexualities*, p. 309.

99. Jay and Young, *The Gay Report*, pp. 248–249; Bell and Weinberg, *Homosexualities*, p. 308.

100. Bell and Weinberg, *Homosexualities*, p. 309. Cf. Pat Califia, "Lesbian Sexuality," *Journal of Homosexuality* 4 (Spring 1979). In Califia's study, 60 percent of the lesbians interviewed said they enjoyed sex without deep emotional commitments. Similar findings are reported by Letitia Anne Peplau, Susan Cochran, et al., "Loving Women: Attachment and Autonomy in Lesbian Relationships," *Journal of Social Issues* 34 (1978). They found that almost one-third of the coupled lesbians interviewed indicated they had sex outside their relationship and valued this as a part of their sexual autonomy.

101. Linda Wolfe, *The Cosmo Report* (New York: Arbor House, 1981), p. 333.

102. Jay and Young, *The Gay Report*, p. 248.

103. Edward William Delphi, *The Silent Community* (Beverly Hills: Sage, 1976); Also see Warren, *Identiy and Community in the Gay World*.

104. Laud Humphreys, *Tearoom Trade* (Chicago: Aldine, 1970).

105. Richard Troiden, "Homosexual Encounters in a Highway Rest Stop," in *Sexual Deviance and Sexual Deviants*, ed. E. Goode and R. Troiden (New York: Morrow, 1974), p. 227.

106. Martin Weinberg, "Gay Baths and the Social Organization of Impersonal Sex," *Social Problems* 22 (Dec. 1975).

107. On casual sex in gay baths, see Michael Rumaker, *A Day and Night at the Baths* (Bolinas, Calif.: Grey Fox, 1979); Tim McCaskell, "Untangling Emotions and Eros," *The Body Politic*, July/August 1981, p. 22.

108. Bell and Weinberg, *Homosexualities*, p. 310. Jay and Young, *The Gay Report*, p.

109. Robert Boyers, "The Ideology of the Steam-Bath," *Times Literary Supplement*, May 30, 1980, p. 604.

110. Martin Hoffman, *The Gay World*, pp. 181–182.

111. Jay and Young, *The Gay Report*, p. 250. Cf. Dennis Altman "How Much Do Gay Men and Lesbians Really Have in Common," *The Advocate*, April 16, 1981. Edmund White and Charles Silverstein, *The Joy of Gay Sex* (New York: Simon & Schuster, 1977).

112. See Arthur Bell, "Bath Life Gets Respectability," in *Lavender Culture*, p. 82. Edmund White, *States of Desire*, pp. 15–16.

113. Dennis Altman, *The Homosexualization of America*, p. 79.

114. Quoted in Arthur Bell, "Bath Life Gets Respectability," p. 82.

115. Jay and Young *The Gay Report*, pp. 249, 324.

116. There is a continuing discussion in the gay and lesbian community on the relation between gender and homosexuality. See, for example, the interesting exchanges in the *Body Politic* between 1976 and 1979; Marie Robertson, "We Need Our Own Banner"; Andrew Hodges, "Divided We Stand"; Charis Bearchell, "Gay Men and Lesbians Can Work Together"; Beatrice Baker, "Confessions of a Lesbian Gay Liberationist"; Brian Mossop, "Gay Men's Feminist Mistake"; Chris Bearchell, "Every Faggot's Dyke, Every Dyke's Faggot," Reprinted in *Flaunting It!* ed. Ed Jackson and Stan Perskey (Vancouver, Toronto: Pink Triangle Press, 1982). There is, of course, a growing academic literature on this topic. See, for example, Deborah Wolf, *The Lesbian Community* (Berkeley: University of California Press, 1979); E. M. Ettore, *Lesbian, Women and Society* (London: Routledge and Kegan Paul, 1980); Jeffrey Weeks, *Sexuality and Its Discontents;* and C. A. Tripp, *The Homosexual Matrix*.

117. Jay and Young, *The Gay Report*, p. 252.

118. Ibid., p. 324.

119. Ibid., p. 252.

120. See, for example, *Heresies*, 3, no. 12, (1981). I will discuss this further in the Epilogue.

121. John Lee, "The Gay Connection," p. 192.

122. Ibid., p. 182.

123. Altman, *The Homosexualization of America*, p. 184.

124. Altman, "How Much Do Gay Men and Lesbians Really have in Common?" *The*

Advocate, April 16, 1981. Cf. the major gay male sex manual by White and Silverstein, *The Joy of Gay Sex.*

125. See McCaskell, "Untangling Emotions and Eros." Bronski, *Culture Clash*, p. 184. This argument has been expanded to viewing gays as pioneers of lifestyle experimentation. See White and Silverstein, *The Joy of Gay Sex*, p. 115; Altman, *The Homosexualization of America*, p. 188.

126. "The Aesthetics of Existence: Listening to Michel Foucault," *New York Native*, July 30–Aug. 12, 1984, p. 12.

127. Arnie Kantrowitz, "Till Death Us Do Part: Reflections on Community," *The Advocate* 1983, p. 26.

128. Richard Goldstein, "Fear and Loving in the Gay Community," *The Village Voice*, June 28, 1983, p. 12. C. A. Tripp, in *The Homosexual Matrix*, reported that one-half of the men he interviewed who had been coupled met their lovers through casual sex. Also see Donald Vining, "Where Coupledom Begins: Meetings in Likely and Unlikely Places," *The Advocate* Nov. 25, 1982.

129. White, *States of Desire*, p. xiii. Cf. Ken Popert, "Public Sexuality and Social Space," *The Body Politic*, July–Aug. 1982.

130. Larry Kramer, *The Faggots*; Andrew Holleran, *Dancer from the Dance: Nights in Aruba* (New York: Morrow, 1983).

131. For example, Seymour Kleinberg, *Alienated Affections* (New York: Warner, 1980); David Sloven and Jeffrey Leiphart, "Coping with the Kid in the Candy Store," *New York Native*, March 16–28, 1982.

132. Jeremy Seabrook, *A Lasting Relationship: Homosexuals and Society* (London: Allen Lane, 1976); Neil Alan Marks, "Sexual Manners, Part One," *New York Native*, May 24–June 6, 1982.

133. Thom Willenbecker, "Quick Encounters of the Closest Kind,: The Rites and Rituals of Shadow Sex," *The Advocate*, March 6, 1980. Thomas Garrett, "Not Play, Not Recreation," *New York Native*, March 15–28, 1982.

EPILOGUE

1. On purity movements in the United States, see David Pivar, *Purity Crusade: Sexual Morality and Social Control, 1868–1900* (Westport, Conn.: Greenwood Press, 1973); Paul Boyer, *Purity in Print* (New York: Charles Scribner's Sons, 1968); and *Urban Masses and Moral Order in America, 1820–1920* (Cambridge: Harvard University Press, 1978).

2. Cf. Jeffrey Weeks, *Sexuality and Its Discontents* (London: Routledge and Kegan Paul, 1984).

3. Willard Gaylin, *Rediscovering Love* (New York: Viking, 1986), p. 11. Among the many articles in mass circulation magazines announcing, indeed celebrating, the end of the sexual revolution, see John Leo, "The Revolution is Over," *Time*, April 9, 1984.

4. See, for example, Andrew Cherlin, *Marriage, Divorce, and Remarriage* (Cambridge: Harvard University Press, 1981).

5. One study of recent sexual mores reports that "by the 1980s, swinging . . . had become a highly organized subculture with more than two hundred clubs, two big annual conventions, dozens of magazines and newsletters, and scores of party

cruises and special events." See Steve Chapple and David Talbot, *Burning Desires: Sex in America* (New York: Doubleday, 1989), p. 6. On the development of S/M communities, see Geoff Mains, *Urban Aboriginals* (San Francisco: Gay Sunshine Press, 1984).

6. E.g., Patricia Morrisroe, "Forever Single," *New York*, Aug. 20, 1984. See the analysis by Barbara Ehrenreich et al., "The Media Fights Casual Sex," in *Re-making Love* (New York: Doubleday, 1987).

7. Caryn James, "Love with Improper Strangers," *New York Times*, Arts and Leisure Section, April 22, 1990.

8. Editors, "Editorial," *National Review*, July 8, 1983.

9. B. D. Colon, "The Gay Plague, Part One," *The Rolling Stone*, Feb. 18, 1983, p. 50. Cf. Jon Nordheimer, "With AIDS about, Heterosexuals Are Rethinking Casual Sex," *New York Times*, March 22, 1986.

10. Michael Callen, letter, *The Body Politic*, April 1983, p. 93. Michael Callen and Richard Berkowitz with Richard Dworkin, "We Know Who We Are," *New York Native*, Nov. 8, 1982.

11. See Steven Seidman, "Transfiguring Sexual Identity": AIDS and the Contemporary Construction of Homosexualty," *Social Text* 19/20 (Fall 1989).

12. See George Leonard, *The End of Sex: Erotic Love after the Sexual Revolution* (New York: Banton Books, 1984). This quotation is taken from "The End of Sex," *Esquire*, Dec. 1982, pp. 74–75. Cf. John Leo, "The Revolution is Over," *Time*, April 9, 1984, pp. 74–83.

13. Leonard, *The End of Sex*, p. 107.

14. Gaylin, *Rediscovering Love*, p. 22.

15. Arthur Bell, "Where Gays Are Going," *The Village Voice*, June 29, 1982.

16. David Goodstein, Editorial, *The Advocate*, Aug. 6, 1985.

17. Dagmar O'Connor, *How to Make Love to the Same Person for the Rest of Your Life and Still Love It* (New York: Viking, 1987), p. xi.

18. Ibid., p. xiii.

19. Ibid., p. 8.

20. Paul Pearsall, *Super Marital Sex: Loving for Life* (New York: Doubleday, 1987), p. xv.

21. Ibid., p. 6.

22. Harold Bloomfield and Sirah Vettese with Robert Kory, *Lifemates: The Love Fitness Program for a Lasting Relationship* (New York: New American Library, 1989), p. 111.

23. Ibid., p. 118.

24. Ibid., pp. 111–112.

25. Ibid., p. 117.

26. Ann Ferguson, "Pleasure, Power and the Porn Wars," *The Women's Review of Books* 3, no. 8 (May 1986) and "The Sex Debate in the Women's Movement: A Socialist-Feminist View," *Against the Current*, Sept.–Oct. 1983. Cf. Steven Seidman, *Embattled Eros: Sexual Politics and Ethics in Contemporary America* (New York: Routledge, 1992), chap. 3.

27. Ann Snitow et al., *Powers of Desire* (New York: Monthly Review Press, 1983);

Carole Vance (ed.), *Pleasure and Danger; Heresies* 3, no. 12 (1981); "Sex Issue", Varda Burstyn (ed.), *Women against Censorship* (Toronto: Douglas and McIntyre, 1985).

28. Joan Nestle, "Butch-Fem Relationships," *Heresies*, "Sex Issue," Gayle Rubin, "Thinking Sex," in *Pleasure and Danger*. Amber Hollibaugh, "Desire for the Future: Radical Hope in Passion and Pleasure," in *Pleasure and Danger*. Paula Webster, "Pornography and Pleasure," *Heresies*, "Sex Issue."

29. Pat Califia, "Feminism and Sadomasochism," *Heresies*, "Sex Issue." Gayle Rubin and Pat Califia, "Talking about Sadomasochism: Fear, Facts, Fantasies," *Gay Community News*, Aug. 15, 1981. Gayle Rubin, "The Leather Menance: Comments on Politics and S/M," in Samois, *Coming to Power* (Boston: Alyson, 1982).

30. See Robin Ruth Linden (ed.), *Against Sadomasochism* (East Palo Alto, Calif.: Frog in the Wall, 1982).

31. Janet Schrim, "S/M for Feminists," *Gay Community News*, May 9, 1989, p. 8. See the essays defending lesbian S/M in Samois, *Coming to Power*.

32. Barbara Ehrenreich, Elizabeth Hess, and Gloria Jacobs, *Re-making Love: The Feminization of Sex* (New York: Doubleday, 1986), p. 191.

33. Ibid.

34. See, for example. M. H. Berker, and J. G. Joseph, "AIDS and Behavioral Change to Reduce Risk: A Review," *American Journal of Public Health* 78 (1988), pp. 394–410; J. L. Martin, "AIDS Risk Reduction Recommendations and Sexual Behavior Patterns among Gay Men," *Health Education Quarterly* 13 (1986), pp. 347–358, and "The Impact of AIDS on Gay Male Sexual Behavior Patterns in New York City," *American Journal of Public Health* 77 (1987), pp. 578–581. L. McKusick et al., "AIDS and Sexual Behavior Reported by Gay Men in San Francisco," *American Journal of Public Health* 75 (1985), pp. 493–496. For a general overview, see "Sexual Behavior and AIDS," in *AIDS: Sexual Behavior and Intravenous Drug Use*, ed. Charles Turner, Heather Miller and Lincoln Moses (Washington, D.C.: National Academy Press, 1989).

35. *The Advocate*, Dec. 20, 1988, p. 134.

36. *Outweek*, June 26, 1989, p. 137.

37. Recently, two reporters have tried to make the case that the commitment to a strong agenda of sexual liberalization is alive and well in the social mainstream. See Steve Chapple and David Talbot, *Burning Desires: Sex in America*, p. xiv.

Index

gers of sex in Victorian era, 31–32; sexual equality, 85. *See also* Feminism; Sexuality, female
Women in the Shadows, 115–16
Woodward, Samuel, 20, 34
Wright, Helena, 89–90

Yarros, Rachelle, 75
Young, Allen, 170
Young Man's Guide, 33
Yourself: The Fulfillment of Female Sexuality, 148–49
Youth culture, 125, 155